BEYOND THE CLASSICS?
Essays in Religious Studies and Liberal Education

SCHOLARS PRESS
Studies in the Humanities

Suicide

John Donne
William A. Clebsch, editor

Tragedy as a Critique of Virtue:
The Novel and Ethical Reflection

John D. Barbour

Lyric Apocalypse: Reconstruction
in Ancient and Modern Poetry

John W. Erwin

The Unusable Past: America's Puritan
Tradition, 1830 to 1930

Jan C. Dawson

The Visual Arts and Christianity
in America: The Colonial Period through
the Nineteenth Century

John Dillenberger

Chaos to Cosmos: Studies in Biblical
Patterns of Creation

Susan Niditch

Melville and the Gods

William Hamilton

The Character of the Euripidean Hippolytos:
An Ethno-Psychoanalytical Study

George Devereux

To See Ourselves As Others See Us:
Christians, Jews, "Others" in Late Antiquity

Jacob Neusner,
Ernest S. Frerichs, editors

Civitas: Religious Interpretations of
the City

Peter Hawkins, editor

The Riddle of Liberty:
Emerson on Alienation, Freedom, and Obedience

Lou Ann Lange

Why Persimmons and Other Poems

Stanley Romaine Hopper

Gregor Sebba: Lectures on Creativity

Helen Sebba,
Hendrikus Boers, editors

Beyond the Classics? Essays in Religious
Studies and Liberal Education

Frank E. Reynolds,
Sheryl L. Burkhalter, editors

BEYOND THE CLASSICS?
Essays in Religious Studies and Liberal Education

edited by

Frank E. Reynolds
Sheryl L. Burkhalter

Scholars Press
Atlanta, Georgia

BEYOND THE CLASSICS?
Essays in Religious Studies
and Liberal Education

edited by

Frank E. Reynolds
Sheryl L. Burkhalter

©1990
Scholars Press

Cover design:
Isometric Systems in Isotropic Space - Map Projections: The Snail,
original ink & charcoal drawing by artist Agnes Denes
© Copyright by Agnes Denes 1974

Library of Congress Cataloging in Publication Data

Beyond the Classics? : essays in religious studies and liberal
    education / edited by Sheryl Burkhalter, Frank Reynolds.
    p. cm. -- (Scholars Press studies in the humanities series :
    no. 14)
    ISBN 1-55540-517-7 (alk. paper). -- ISBN 1-55540-518-4 (pbk. :
    alk. paper)
    1. Religion--Study and teaching (Higher) 2. Education,
Humanistic. I. Burkhalter, Sheryl. II. Reynolds, Frank, 1924- .
III. Series.
BL41.B49 1990
200'.71'1--dc20   90-46976
                                                     CIP

Printed in the United States of America
on acid-free paper

THE BERKELEY-CHICAGO-HARVARD PROGRAM: RELIGIOUS STUDIES IN THE LIBERAL ARTS

This volume is a product of the Berkeley-Chicago-Harvard Program, a five-year series of institutes, workshops and related projects aimed at enlarging the role and scope of religious studies in the undergraduate liberal arts curriculum. The objective was to collect resources to assist teachers of undergraduate courses in religious studies—especially those teachers whose training has been limited to only one religious tradition—and to provide reflection on the changing nature of the liberal arts curriculum, and the role that religious studies plays within it.

These two objectives are linked. The basic courses in religion have within recent years begun to move away from the periphery of the liberal arts to which they have been banished for over a century. Increasingly they have come to occupy a more central location in the college curriculum. In many schools the "world religions" and "introduction to religion" courses serve as integrators for the humanities and the social sciences. These courses give an overview of the history of world civilization, provide a window on the cultural dimensions of global politics, and supply a way of perceiving many of the modern quests for personal meaning. This three-volume sourcebook and other projects related to the Berkeley-Chicago-Harvard Program were created to facilitate this new and expansive vision of religious studies in the liberal arts.

The Berkeley-Chicago-Harvard Program was funded by grants from the National Endowment for the Humanities and was sponsored by the Office for Programs in Comparative Religion at the Graduate Theological Union, Berkeley; the History of Religions Program in the Divinity School of the University of Chicago; and the Center for the Study of World Religions at Harvard Divinity School. The codirectors were John Carman (Harvard), Mark Juergensmeyer (Berkeley), and Frank Reynolds (Chicago).

Contents

THE CONTRIBUTORS

Judith A. Berling
Dean, Graduate Theological Seminary

Sheryl L. Burkhalter
Ph.D. Student, The University of Chicago

W. Royce Clark
Professor, Pepperdine University

William R. Darrow
Professor, Williams College

James H. Foard
Professor, Arizona State University

Charles H. Long
Professor, Syracuse University

Robin W. Lovin
Professor, The University of Chicago

George W. Pickering
Professor, The University of Detroit

Frank E. Reynolds
Professor, The University of Chicago

Lawrence E. Sullivan
Professor, Harvard University

Lee H. Yearly
Professor, Stanford University

INTRODUCTORY COMMENTS

The collection of essays that follows is the product of a five-year project devoted to "Religious Studies and Liberal Education: Toward a Global Perspective" jointly sponsored by the University of Chicago, Harvard University and the Graduate Theological Union, and funded by two major grants from the National Endowment for the Humanities. More specifically, it is the result of the intense collaborative efforts of a subgroup that was originally formed to take responsibility for the first of the project's three Summer Institutes for College Teachers. Entitled "Religious Studies and the Liberal Arts: Opportunities and New Directions," this Institute was held at the University of Chicago in the summer of 1986.

The majority of the contributors to the present volume (Reynolds, Long, Sullivan, Burkhalter, Yearley, and Berling) were members of this original "Chicago group."[1] They played a central role in planning the 1986 Institute and provided the core of its administration and faculty. Since 1986, they have actively participated in several specially organized conferences and colloquia. Three other contributors (Lovin, Clark and Foard) joined the original group as a result of the distinctive contributions that they made during the course of the Chicago Institute.[2] William Darrow was drawn into the discussions

---

[1]Marilyn Waldman was also a member of the original group and one of the prime movers of the project in general and the Chicago Institute in particular. Without her ideas and enthusiasm, the entire project would have been greatly impoverished. Robert Cohn participated in the original discussions, was a member of the Institute faculty, and led several important sessions. Robert Campany, who served as an administrative assistant in the early phases of the project, compiled an impressive bibliography that greatly facilitated the work of the Institute.

[2]Others who were involved in the Chicago Institute injected important ideas into the ongoing discussion and deserve much of the credit for whatever strengths this volume may have. The twenty-four regular participants were intensely involved in the conversations that developed; and five of the participants contributed papers that were published—along with an essay by the editors of this volume—in a special issue of *Criterion* entitled, "Religious Studies and Liberal Education: Opportunities and New Directions" 26:2 (1987). Wendy Doniger,

during the project's final Workshop that met in Berkeley for a week in June, 1989.[3] Though George Pickering did not participate in any of the project discussions, his contribution was included because of its relevance to the topic and the extent to which it carried further the concerns raised in several of the other essays.

The level of creative involvement that the members of the Chicago group have maintained over an extended period of time has been unusual to say the least. For example, with the exception of Pickering's essay and Foard's second article, all the papers included in this volume have been written, discussed and criticized in a variety of contexts by participants in the project, and then revised at least once.

The group has been able to attract the enthusiastic, long-term participation of its members at least in part because those who have been involved share common commitments and a common perspective. All of the contributors to the present volume share strong commitments to the cause of liberal education, to the teaching of religious studies and to the belief that these two arenas must be mutually supportive if either one is to realize its full potential in the contemporary academy. Over the course of the project, the contributors grew in their conviction that if liberal education and religious studies are to make significant contributions in the 1990s and beyond, both arenas must undergo major reforms—reforms that recognize and support the positive possibilities that are inherent in the new intellectual and social developments that are presently occurring in the academy and in society as a whole.

The vitality that the Chicago group has been able to maintain is also closely related to the fact that it has provided an appropriate context for a creative encounter among religious studies scholars and teachers who—despite their common commitments and perspective—brought a wide variety of experiences and judgements to the discussions. They have put forth different ideas concerning the way in which the contemporary situation has developed; they have expressed different views concerning the specific reforms that deserve priority; and they have proposed the use of different strategies and tactics. In some cases, this disparity can be traced to differing notions of liberal education and/or religious studies. In other instances, they can be attributed to the very different institutional settings in which the ideas have been formulated and tested. But whatever the basis of

---

John Carman and Mark Juergensmeyer were a part of the regular faculty and led several sessions. Jonathan Z. Smith, Carol Schneider and David Tracy delivered special lectures.

[3]William Graham also made important contributions to the discussions of the Chicago group during this Workshop.

the differences may be, they are very real, and the debates they made for were often intense.

Taken as a whole, the essays in this volume convey the basic commitments and perspective of the Chicago group. It is our hope that when the essays are read as a unit, these basic commitments and perspectives will prove convincing not only to those involved in religious studies, but to administrators and teachers in other areas as well.

Taken *ad seriatim,* these essays present a wide range of differing theoretical positions and practical strategies for reform. It is our hope that, when read from this point of view, they will evoke the kind of very specific discussions, debates and actions that will be required if real change is to occur.

> Sheryl Burkhalter
> Frank Reynolds

PART I: PERSPECTIVES

RECONSTRUCTING LIBERAL EDUCATION:
A RELIGIOUS STUDIES PERSPECTIVE[1]

Frank E.Reynolds

In reviewing current trajectories in liberal education, J. W. Corder
has characterized the situation in terms that are accurate but depress-
ing. "So there we are," he writes, "despairing, a little afraid, and the
dark coming down; and no programs, no curricula, no saving authority to aid us. . . . The tone of lamentation dominates and that's a wor-
risome, perhaps perilous thing. Many things have gone to hell. And
more will go to hell tomorrow . . . ." Yet, Corder warns, "if the cavalry
comes in aid of those who yearn for a saving authority, it may not be
the cavalry they expect. Things are not the same as they were in
former times."[2]

Yes, Corder is right in that there is, these days, a great lament
among those who are committed to the cause of liberal education.
This lament has been articulated from many different perspectives,
and it has been expressed by those in diverse academic disciplines.
But the theme remains constant: there is a crisis in liberal education.
Moreover, the more insightful commentators and participants recognize that this crisis cannot be passed off as one that has been generated by external factors alone. Financial problems are real, but—up to
this point at least—they have not been determinative in most situations. Nor can the crisis be attributed simply to an erosion of administrative support. In many instances, where universities have become

---

[1]An earlier draft of this paper was presented as one of two Wickenden Lectures
at Miami University in Oxford, Ohio. Later versions have been presented at the
National Endowment of the Humanities Summer Institute on "Religious Studies
and the Liberal Arts: Opportunities and New Directions" (Chicago, 1986) and at
Knox College, Western Kentucky University, St. Joseph's University, and
Monmouth College. In each case, I have profited from comments offered in the
discussions that followed. I have also been greatly aided by suggestions made by
Sheryl Burkhalter.

[2]"The Time the Cavalry Didn't Come, Or the Quest for a Saving Authority in
Recent Studies in Higher Education," *Liberal Education* 71:4 (1985) p. 310.

big businesses overseen by fund raisers and managers, administrative support for the liberal arts has declined; but a lack of administrative support is often more a result, than the cause, of the crisis. Thus, there is every reason to suspect that the malaise the we are experiencing in liberal education has deeper roots. Corder is also right in his assertion that there is a yearning for the arrival of a cavalry capable of rescuing the beleaguered defenders who still man the barricades of the liberal education establishment. Indeed, the rhythms of such a cavalry can now be heard, and the hoofbeats are becoming much more audible than they were when Corder published his article in 1985. In the present situation, we are being summoned by highly placed and well-financed individuals and groups to emerge from the present educational crisis through a nostalgic return to traditions that have sustained us in the past. What is more, the messages that these individuals and groups are bearing have touched a responsive chord, both among educators and among the public at large.

Consider, for example, the widespread influence of William Bennett who served as the head of the National Endowment for the Humanities and later as Secretary of Education in the Reagan administration. Bennett has written a government-sponsored report quite appropriately entitled "Reclaiming a Legacy,"[3] and has delivered many speeches including a number that have recently appeared in a collection called *American Education: Making It Work*.[4] In these and other contexts, he has very effectively highlighted the crisis that exists, and has proposed to meet that crisis with a "return to basics." In addition to a highly commendable emphasis on the primary skills of reading, writing and arithmetic, he has proposed a return to a traditional humanities curriculum that focuses on the kind of American history and values that have, in his view, been characteristic of the best American education in the past.

To cite another rather different example, consider Allan Bloom's well-financed best seller, *The Closing of the American Mind: How Higher Education Has Failed Democracy and Impoverished the Souls of Today's Students*.[5] Bloom, in an impassioned critique of almost everything that has happened in higher education since the early 1960s, has identified many of the problems that have contributed to the present crisis. Then, with this critique as background, he goes on to propose a return to his own brand of fundamentals—namely, the serious study

---

[3]*Chronicle of Higher Education* 28 (1984) pp. 16-21.

[4]Washington: Department of Education (1988). Regarding Bennett's position on the teaching of religion in public education, see his essay, "Religious Belief and the Constitutional Order," in *Religious Beliefs, Human Rights and the Moral Foundations of Western Democracy: 1986 Paine Lectures in Religion*, ed. Carl H. Esbeck (Distributed by the University of Missouri at Columbia) pp. 1-11.

[5]New York: Simon and Schuster, 1987.

of a particular series of western classics beginning with the dialogues of Plato and culminating in the writings of Rousseau.

There is much to be learned from Bennett, Bloom and others of their ilk. At the very least, we must be grateful to them for focusing public attention on the plight of liberal education, and on the need to engage in a process of reconstruction. But before we become too euphoric about the rescue effort that they are mounting to meet the present crisis, we would do well to recall again the cautionary note that is included in Corder's comments quoted above. "Things," he very accurately observes, "are not as they were in former times."

In the discussion that follows, I would like to suggest an alternative to the emphasis on "returning," "reclaiming," and "recovering" that characterizes the "cavalry of lost authority." There *is* a crisis in liberal education. But the conditions that have brought it about are much more deeply rooted and much more irreversible than Bennett and Bloom are willing or able to recognize. Yes, the intellectual and educational traditions that we have inherited from our pre-modern and more immediate predecessors are truly great traditions that we ignore at our peril; but these traditions must not be reified into a monolithic and idealized past to which we repentantly return. Rather, these intellectual and educational traditions must be seen as earlier phases of a very ambiguous historical process that we, in the last decade of the 20th century, are called upon to appropriate and to transform in the light of our own very different contemporary situation.

In order to clarify my position more precisely, I will identify three quite different, though closely interconnected, patterns of liberal education. The first I term the early-modern, classically oriented pattern; the second I label the late-modern, critically oriented pattern; the third, I name the post-modern, pluralistic pattern. From one point of view, these three quite distinct patterns of liberal education have succeeded one another in chronological succession. But from another equally valid perspective, these patterns are historical types that co-exist in our present situation. The first two patterns are remnants from a further and a nearer past that are still very much with us; they persist in our midst, but as the remnants of worlds that have essentially passed away. The third is also with us, but in a very different way: this post-modern, pluralistic pattern is present as a possibility for the kind of creative future that we are just now beginning to envision. In the discussion of each of these patterns, I will place special emphasis on the role of theology and/or religious studies.

There can be little doubt but that the basic pattern of liberal education from which our contemporary forms have developed was a pattern originally constructed (or better: reconstructed from its Greek and medieval roots) in the 17th and 18th centuries. This early-modern pattern of liberal education was formulated to serve as an initiation for the intellectual and cultural elite that dominated the western world and gave it leadership and direction. Initiants were from the upper echelons of bourgeois society; and since they were assured of at least a moderate degree of economic security, they did not have to prepare themselves for the grossly "practical" pursuits of a personal nature. They were being initiated to be gentlemen and leaders in the social world of their times. But what was the content of their initiation? What were the forms of their initiatory training? And what were the initiatory "secrets" imparted to them?

Putting the matter very briefly, there were two primary foci of the early-modern initiation process that coexisted in a state of creative tension. The first focus of the elliptical pattern that characterized liberal education in this period was the so-called "scientific" mode of Enlightenment rationality. Reason, in the Enlightenment sense of a supposedly objective and disinterested means of ascertaining truth, became the preeminent means for obtaining knowledge about the natural world. And it became a preeminent criteria for establishing and validating knowledge in other areas as well. Thus Reason, in its specifically Enlightenment expression, served as the intellectual and epistemological basis for the development of early-modern culture in the West.

Within the western world itself, the Enlightenment notion of Reason provided an intellectual and epistemological basis for transcending the diversity of religious traditions that had come into conflict, and had fueled the devastating wars that ravaged European society in the 16th and 17th centuries. At the same time, it provided an ideal intellectual and epistemological basis for establishing and legitimating the hegemony of the West over against the non-western traditions which Europeans were beginning to encounter in Asia, in Africa, and in the Americas.[6] Given these facts, it is not surprising that Reason, as the Enlightenment had come to understand and practice it, became a primary focus in the process of liberal education through which the leaders of early American society were initiated and trained.

The second focus of the elliptical structure that characterized the early-modern pattern of liberal education was classical study. Such classical study began with the discipline of learning classical languages such as Greek, Latin and sometimes Hebrew. Some interpreters have seen this discipline of language study as an exercise designed to provide the educated class with a special kind of cultural adornment, a badge of status that would distinguish the elite from

---

[6]There were, of course, Enlightenment figures who idealized the "noble savage" and recognized an Enlightenment-type orientation outside the West—especially in China. But the fact remains that the Enlightenment rendering of Reason became closely associated with a very strong affirmation of western superiority.

the masses. And this is certainly one of the purposes that was achieved. But at a deeper level, this kind of study was also intended to train the mind; and in so doing, to establish a basis for controlling the passions. It is not by chance that in the books of the period, sexually explicit or pornographic passages were rendered in Latin. Clearly the rationale for this seemingly strange practice was to assure that only those who had undergone an appropriate discipline would be exposed to the dangers that might overwhelm an unprepared reader.

Beyond the basic discipline of language study, classical study also involved the reading of a circumscribed corpus of so-called classical texts that included explicitly religious texts such as the Bible and later works of Christian theology and literature, in addition to Greek and other western texts of a philosophical, historical and literary nature. Again, the purpose was to some extent cultural adornment and the attainment of a badge of cultural and social status. But this played alongside a conviction that the study of classical texts, including specifically religious texts, served to train the mind and to cultivate the virtues that were needed by those who would assume leadership roles in the state, in the Church, and in society as a whole.

It is true that there was a good deal of tension between the prominence and cultivation of Enlightenment rationality on the one hand, and the disciplines associated with classical, Biblical and theological studies on the other; but the inherent tension proved to be very creative indeed. For at least two centuries during the early-modern period, liberal education—operating in terms of this elliptical pattern—proved to be an effective vehicle for initiating the intellectual and social elite that dominated western society.

By the end of the 19th century, however, this early-modern pattern of liberal education had spent its force, and a new pattern had begun to appear. This new pattern had much in common with its predecessor. But there are some very important differences that make it appropriate to characterize it as late-modern in contrast to the early-modern pattern that I have already described.

In the latter half of the 19th century, American society was becoming increasingly caught up in the dynamics of modernity. At this time, two different tendencies can be discerned within colleges and universities. On the one hand, many institutions of higher education, particularly the new state universities, put an increasing and sometimes exclusive emphasis on providing technically oriented training for those who were destined to assume particular roles in agriculture, industry, commerce and the like. Thus, many technically well-trained graduates received little, if any, serious introduction to the liberal arts.

At the same time, the group of students who did participate in the process of liberal education became considerably more diverse than it had been in the past. The most dramatic change was, of course, the greater inclusion of women, although other kinds of folk were also appearing on the scene. Liberal education was still an initiation process carried on by and for a cultural and social elite; but that elite was itself undergoing a transforming process of expansion and diversification.

The late-modern pattern of liberal education that began to emerge in the 19th century was clearly a variant of the older pattern. A very important structural change, however, had taken place. This change involved the emergence of the social sciences as a set of distinctive disciples that claimed to apply the supposedly objective mode of Enlightenment rationality to the study of human phenomena: to psychological phenomena through the science of psychology, and to social phenomena through the sciences of critical history, political science, sociology and anthropology. Thus, the initiatory process of liberal education came to involve training in the Enlightenment-oriented natural sciences, in the Enlightenment-oriented psychological and social sciences, and (at least for those few who were still interested) in a diluted and severely down-graded version of classical studies—a version that came to be labelled "the humanities."

In this situation Biblical, theological and religious studies lost the prominent position that they had held in the early-modern period. Alongside the new sciences that focused on various aspects of human culture, politics and society, a parallel discipline known as *Religionswissenschaft* (translated into English either as "the Science of Religions" or "the History of Religions") *did* appear on the scene. But this discipline had great difficulty establishing its scientific credibility. As a result, it was not able to carve out for itself a viable space within the institutional structure of American universities.[7] Within the humanities, moreover, Biblical studies, theology and religious studies came to be perceived (often, quite accurately) as inappropriate expressions of religious confessionalism. In non-sectarian, private universities and colleges, programs in the humanities gave short shrift to the study of religion; and in many state universities, programs in the humanities either ignored the study of religion completely, or subsumed it under the study of history, literature or the like.

In addition to this change in the structure of liberal education, there was a closely related change in tone that was at least as important. This change in tone can perhaps best be characterized as a critical turn in educational style. Previously, liberal education had been

---

[7]For an interesting discussion of the aborted attempt to establish *Religionswissenschaft* in American universities at the end of the 19th and the beginning of the 20th centuries, see Robert Shepard, "The Science of Religion in American Universities 1880-1930: A Comparison of Six Universities," (University of Chicago Doctoral Dissertation, 1988).

basically supportive of the religious, social and economic institutions of western, bourgeois society. Now, those involved in liberal education began to bring a more critical judgement to bear on established institutions. Some of these critiques were democratic and egalitarian critiques; some were Marxist critiques; some were Freudian critiques; some were militant secularist critiques; and more recently, some have been feminist critiques. The list could be continued. But the point is that knowledge communicated in the context of the initiatory process was increasingly seen as a means of unmasking various forms of false consciousness on which traditional religions and societies, including western religions and societies, had supposedly been based.

In the early-modern period, the "liberal" in liberal education had been taken to specify the kind of education that would appropriately train the "free men" who constituted the elite of the early-modern world. It was an education designed to inculcate well-established religious and cultural values in initiants who were expected to become leaders responsible for the maintenance and development of inherited traditions and institutions. With what I have called the critical turn in the late 19th and early 20th centuries, the adjective "liberal" came to signify something rather different. It came to signal primarily the kind of freedom from inherited religious and cultural prejudices which a critical education could supposedly accomplish. It was assumed that students came to colleges and universities with inadequate values and standards derived from their bourgeois backgrounds; it was the function of a liberal education to submit those values to critical scrutiny and to bring them under the supposedly objective judgement of scientific scholarship.

This triadically structured, critically oriented, late-modern form of liberal education has—over the past century or so—served a very useful purpose. Most of the faculty presently teaching in liberal arts programs across the country received their own educations in institutions where this pattern played a significant role; and it is still playing a significant role in most top-rate liberal arts programs in America today. Moreover, it is a pattern that has been instrumental in fostering some of the most positive developments that have recently occurred in American religion and society. Without question, components derived from this pattern still have a significant contribution to make. But, unless I am woefully inaccurate in my reading of the present crisis, its most creative force has been spent. The social and intellectual presuppositions on which this late-modern pattern of liberal education have been based are disintegrating, and a new vision is required.

This leads, then, to a discussion of the third pattern of liberal education. I will begin by commenting more specifically on some of the developments that have brought about the demise of the earlier pat-

terns, developments that provide the context for a new pattern that
we see beginning to emerge. I will then go on to consider some of the
already visible components of a new, and more viable, alternative.

The reasons for the contemporary crisis in liberal education are
legion. But there are three closely related developments that are absolutely basic. The first of these is the emergence, in recent decades, of a
global order which we, as Americans and westerners, can no longer
control purely on our own terms, purely for our own purposes. We
are now living in a world in which we must continually confront, in
very immediate and practical ways, the intractable reality of "others"
as diverse as the South Africans, the Russians, the Iranians and the
Japanese. In this new situation, we require a global perspective and
understanding which neither the early-modern nor the late-modern
pattern of liberal education is able to provide.

The second major factor that has led to the present crisis in liberal
education is the process of pluralization that has occurred within
American society itself. The first, tentative steps in this direction occurred during the 19th century; but since World War II, the process
has become increasingly radical and pervasive. At one level, this process of pluralization has resulted from the fact that native Americans,
blacks, women and other previously silenced groups already present
in American society have found a more public voice; and thus, the
various kinds of "otherness" that they represent have come to be expressed and heard within the arena of public discourse and debate.

At another level, this process of pluralization has been fueled by
the fact that many minority communities that were once small and
isolated have begun to emerge as extremely important factors in the
structure and dynamics of American life. Here, the first group that
comes to mind is the Hispanic community which continues its extremely rapid growth, both in terms of its size and its influence. But
in addition to the Hispanics, there are also a wide variety of non-Eu-
ropean, predominantly non-Christian groups that are rapidly expanding their numbers and very quickly making their way into the
mainstream of American society. These include, among many others,
the Japanese, the Southeast Asians, the Indians and the Arabs.

At this point, there is no way in which the rise of previously
marginalized and newly immigrating groups can possibly be re-
versed. In this situation liberal education—if it is to be at all relevant
to the experiential realities of American life—must obviously take this
new ethnic and religious pluralization seriously into account. It must
attend, in other words, to the new kind of "mutual otherness" that is
coming to characterize the relationships that pertain among the many
ethnically and religiously diverse segments that now constitute the
American republic (and that will increasingly constitute it in the fu-

ture). In this situation, the early-modern and late-modern patterns of liberal education are simply not adequate to the task at hand.

In addition to the new global context in which we live, and the ethnic and religious pluralization of our own American society, there has been a major intellectual transformation that must also be taken into account. As we have seen, the early and late-modern patterns of liberal education have depended to a great extent on the acceptance of the Enlightenment conception of Reason, and on a strong faith in its power to generate theories that are taken to be universally true and socially efficacious. These inherited patterns of liberal education depended heavily on the conviction that the Enlightenment mode of rationality provides a prejudice-free mechanism for discerning and exploring the factual truth about the one purely objective natural and social world in which all human beings, whether they know it or not, are destined to live. The problem, of course, is that in a post-modern, pluralized world, this Enlightenment conception of Reason is rapidly losing its credibility.

The breakdown of the Enlightenment rendering of Reason first became apparent in the arena where the Enlightenment perspective had gained its greatest currency and won its greatest victories— namely, in the natural sciences. The story began to unfold with the introduction of new notions of relativity, indeterminacy and observer-impact by physicists such as Einstein, Heisenberg and Bohr. The plot unfolded further in the works of philosophers of science such as Thomas Kuhn, works that have demonstrated that Enlightenment rationality in general, and scientific theories in particular, are—like all other renderings of human reason—a historical product subject to various kinds of historical limitations and contingencies.[8] What is more, contemporary social scientists have long since joined the chorus. Witness, for example, the very different critiques of various aspects of the Enlightenment rendering of Reason that have been mounted by Edward Shils[9], Clifford Geertz[10], and (most recently) Renato Rosaldo.[11]

With the disintegration of the Enlightenment myth of Objective Reason, educators caught up in the early and late-modern patterns of liberal education face a very uncomfortable set of alternatives. They can ignore the changing intellectual climate and proceed with business as usual. They can adopt, or at least implicitly countenance, a

---

[8]*The Structure of Scientific Revolutions* (2nd ed.; Chicago: University of Chicago Press, 1970).

[9]*Tradition* (Chicago: University of Chicago Press, 1981).

[10]*Local Knowledge* (New York: Basic Books, 1983), or his more recent book, *Works and Lives: the Anthropologist as Author* (Stanford: Stanford University Press, 1988).

[11]*Culture and Truth* (Stanford: Stanford University Press, 1989).

kind of cheap relativism that despairs of finding any intellectually defensible procedures for making real life decisions—a kind of cheap relativism that implies that, at least as far as the academy is concerned, anything goes. Or they can resort to some kind of half-disguised dogmatism that supports their preconceived prejudices or assuages their pent-up guilt. But none of these responses to the demise of the Enlightenment rendering of Reason has proved to be convincing to educators themselves, to their students, or to the public at large. Hence, the intellectual malaise and frustration that characterizes so much that presently goes on in the name of liberal education.

If the foregoing analysis of the social and intellectual situation that has brought about the crisis in liberal education is basically correct, then the crucial question that faces liberal educators can be specified quite precisely. That question goes as follows: What must we do in order to establish an a truly new pattern of liberal education that can provide a relevant initiation and training for the leaders of a new kind of society that is globally oriented, ethnically and religiously pluralized, and post-modern in its intellectual orientation? I have no final answers, but I do have some suggestions.

Conservatives such as Bennett and Bloom have attempted to depict the contemporary debate in liberal education as an encounter between the defenders of intellectual standards and those who are willing to sacrifice intellectual principles in order to accommodate political pressures from irresponsible or disgruntled segments of the population. In contrast, my contention—and that of the other authors contributing to the present volume—is that the establishment of social relevance in our increasingly globalized and pluralized society, and the achievement of intellectual integrity in an increasingly post-modern intellectual environment, can and must be two aspects of a single reconstructive process.

At the level of context, a more diversified constituency must be actively recruited not only in higher education in general, but (and I am convinced that this will be a much more difficult goal to accomplish) in liberal education in particular. It is important that the members of new groups that are coming to play a greater role in the mainstream of American life be encouraged to take advantage of the economically rewarding opportunities that the vocational and professional aspects of higher education in America have provided in the past, and will continue to provide in the future. But it is equally important for the health and well-being of the society as a whole that members of these groups participate with members of already established groups in a new kind of process of liberal education: that they become involved, along with their contemporaries from more established backgrounds, in a new form of educational initiation and training that will prepare everyone concerned for creative participation in the leadership of various political, religious and social aspects of a post-modern, pluralized society.

But recruitment efforts in themselves are obviously not sufficient. At the same time that our recruitment efforts are being pursued, we must also carry forward the process of discerning and implementing a post-modern, pluralistic pattern of liberal education that will evoke and justify the participation that we seek. At this point, the details of the structure of a new pattern of liberal education that will be equal to the challenge have yet to be specified. The intellectual basis for such a pattern, however, is already being established; and the tone that needs to characterize the educational process is already evident.

The way towards a pattern of liberal education that will be appropriate for students who will be living in a post-modern, pluralized world has been opened up by new intellectual developments that are rapidly gaining ground in the academy.[12] These new developments include the increasing recognition of the implications of the historical embeddedness of all human individuals and groups, including not only "others," but ourselves as well. They include an increasing recognition of the importance of the fact that all human individuals and groups, including both "others" and ourselves, construct or discover a multiplicity of historically conditioned worlds in which they live and think. And they include an increasing recognition of the importance of the fact that all individuals and groups (again including both "others" and ourselves) create and recreate these historically conditioned worlds through many diverse processes in which various types of human imagination and various styles of human rationality coalesce in a wide variety of different ways.

This new understanding of the human enterprise as the historically conditioned creation and recreation of multiple worlds in which to live and think is presently being explored by many of the best scholars in a wide variety of disciplines. In philosophy, for example, Nelson Goodman has written an important book entitled *Ways of World Making* in which he takes both aesthetic sensibilities and rational processes seriously into account.[13] And in psychology, Jerome Bruner has recently published an analysis of the imaginative and reflective aspects of world construction under the equally intriguing title, *Actual Minds, Possible Worlds.*[14]

Other scholars are analyzing the dynamics and results of this process of world creation in more specific contexts. Stephen Toulmin has

---

[12]For a discussion of a number of very important aspects of the situation not highlighted below, see the excellent essay by Thomas A. Byrnes entitled, "Dialogical Rationality: A New Context for Religious Studies and Liberal Education," *Criterion* 26:2 (1987) pp. 11-14.

[13]Indianapolis: Hackett Publishing Company, 1978.

[14]Cambridge: Harvard University Press, 1986.

described the closely correlated roles of imaginative hypotheses and practical reason in the formation and maintenance of scientifically defined worlds.[15] Paul Ricoeur has analyzed various ways in which human imagination and human reason work together in creating and recreating the worlds that are constituted by literary texts.[16] David Tracy and I have edited a forthcoming book entitled *Myth and Philosophy* which includes essays that describe the integral and ongoing coalescence of imaginative and more discursive modes of thought in the creation and communication of religious worlds from ancient Greece and Japan, to contemporary New Zealand and the modern west.[17] In a rather different mode, Mark Johnson (a philosopher) and George Lakoff (a cognitive scientist) have joined together to examine ways in which the metaphoric imagination combines with rational reflection in the process of constituting the everyday worlds in which ordinary people pursue their ordinary lives.[18]

This new, post-modern emphasis on the human enterprise as a historical process in which culturally embedded individuals and communities continually construct and reconstruct various kinds of worlds opens up the possibility for a new, post-modern pattern of liberal education that can be both intellectually sound and socially efficacious. In terms of its basic intellectual structure, this new post-modern pattern of liberal education would be much more unified than either its early-modern or late-modern predecessors. To be sure, the triadic structure that differentiates the natural sciences, the social sciences and the humanities might well be retained for pragmatic purposes. But there would be no unbridgeable gap between the three segments; nor would there be an implicit hierarchy that ranked them in terms of their conformity to a single ideal of purely "objective" rationality. Rather, the major divisions of the liberal arts curriculum, and the various disciplines within them, would be recognized as dif-

---

[15]*Human Understanding: The Collective Use and Evolution of Concepts* (Princeton: Princeton University Press, 1977).

[16]For one of Ricoeur's many treatments of the subject, see his *Interpretation Theory* (Fort Worth: Texas Christian University Press, 1976).

[17]Albany: State University of New York Press, forthcoming 1990. This book is the first volume in a new series entitled *Toward a Comparative Philosophy of Religion*. Volume III, which is another collection of essays that David Tracy and I are editing (*Discourse and Praxis*, forthcoming from SUNY Press is 1991), will also contain a number of contributions that are directly relevant to the present discussion.

[18]*Metaphors We Live By* (Chicago: University of Chicago Press, 1980). The philosophical basis and implications of the ideas put forward in this book are much more fully developed by Johnson in *The Body in the Mind* (Chicago: University of Chicago Press, 1987). See especially his chapter on "Kant and the Imagination." The cognitive science side is more fully developed by Lakoff in *Women, Fire, and Other Dangerous Things* (Chicago: University of Chicago Press, 1987).

ferent kinds of humanly constructed or discovered (and therefore historically conditioned and limited) worlds of thought. In this situation each of these segments and disciplines would have to justify the processes of imagination and rationality through which it generates and maintains its particular world; and to defend the value of that world for individuals and for society as a whole.[19]

At the same time that this new, post-modern pattern of liberal education would have a more unified intellectual foundation than its predecessors, it would be much more flexible in its subject matter. Liberal education, in this new format, would include the study of a variety of different kinds of worlds constructed or discovered by a variety of different kinds of people. It would include the study of natural-scientific worlds, fictional worlds, religious worlds, aesthetic worlds, and social worlds. It would include the study of worlds constructed or discovered by privileged elites, and worlds constructed or discovered by peoples relegated to the margins of society. It would include worlds constructed or discovered by Europeans, and worlds constructed or discovered by the peoples of Asia, Africa and the Americas. It would include worlds that have been generated and communicated in and through classic texts, and worlds generated and communicated through popular story-telling, music, architecture and dance. It would include the study of worlds that have been generated in the past, and worlds that are being generated in the present. And—perhaps most important of all—it would include studies of worlds familiar to the students (including worlds they themselves live and think in), as well as the unfamiliar worlds of "others."

Obviously, no particular institution or individual student would be in a position cover all of the areas suggested here, much less the even fuller range that would be included within a liberal education that might be considered in some sense "complete." Particular institutions and individual students would necessarily have to make choices relevant to their own distinctive situation—choices that would combine appropriate amounts and types of diversity with an appropriate opportunity for studies-in-depth.[20]

---

[19]See Kenneth Bruffee's essays on, "The Structure of Knowledge and the Future of Liberal Education," *Liberal Education* 67:3 (1981) pp. 177-86; and, "Liberal Education and the Social Justification of Belief," *Liberal Education* 68:2 (1982) pp. 95-114. Though Bruffee's position is in many respects rather different from the one set forth here, these essays were ground-breaking when they appeared and remain important resources for those interested in the subject.

[20]This having been said, it should also be noted that it is possible to incorporate a considerable amount of this kind of diversity within a single, well-organized and well-focused course. A number of useful suggestions for such course can be found in the two other volumes published in the *Religious Studies and Liberal Education* series. The interested reader should also consult James Dalton's proposal in his essay on "Theory and Practice in the Teaching of American Reli-

In order for this more unified, yet more pluralistic pattern of liberal education to function creatively in initiating and training students for leadership in a post-modern, pluralized society, it must be characterized by an appropriate pedagogical tone. It cannot have the essentially conservative tone of its early-modern predecessor. Nor can it have the essentially critical tone of its late-modern predecessor. Nor can it condone the kind of cheap relativism that ignores the necessity of evaluation, choice and judgement.

On the contrary, this new, post-modern pattern of liberal education will have to exhibit and cultivate a pedagogical style that can perhaps best be characterized as hermeneutical or dialogical. In this new context, teachers and students alike must use their own powers of imagination and rationality to discern and reform, to expand and integrate, the various worlds in which they themselves live and think. And they must do this in and through creative encounters and interactions with new people(s) and new worlds that they confront, both directly and indirectly, in the course of their teaching on the one hand, and their studies on the other. Thus, the "liberal" in liberal education must come—in this new context—to mean the freedom that individuals and groups achieve as they learn to create, in and through their imaginative and actual encounters with other people(s) and other worlds, new realities that will be of benefit both to themselves and to society as a whole.

The possibility of actually implementing this new kind of post-modern, pluralistic pattern of liberal education poses a challenge to the entire academy. Potentially, at least, each and every discipline associated with the liberal arts has a distinctive contribution to make, and a distinctive role to play. For a variety of reasons, however, both intrinsic and accidental, religious studies has a special responsibility and a special opportunity.

Because of its distinctive history within the modern academy, religious studies is in a position to play a significant role in developing the intellectual foundations that are needed, and in cultivating the hermeneutic/dialogical tone that is required. Much earlier than most other disciplines, religious studies experienced the collapse of traditional norms. As a result, it was one of the first disciplines to face the necessity of searching out a middle way between a return to dogmatism on the one hand, and a cheap relativism on the other. Also, because of its distinctive history, religious studies has been forced to confront, more seriously than most of its sister disciplines, the historical embeddedness of all human expressions, including the interpre-

---

gion," *Criterion* 26:2 (1987) pp. 19-21. For suggestions concerning a Bible course that could (with some refinements) meet this criteria, see Raymond Williams' essay, "The New Testament and the Liberal Arts" that is published in the same collection.

tive expressions formulated by academics themselves. Certainly no one would claim that religious studies scholars have produced any definitive answers in either of these very difficult and complex areas. They have, however, over the years generated a variety of insights that can be helpful in grounding and implementing the new pattern of liberal education that is beginning to emerge.[21]

Religious studies is also in a very distinctive position by virtue of the particular kind of subject matter that comes within its ken. Religious worlds have been (and continue to be) prominent in virtually all times and places, among virtually all types of people. These religious worlds provide profound and fascinating examples of how human beings employ various modes of imagination and rationality in various combinations and contexts. And they are worlds that pose and answer questions about the most fundamental and controversial issues of individual and social life. Thus, those who present and interpret these religious worlds have an ideal opportunity to attract and engage a very diverse group of students; to confront those students with a wide range of data that is both challenging and interesting; and to cultivate, with them, the necessary virtues of appreciative awareness on the one hand and critical judgement on the other.

Given the present political, economic and social climate in America, I am not certain to what extent it will be possible to convince colleges and universities across the country to build comprehensive programs of liberal education that will more fully embody and implement the kind of new, post-modern, pluralistic pattern of liberal education that I have tried to envision. Nor am I certain to what extent it will be possible to convince departments of religion to offer courses and construct majors that will exhibit the kind of intellectual and pedagogical dynamics that I have tried to describe. However, in this very uncertain situation, there are at least four points that *are* certain and that need to remain to the fore as we look to the future.

The first is that American society, in the 1990s and beyond, will need leaders in many different fields of endeavor who are capable of operating confidently and cooperatively in a post-modern, highly globalized and pluralized environment. The second is that in America, liberal education programs in colleges and universities provide the only institutional setting where such leaders can be given the kind of intellectual initiation and training that will prepare them for this kind of task. The third is that conditions presently exist that make it possible to reconstruct liberal education in such a way that an appro-

---

[21]For a sketch of the historical development of religious studies that focuses on the early introduction and impact of these issues in religious studies discourse, see Sheryl Burkhalter and Frank Reynolds, "Privileging the Periphery: Reflections on Religious Studies and the Liberal Arts" *Criterion* 26:2 (1987) pp. 2-6.

priate kind of intellectual initiation and training can, in fact, be provided. The fourth is that those of us who are engaged in the practice of religious studies have a very special opportunity (and, therefore, a very special obligation) to participate creatively in this reconstructive process.

THE UNIVERSITY, THE LIBERAL ARTS, AND THE TEACHING AND STUDY OF RELIGION

Charles H. Long

This essay places the issue of liberal education within the context of exchanges. I have approached the issue in this manner rather than the more abstract, and perhaps more familiar, discussion of "What constitutes an educated person?" because I believe the problem of education as cultural formation requires a broader and more concrete framework for its discussion. In one sense, I do address the issue posed by the above question, as education in any culture has to do with the empowering of individuals to enhance and contribute to their specific cultural milieu. But I move beyond the traditional parameters of the question in discussing the extent to which processes of formation involve knowing the order, structure and dynamics of a variety of exchanges within a social situation, whether these exchanges be intellectual, social, material or political in nature.

My perspective in discussing this dimension of liberal education has been informed by meanings related to my grammar and high school education in Little Rock, Arkansas. It was in the 1930s that the parents of black students had to fight through the wide range of problems related to the communicative orders of our society in the establishment of a high school for African-American youth. This debate was carried on between the African-American citizens and the Little Rock Board of Education. The rhetoric of the debate was defined by the competing philosophies of education as espoused by W. E. B. DuBois and Booker T. Washington.

Stated in most general terms, the issue of contention had to do with whether the proper education for African-American youth should emphasize vocational/technical training, or whether high school education should be devoted to the liberal arts curriculum. Two differing notions of the functioning of reason and the nature and understanding of exchanges lay behind these opposing philosophies. Washington's notion was a more strategic one: the training in vocational/technical crafts would enable the African-American minority to realize a viable economic position. He recognized the relationship between economic and political social power; the goal of education was the enhancement of technical/vocational skills which would enable his community to find its legitimate place in American society. DuBois' position did not negate the necessity of vocational training; however, he thought that the primary goal of education, especially for a persecuted racial minority in the United States, should be the creation of an intellectual perspective on the cultural situation as a possibility for a truly democratic republic. This brought the issues of reason to the fore as a critique of the status quo on the one hand, and as the necessary creative structure in the constitution of a just society on the other.

In my mind, the two conflicting philosophies of Washington and Dubois are now mirrored with reminiscent intensity in the more general debate over the future of liberal education for the country as a whole. Washington's emphasis on technical/vocational competence is currently played out on a much broader scale with the priority now given to pre-professional competency and skills as the basis for a college degree. DuBois' position currently finds expression by those who continue to hold to an Enlightenment vision of reason as a basis for formation through education. Although this 1930s debate has fundamentally informed my perspective on current issues in liberal education, it is clear that one can not turn to the vision of either leader for an answer to our current dilemma. All the same—and, perhaps, more importantly—it is equally clear that neither answer can be ignored.

We must work through the kind of materiality represented by Washington's position, as well as the more ideational and spiritual meaning of formation as represented by DuBois. Only then, I believe, will we be in a position to recognize the relationship between reason as a primary orientation to our body politic and national community, and reason as the ordering power of the university.

Addressing the interface of the debate in this manner requires that contextualization be given our notions of reason as the organizing principle of the university. I address this issue of context by focusing on the various exchanges operative within our society. First of all, the exchange between society and organized knowledge as expressed in the university; second, the exchange within the structure and order of reason itself; and third, the exchange between reason and the ground of reason. The sections dividing this paper reflect these three moments in this discussion of exchange. I begin by setting forth some of the formative notions present in the emergence of the American university in the latter quarter at the turn of the 20th century. I attempt to address the emergence of higher education in this period at it relates to the technologization and industrialization of American society. I then turn to a discussion of how reason within the university organizes knowledge on the one hand, but in its critical capacity it undertakes a critique of reason itself. Finally, I relate the critique of reason both to the study of religion and to the materiality and historicity of our cultural modalities.

History and Context of the American University

The problem of a general education and the liberal arts, along with the more specific issue of the meaning of the teaching and study of religion within these contexts, is coterminous with the rise of the modern American university. Seldom do discussions of liberal or general education pay attention to the historical dimensions of this development. Consequently, discussions and proposals for reform in liberal education tend to be delimited by a rather abstract or philosophical discourse. Historical perspective does not afford a more definite answer to the current dilemma of where to go with liberal education; but it does open up the arena of possible solutions and strategies by providing them a quite different context for discussion. I therefore begin this discussion with an outline of the American university in its formation. Addressing the theoretical considerations that arise from the history and practice of the university will afford a quite different vantage point for discussing a theory of university education, and an argument for the organization of knowledge and a pedagogy appropriate for it, which I take up with the second section of this paper.

One possible date for marking the beginning of a new and decisive role of the American university as a cultural force on the national scene is 1862. In this year, Congress passed the Morrill Act which granted federal aid to states for college instruction in agriculture and mechanics. Shortly after this, in 1868, Ezra Cornell's aspiration to, "found an institution where any person can find instruction in any study" was instituted as Cornell University; and in 1869, Charles W. Eliot was elected president of Harvard. It was Eliot who led Harvard from a college to a university, encouraging graduate study and abandoning the traditional, fixed classical curriculum in favor of a system of free student electives.[1] Johns Hopkins opened its doors in 1876 as

---

[1]The history of the American research university came from a very good book, *A City and Its Universities* by Steven J. Diner (Chapel Hill: University of North Carolina Press, 1980). The city referred to is Chicago. I obviously had the University of Chicago in mind in the writing of this section. I do not know of another University that has carried on such a sustained and intense discussion of the issues involved in university education in general and the liberal/general education in particular. In this regard, I also consulted *The Idea and Practice of General Education. An Account of the College of The University of Chicago*, ed. F. Champion Ward (Chicago: University of Chicago Press, 1950); *The Idea of the University of*

the first institution with a graduate program; and in 1881 Columbia began its first graduate program. Clark University, in 1889, was the first American university organized as only a graduate school. And the University of Chicago was inaugurated in 1892.

The period that witnessed this activity among the most prominent of America's educational institutions is synonymous with what has been characterized as the Gilded Age in American cultural history. The organization and institutionalization of higher education as represented by these universities mirrors a potpourri of meanings, intentions, and hopes—a potpourri that in large part continues to form the context of discussions devoted to the educational mission of American higher education.

In the post-Civil War period, industrialization, and the accumulation of wealth by those who had amassed of vast amounts of capital in the process, would have a profound effect on American higher education. Industrialization also led to training in those new knowledges and skills that would enhance and allow the population to cope with these changes. On the one hand, higher education in the land-grant colleges (thanks to Senator Morrill), and in the private universities such as Cornell, vied for support from the industrial sector by offering practical courses in agriculture, engineering, and mechanics—a curricula directly related to the demands inherent in the technologization of society. On the other hand, universities such as Johns Hopkins, Clark and Chicago were seeking support for a form of higher education that championed rigorous academic study and methods of pure research, while eschewing more practical, technical, utilitarian ends.

These two kinds of universities, or the two kinds of aims represented by those universities that had their origins in the Gilded Age, posed the issue of the liberal arts in a rather stark manner. There were, to be sure, problems of liberal education internal to the constitution of all the new university models; but a prior issue of liberal education had already been posed in the myriad of colleges and universities that had come into being before the Civil War. In this group must be included many private schools, state universities, and denominationally oriented institutions of higher learning throughout the country. For one reason or another, these schools were not confronted—or refused to confront—the issues of industrialization and culture as posed in the organization and structure of the new universities. To the extent that the problem arose, more often than not they expressed a reactive or counter meaning of the nature of the human

---

Chicago, eds. W.M. Murphy and D.J.R. Bruckner (Chicago: The University of Chicago Press, 1976); and Richard J. Storr, *Harper's University, The Beginnings* (Chicago: The University of Chicago Press, 1966).

and society. For most of them defined liberal education as the education of a gentleman or the forming of a "cultured" individual.

Given this history, the discussion of liberal education was defined by three distinct arenas: 1) by the new research and graduate private universities where it took on the rhetoric and practice of specialization and/or professional education as over against a liberal education; 2) by the land-grant colleges where the issue was defined as liberal education as over against a technological training; and 3) by the liberal arts colleges which placed the liberal arts in tension with the vulgarization of culture by either technology or specialization. In many cases, the liberal arts colleges were attempting to form an educated person in contradistinction to the specialized scholar or the technically trained individual.

These three contexts for the discussion and organization of higher education were not exerted with equal force on the American scene. The high ground was taken by the new research universities, and this for several reasons. First of all, they were all inspired by the novelty of creating a new kind of American University; second, they tapped into the coffers of the new financial resources of entrepreneurial capitalism; and third—and probably most important as it relates to the internal ordering of the university—the new universities were forced to create a new theoretical and practical meaning of reason that represented a continuity with the dynamics of society on one hand, and a discontinuity and distance from its presuppositions and goals on the other.

For example, while Johns Hopkins and the University of Chicago made much of the rigorous scientific and intellectual structure in their research, the leaders of these institutions from their inception carried on a high-powered public language of involvement in the social and cultural meanings of their respective local communities and the general problems of the nation. Furthermore, it is significant to note that though the University of Chicago has always possessed excellence in the physical and natural sciences as well as in those areas that have come to be known as the Humanities, from the very beginnings of the University the public service languages and those departments and schools related in a direct manner to the sociological aspects of culture—sociology, social work, education, political science, etc.—remained to the fore. Significantly, the first university building ever dedicated to the study of society as a scientific endeavor was the Social Science Building at the University of Chicago.

Daniel C. Gilman, the founding president of Johns Hopkins, toyed with the idea of limiting the university to graduate study and research; but he was dissuaded from this course by several of his advisors who warned him that such a notion smacked of elitism and would probably cause public alienation. Gilman was attentive to his advisors and created a college as well as a graduate school. But more than this, he and his colleagues actively engaged in a wide range of community activities, from public education and serving on state commissions, to engaging in matters dealing with safe water supply and wrestling with issues of social medicine.

Clark University, which opened as a graduate school in 1880, foundered in the early 1890s. This was due in part to the idiosyncratic actions of its founder and benefactor, Jonas Clark. It was equally due to the fact that Clark University never established the wider arena for the expression of the ranges of reason, practical and theoretical, for the proper ordering of the university in this period. No provisions were made for a more general discussion of the meaning of the university within the structures of society, or for a discussion of the proper pedagogy incumbent upon the university in the training of youth.

It could be argued that the Universities of Chicago and Johns Hopkins were simply following the equally idiosyncratic styles of their founding presidents. And, in part, this is true. William Rainy Harper was an activist academic. According to Joseph E. Gould, he was "a young man in a hurry." Many of the educational activities of a public sort had grown out of his experience with the Chatauqua movement and the generalized notions of the necessity for education in a democratic country. There is, however, an additional and deeper level manifested in the peculiar circumstances of the new research universities and the opportunities for new intellectual approaches to the problem of knowledge itself and the expression of knowledge in teaching, research, and as a beneficent meaning in society at large.

I have already alluded to the fact that though the University of Chicago has always shown excellence in the natural physical sciences and the Humanities, its earliest and abiding rhetorics stemmed from and related to the scientific and practical meaning of the "sociological sciences." Louis Wirth's classic essay, "Urbanism as a Way of Life," is a symbolic expression of the basis and principle for the possibilities of a new form of knowledge and its organization in the new universities and in the university reforms of the Gilded Age. Michel Foucault addressed this development in the human sciences with the following:

> The first thing to be observed is that the human sciences did not inherit a certain domain, already outlined, perhaps surveyed as a whole, but allowed to lie fallow, which it was then their task to elaborate with positive methods and with concepts that had at last become scientific . . . for man did not exist (anymore than life, or language, or labor); and the human sciences did not appear when, as a result of some pressing rationalism, some unresolved scientific problem, some practical concern, it was decided to include man (willy-nilly, and with a greater or lesser degree of success); . . . [the human sciences] appeared *when man constituted himself in Western culture as both that which must be conceived of and that which is to be known*. There can be no doubt, certainly, that the

historical emergence of each one of the human sciences was occasioned by a problem, a requirement, an obstacle of a theoretical or practical order: the new norms imposed by industrial society . . . were certainly necessary before psychology, slowly, in the course nineteenth century, could constitute itself as a science.[2]

The new universities, as research institutions, implied a new structure in the order of knowledge on both theoretical and practical levels. The meaning of nature and human effort as work and culture form the contours of a new debate within the structures of knowledge itself. The urban setting is the context for the setting forth of this debate as theoretical and practical, as the city is a microcosm of the communicative systems of material and ideational exchanges which are national and international in scope. Research as a defining characteristic of the university implies a theoretical "world" capable of providing the clues and traces which would enable this new world to become habitable and beneficial to the human community.

At a somewhat later period, similar developments took place along more or less the same lines in several of state universities, such as the Universities of Minnesota and Wisconsin. I know more of this history at my former university, the University of North Carolina. It was through research in the sociological sciences that a break was made from the university being a place for the formation of the gentry into the university as a place for the exercise of a critical cultural consciousness. In this case, the options were clear-cut. The agrarians of the literary tradition had set forth a self-conscious ideology for the "fashioning of a gentlemen" as a model for Southern education. It possessed even greater power because it fed into southern values and the ideology of the South. The empirical research and the critical cultural languages stemming from the researches of Howard Odum and Guy B. Johnson made an end run around this ideology and placed the University within the structures, languages, and procedures of the new university as a research institution.[3]

The economy, ecology, and ecumenical meanings of the American research university are touched upon in these dimensions of its history. The economy, in its vulgar material sense, may be seen in the relationship of the university to its patrons, the new capitalists. Again, this economy leads to the deployment of university resources to enhance and criticize the structures of urban society. The univer-

---

[2]Michel Foucault, *The Order of Things: An Archeology of the Human Sciences* (New York: Vintage Book, Random House, 1970) pp. 344-45.

[3]Daniel Joseph Singal, *The War Within: From Victorian to Modernism, 1919-1945* (Chapel Hill: The University of North Carolina Press, 1982). This work is a kind of analogue to Diner's work cited above. While Diner discusses the university and the urban situation, Singal's work treats this same kind of problem in the context of agrarianism and its implications—economic, cultural, and literary.

sity is thus continuous with the forms of its society in its public service aspect, and discontinuous with it in its theoretical structures. The physical location of many of these universities at the time of their founding was more often than not far removed from the heart of the activities of its patrons, the business community, and its clients, the indigent—the poor, women, blacks, laborers—all victims in one way or another, of the new urban world. The physical separation between the university and the urban centers thus might be seen to reflect the gap we have discussed in the meaning of knowledge as a cultural production.

In this section, I have attempted to do several things: first of all, to locate issues of higher education in America within a historical context; second, to show how the problems and tensions of curricula and the organization of knowledge arose in the American research university; and third, to draw out implications regarding the meaning of organized and institutionalized knowledge as a structure of society. This discussion brings us to acknowledge that although issues of liberal education are part of a curricular structure at the undergraduate level, the debate about it was, and continues to be, dominated by the more comprehensive theories and practices of the research university. To the extent that these universities express the wider meanings of the nature and function of reason, they afford a requisite perspective for addressing the notion of a liberal education in its relation to reason.

The Economy of Reason in the University

I raise this more comprehensive meaning of the systematic ordering of knowledge within the university in the terms of the "economy of reason." I have already alluded to the gross, material, financial, and conventional meaning of the economy and the rise of the research university in the United States in the section above. In this section, I shall be speaking of those levels of meaning in the term "economy" that refer to its more archaic derivation as the systematic dispensation of power over a field or area. This meaning implies another Greek term, "oecumene," or ecumenical as relating to that field or area over which the power is dispensed. I will therefore be speaking of the power of reason as a production, as an activity and a product which can be used within and without the confines of the university. And then I must of necessity speak of reason as a mode or capacity in itself and for itself.

Obviously, reason and its practice are not confined to the university community. The university is, however, that institution that recognizes, orders its life, and carries on its activities as an expression of the principle of reason. Reason is the active principle in its practical activities and goals, as in the rhetorical and theoretical justification for its being. This does not mean that the principle of reason is equally exemplified in all universities; all the same, it is difficult to find a university that has constituted itself against the notion of reason. Let me begin this discussion with a statement from the venerable Aristotle—from the *Metaphysics*.

> All men by nature desire to know. An indication of this is the delight we take in our senses; for even apart from their usefulness they are loved for themselves; and above all others the sense of sight. For not only with a view to action, but even when we are not going to do anything, we prefer seeing (one might say) to everything else. The reason is that, most of all senses, makes us know and brings to *light* many differences between things. By nature animals are born with the faculty of sensation, and from sensation, memory is produced in some of them but not in others. And therefore the former are more intelligent and apt at learning than those which cannot remember; *those which are incapable of hearing sounds are intelligent though they cannot be taught, e.g., the bee, and other races of animals that may be like it; and those which besides memory have this sense of hearing can be taught.* [*Metaphysics*, 980-980b]

This is as good a place as any for beginning a discussion of the principle of reason and the various forms it takes in the organization of knowledge, for Aristotle's *Metaphysics* not only delineates the forms of knowledge, their bases and processes; it also sets forth the meaning of reason as a universal attribute of the human and systematic reason as philosophy. More than this, Aristotle introduces the empirical and metaphorical meanings of knowledge as seeing and hearing as defining the possibility for learning.

The principle of reason within the university thus yields at least two kinds of expressions: one pertains to practical knowledge, knowledge for the sake of doing; the other, to the desire to know for the sake of knowing, the desire for knowledge for no practical purpose. Both expressions of the exercise of reason, however, constitute modes of social power. The practical meaning of knowledge as power is self-evident. Knowledge for no purpose, however, also constitutes an expression of social and cultural power. Hannah Arendt's point regarding the origin of the Royal Society is indicative of this meaning. Of this organization she writes,

> When it was founded, members had to agree to take no part in matters outside the terms of reference given it by the King, especially to take no part in political or religious strife. One is tempted to conclude that the modern scientific ideal of 'objectivity' was born here, which would suggest that its origin is political and not scientific. Furthermore, it seems noteworthy that the scientists found it necessary from the beginning to organize themselves into a society, and the fact that the work inside the Royal Society turned out to be vastly more important than work done

outside it demonstrated how right they were. An organization, whether of scientists who have abjured politics or of politicians, is always a political institution; where men organize they intend to act and to acquire power. *No scientific teamwork is pure science, whether its aim is to act upon society and secure its members a certain position within it or—as was and still is to a large extent the case of organized research in the natural sciences—to act together in concert to conquer nature. It is indeed, as Whitehead once remarked, "no accident that an age of science has developed into an age of organisation."*[4]

The power of organized reason as research in the contemporary universities blurs the distinction between pure and practical reason. The power of knowledge on both the theoretical and practical levels is now deployed within a cultural context of informational or communicative systems. It is difficult to locate a clear distinction between practical or instrumental reason from "useless" or theoretical reason. As Jacques Derrida states the case,

> At the service of war, of national and international security, research programs have to encompass the entire field of information, the stockpiling of knowledge, the workings and thus also the essence of language of all semeiotic systems, translations, coding and decoding, the play of presence and absence, hermeneutics, semantics, structural and generative linguistics, pragmatics, rhetoric.

And he continues,

> I am accumulating all these disciplines in a haphazard way on purpose, but I shall end with literature, poetry, the arts, fiction in general: the theory that has these disciplines as its object may be just as useful in ideological warfare as it is in experimentation with variables in all-too-familiar perversions of the referential function.[5]

Derrida is not speaking here of the overt control or subversion of the research and practice of the university by the State. He is referring, rather, to the more comprehensive and pervasive decentralized orders of our culture as they relate to the funding of projects, the legitimacy of course offerings—the totality of evaluative structures operative in a given situation as they relate to the broader cultural context. These kinds of relations were certainly present in the rhetoric

---

[4]*The Human Condition* (Chicago: University of Chicago Press, 1958) p. 271.

[5]Jacques Derrida, "The Principle of Reason: The University in the Eyes of Its Pupils," *Diacritics* 13:3 (1983) p.13. It is clear that I have been influenced, if not convinced, of Derrida's position in this essay. If it was not absolutely incumbent upon me to write an essay, I might have simply submitted his essay for our discussion. The essay is much less idiosyncratic than many of his other writings. Of course, the double entendre in the use of the word "pupils," as referring both to students and the pupil of the eye that refers us back again to Aristotle's discussion of hard-eyed and blinking eyes is a pure Derridian delight.

and strategies employed at the beginnings of the American research universities. In our time, they have simply become more intense.

The rise of the new research university in the United States during the industrial age was the harbinger of an intense symbiotic relationship between the university and its culture, a relationship that directly involves issues of the kind of person the university can or may form through its processes and principles. Again, Derrida remains to the fore with his discussion of this meaning of informational structures.

> Information does not inform merely by delivering an information content, it gives form, 'in-formiert,' 'formiert zugleich.' It installs man in a form that permits him to ensure his mastery on earth and beyond. All this has to be pondered as the effect of the principle of reason, or, put more rigorously, has to be analyzed as the effect of the dominant interpretation of that principle, of a certain emphasis in the way we heed its summons.[6]

In specifying this range within the economy of reason, I am not suggesting a nostalgia for the pre-research university, nor for some pure and pristine understanding of reason, knowledge, or the university that would not have to come to terms with such contextuality. Rather, I present these considerations to give a quite different background for discussing liberal education as an element of the processes and structure of the university.

Such contextualization of reason within its cultural milieu—as exemplified within the university's various departments and schools, and expressed on the theoretical and practical levels of its life—cannot be avoided. There is something to be admired in this function of reason; indeed, there is something internal to the principle of reason itself evidenced in this deployment. It is a fact that reason can and ought to be *rendered*. The verb "to rend" in this context should be seen in terms of its two related meanings: with meaning given "to exchange, circulate, borrow, donate, debt, etc."; but also, with its meaning "to tear or be torn." The university is an arena for the *exchange* of ideas, and the public beyond the university participates in this exchange through the re-presentation of meanings and ideas that constitute the "universe of discourse" that is the university.

But the university is more than the generator of rendered reason. It is incumbent upon the university to at least ponder the most basic issue of reason: On what does the principle of reason—as constitutive of the university, as rendered in its practical and theoretical modes, and as the basis for public debate—on what does this principle of reason ground itself? Can one, as Charles Sanders Peirce asked,

---

[6]Derrida, *op. cit.*, p.14.

"demand a reason for reasonableness itself?"[7] I raise his question at this juncture, as it relates to more recent calls for reform of liberal arts curricula at numerous universities. Many of these reforms are responding to the rendering of reason pervasive within the general culture, and more specifically to the extent to which these forms of rendered reason lay claim to objectivity, authority, and justification within the structures of the research university.

Gerald Grant and David Reisman have researched this problematic with their work, *The Perpetual Dream: Reform and Experiment in the American College*.[8] In defining four different types of educational reform in our recent history, Grant and Reisman make a distinction between what they call "popular reforms" and "telic reforms." Popular reforms are a partial response to meritocratic discontents that came to characterize student life in most selective colleges and universities in the 1960s. Students sought relief in a number of reforms that gave them a greater degree of autonomy by granting them considerable freedom in their choices of curricula and courses. The most popular of these reforms—student-designed majors, free-choice curricula, the abolition of fixed requirements—sought not to establish new institutional aims, but to slow the pace and expand the avenues of approach. That is, these popular reforms simply modified the means of education within the constraints of existing goals traditionally sought by the research-oriented universities.

Telic reforms, on the other hand, attempted to reconfigure the goals themselves. As discussed by Grant and Reisman,

> To some degree, they represent an attack on the hegemony of the giant research-oriented multi-universities and their satellite university colleges. In one sense, these telic reforms could be thought of as counter-revolutionary, that is counter to the rise of the research oriented universities . . . [9]

The authors discuss a number of college reforms, but their work focuses on the detailed analyses of four colleges: St. John's, Kresge College of the University of Santa Cruz, The College of Human Services (CHS), and Black Mountain College.

All of these colleges are characterized as "transdisciplinary." That is, all attempt to realize some end or good to which they recognize academic disciplines and their processes to be subordinate. This is

---

[7]Charles S. Peirce, *Selected Writings, Values in a Universe of Chance,* ed. Philip P. Wiener (New York: Dover Publications, 1958) p. 332. This quote is taken from the essay in the collection entitled, "Definition and Function of the University," and it is the only other essay as perceptive as Derrida's about this matter.

[8]Gerald Grant and David Reisman, *The Perpetual Dream, Reform and Experiment in the American College* (Chicago: The University of Chicago Press, 1978).

[9]Grant and Reisman, *op. cit.,* p. 17.

reflected in their respective forms of teaching. At St. John's, disciplines are believed to serve as falsifying lenses through which students preconceive, or are likely to misconceive, the "natural articulations of the intellectual world." They attempt to remedy this with their Great Books curriculum. At Black Mountain, mixed media events—where poets, musicians, dancers, actors, etc. form the structure of production—attempt to draw theory and practice together on a more egalitarian level. At Kresge, the disciplines are viewed as subordinate to the task of building a community; and at CHS, they are subordinated to the aim of discovering the generic competencies of a humane professional.

I will not continue an analysis of "telic" reforms at these institutions. Suffice it to say that all of them, with the exception of St. John's, fail to come to terms with the centrality of the organizing principle of the university. In one way or another, they mount attacks or form themselves in reaction to one form or another of the rendering reason within the university (the disciplines), or within society (authorities and the professions). In this sense, they mount effective critiques and their goals are admirable; but if one fails to come to terms with more basic issues, reforms of this sort contribute little to the ongoing discussion, with the uniqueness of these reforms precluding generalizations that would be applicable to other situations.

The curriculum at St. Johns' might likewise be critiqued in that it assumes—rather uncritically—the notion of "classical texts" as the embodiment and substance of knowledge and virtue. There does not seem to be any one text or group of texts that would enable the student to undertake a critique of the notion of the "classical" or of the "book" and writing in relationship to reason and knowledge. In addition to this, the history, the size of the student body and the general cultural milieu express an unearned notion of elitism on the class level that is perpetuated with an equally unearned curricular structure.

What all of these reforms have in common is a reaction to the domination of the modes and styles of the research university: Kresge, CHS, and Black Mountain attempt to form individuals outside of what it considers to be the oppressive, objectifying, and authoritative structures operative within the university and beyond. St. John's curriculum, on the other hand, reacts to the specializing and disciplinary archetypes of research universities and graduate schools. Yet in both cases, the notion of community is drawn to the fore. Black Mountain, CHS, and Kresge envision community in futuristic and utopian terms; St. Johns' community presumes the class orientation of a cultural and historical ideal.

Although we might object to the specific telic reforms discussed by Grant and Reisman, these reforms leave us with much to ponder if we recognize them as symptomatic of—rather than solutions to—real problems. I discern in these reforms four areas of concern: 1) the desire for knowledge that is historically and culturally substantive; 2) the desire for knowledge that allows the student to participate in a past, present, and future community; 3) the desire for a form of knowledge that affords a critical stance to other modes of the organization of knowledge in the university and the public arena; and 4) the desire for knowledge as personal growth. At the periphery of all of these desires is the integration of practical and theoretical modes of knowing. Are these legitimate concerns for a liberal education? And if so, how might they be accomplished?

Since the 1960s, we have been confronted with a quite different situation in the discussion of liberal education. The fact that thousands of students graduate from high school without knowing how to read or write is an indication of the meaning that education now has in American culture. It is clear that several of the former gaps and distinctions are no longer present; and where such junctures are present, they are located in different places. For example, the gap defining the physical space of the university as separate from the urban space of its patrons and clients has changed: these physical spaces now merge and interpenetrate, destroying the symbolic space of knowledge as reflection and leisure on the one hand, and a haven for a certain class on the other. The present continuity of spaces presents us with the necessity of finding a concomitant meaning of knowledge within our society.

Now, new kinds of students have appeared on our campuses in large numbers. The college degree has become a form of "citizen legitimation," serving in the way a high school diploma did for previous generations. The generalized meaning of a college education has not been matched by equal attention given to the meaning of a general education. The cliché of a college education as preparation for the "job market" has blurred the distinction between professional and nonprofessional education at the college level. And looming alongside these factors is the specter of "big sports." The actuality and symbols of these sports teams define the relationship of many students to the university; and for a significant alumni the meaning of the university is synonymous with "the teams." The university as an institution in American society is caught up in the communicative, informational, and material randomness of our culture.

This situation demands that the liberal arts address in a new way two aspects of reason as it defines subject matter and pedagogy: 1) how reason is rendered—to explain effect through its causes, and to rationally justify according to roots and principles; and 2) to investigate the grounding of reason itself. It is not enough that reason is rendered, for in the disciplines and forms of knowledge, the principle of reason must imply and express its own inner tension regarding its grounding. That upon which reason is grounded is not itself reason.

Several implications follow from this observation. It provides a quite different perspective from which to address the ways liberal arts curricula seem to alienate many students. To be sure, disciplined modes of thought in the academy are different from those to which students are accustomed: there is a necessary distancing between the activity of thought in the university and other places. But all too often, the reason for this alienation is not in the modes of thought as such, but in the subject matter that is configured to be a *representation* of that which is superior—historically, culturally, structurally, and phenomenologically—from anything in a student's own background. This presupposition of education as the transmission of knowledge which is alien, superior, and objective forces the student to respond to it as little more than packaged information; it, in turn, allows instructors continually to obscure the more fundamental problem of the grounding of reason itself. All of this is aided and abetted by sundry textbooks and the rhetorics they employ to emphasize this mode of passing on information.

I do not think that the issue of the grounding of reason can be postponed to another level: it cannot be left to the more "theoretical" problematics taken up with a graduate education. The basic premise of a liberal education is learning how to know and knowing how to learn. In this arena, the quality and intention of faculty at the undergraduate level is of utmost importance. The kind of faculty I presuppose may well be found at a small liberal arts college, though I find it easier to imagine this kind of faculty at a large research university. I admit to a prejudice for the latter situation, as questioning the grounds of reason can take place most effectively where a community of scholars in their disciplined researches into theoretical and practical reason find ample scope for an honest, skeptical attitude regarding the self-sufficiency of the reason that undergirds their enterprise, and who are then open to the possibility of a mode of thought that is not identical with reason.

The planning of a liberal education should be informed by listening, and a discernment of that which is obscured by reason. The subject matter, whatever it is or may be, should be presented as clearly as possible within the pedagogy of rendered reason (disciplinary orders); but in addition, the instruction should be aware of issues beyond those directly addressed. How does the problem arise as an issue and object of study? What is the context of the issue at stake? What are the broader ramifications of accepting a certain point of view regarding specific issues as the truth?

Questions of this sort are related to listening and discernment at the level of subject matter. Another mode of listening and discernment has to do with the context of teaching—the university, the class-room, the student. Who are the students in your course? Why are they in this course? What contradictions are present in the curricular structure and in the lives these students represent as members of the university community? What might they expect from their education? And finally, what resources do they bring to the task at hand? Some of these issues were represented in the telic reforms at Kresge, CHS, and Black Mountain; but these reforms attempted to make sense of issues of this kind through a denial, or subversion, of reason as the organizing principles of the university.

In asking these questions, I am attempting to suggest a notion of liberal education that goes beyond the forms of rendering reason on both the theoretical and practical levels. *Knowing how to learn, and learning how to know, imply that there are modes of thought that are not limited to the exercise of reason; and it is these modes that place reason within the structures of life itself.* In stating this, I am not speaking of the "irrational" or of obscurantism. I am pointing to the university not simply as a community of scholars, but also and more importantly as a community of thought. Such a community would interrogate the very basis of reason, the arche and radicality of the grounding of reason itself. It is only in this manner that we will be able to educate students who will undertake new analyses in order to evaluate the ends and means of community, and be able to make judicious choices about life.

As this notion has come to me through Derrida, let me cite him again at this point.

> It [the community of thought] would be open to types of research that are not perceived as legitimate today, or that are insufficiently developed in French or foreign institutions, including some research that could be called "basic"; but it would not stop there. We would go one step further, providing a place to work on the *value and meaning* of the basic, the fundamental, on its opposition to goal-orientation, on the ruses of orientation in all its domains. As in the seminar I mentioned earlier, the report confronts the political, ethical, and juridical consequences of such an undertaking.[10]

Clearly Derrida is not referring here to the liberal arts curriculum itself. He is speaking of a community of scholars who would constitute a community of thought that might inform such a curriculum. This could take place in small colleges, but as I have noted above, the optimum place for such a community might be the research-oriented university. Yet seldom is such attention given to this dimension of the liberal arts curriculum in most institutions of higher learning.

---

[10]Derrida, *op. cit.*, p.16.

The Teaching and Study of Religion in a Liberal Arts Curriculum

The teaching and study of religion as a component of a liberal or general education curriculum presents some problems and some real opportunities. First of all, some of the problems. Religion is the only subject matter that is not in continuity with other forms of subject matter in previous secondary formal education. (A possible exception might be made of those students who attended parochial schools, although even this kind of education is not an adequate basis for what they confront at the college level.) It is true that certain disciplines such as sociology and psychology may not be taught in the formal sense on the secondary school level; but their relationship to other disciplines is apparent on the secondary school levels. This means that students do not really know what to expect when they come to a religion course on the college level. Most students' understanding or knowledge of religion is held, whether positively or negatively, in a rather personal manner; and this is usually related to some experience and meaning given to religion by their families and communities. For the most part, their notions of religion have never been subjected to any form of critical thought or reflection.

Second, the teaching and study of religion has a dubious career within the university community. It has been understood as necessary for the faith and morals of the students; it has been denied status as a topic that could or should be taught in the university; and, if such teaching did occur, the faculty and students in such programs were often thought to be "soft-headed" and devoid of the rigor demanded by other forms of study in the university.

Third, in an attempt to prove that their subject matter and methods were just as rigorous as those of other disciplines, scholars and teachers in religion often reduced the meaning of religion to methods, techniques, and modes of thought and analysis that were compatible with other disciplines in the university, thus losing anything unique that such study might have added to the meaning of the curriculum. All of these factors have to do with the even stranger meaning that religion carries within the cultural context of the American constitution and culture. Constitutionally, we are a non-religious nation; culturally, we are a "nation with the soul of a church."

The study and teaching of religion in the university present the opportunity for students to understand *human modes of thought that are of ultimate importance but may be more or less than reason.* Notice I insist that religion involves modes of thought. The modes of thought in religion are not simply extraordinary. There are dimensions of religion that are the same as, or analogous to, the forms of rendering reason; but the totality of the meaning of religion is not expressed in its attempt to set forth the proper modes of rendering reason. It is not incidental that theoretical studies in religion are replete with such terms as "the non-rational" or *"mysterium tremendum fascinans et augustum"* (Otto), or of "mana" (van der Leeuw), or "hierophany" or "symbol" (Eliade). All notions such as these are attempts to get at a meaning of this form of life that cannot be grasped immediately by rendering reason, but by other modes of thought. From the point of view of rendering reason, *"religion is for no reason."*

Now, to be sure, this is not something that can be easily taught at any level of the curriculum. It is possible, through the positivity of rendering reason, to set forth the meaning of religion in general and particular religions and religious forms within the context of rendered reason. And I believe this is precisely what should be done in the teaching of religion. Indeed, as noted above, there are aspects of all religion that are quite conducive to this mode of explication. The very study of religion since the latter part of the 19th century shows the tension between various forms of rendering reason and the specific modality of religion in methodological studies. This is seen as much in Max Müller and the studies he fostered, as in Durkheim.

All of these kinds of studies of religion, especially as they relate to non-Western religions were aspects of a broader intellectual and cultural milieu as these religions were presented and *represented* to the world of western scholarship and culture. They were objects presented and placed before a subject (the West). In such presentation and representation, the mastery and dominance over the object is assured: it is rendered in the form of reason by its presentation before the knowing subject. This is seen in the center/periphery structure of geographical and cartographical modes, as well as in the broader ramifications of colonialism as the context for the origin of scholarly questions. Issues of this sort are hidden in the rendering reason as marked by the history of the study of religion.

I am not rejecting this kind of knowledge. I only wish to interrogate it. I seek to find the principle of reason that is obscured in it, to seek out that reason that is in tension with its clarity. The knowledge of other religions must be listened to and seen, and before this knowledge we must "blink."[11] Aristotle states, "All men by nature desire to know." Desire is the relationship to otherness necessary for the articulation of identities and structures. Therein lies the double threat of desire. What is hardly, if ever, spoken about in our search for religious knowledge of the others is the issue of contact with them. In an ironic manner, those notions that could express the meaning of the actuality of the contact that led to our knowledge are usually taken to be conceptual forms that are used to give an objective analysis (scientific rendering of the structures of their religion): mana, taboo, gift exchange, symbol, myth, etc. I am not saying that

---

[11]See note #5 above.

these notions are not adequate as interpretive concepts; I am saying that they need to be explored in terms of the meaning of the situation of knowledge itself.

In this regard, I have been thinking of the notion of "cargo cults" as a paradigm for a kind of knowing that might be possible in religious studies. Cargo cults have been referred to by Weston LaBarre as constituting what he calls "crisis cults." He understands these cults to be "responses to extreme cultural disruptions within a culture—these disruptions, in the case of crisis cults, are caused by the radical impingements of alien forms upon a culture."[12] The cargo cult symbolizes a crisis on all levels of the culture and most especially, a crisis of knowledge and of ontology. The leader or founder of a cargo cult responds to the crisis through a decipherment of the situation to the end of providing those rituals that will allow new human beings to grow out of this crisis. In so doing, the myths of the cult relate how the western cargo was sent to them in a providential manner. Somewhere en route, the cargo that was originally sent to them was interrupted and the cargo stolen by the western people who now make use of it to alienate them from the cargo and from themselves (the westerners), and from their own traditions. In the cargo cult, new rituals are practiced to place the cargo back into the proper circle of beneficent exchange. The cargo cult is an attempt to establish reciprocity and to reinstate the meaning of *exchange* as gift.

Marcel Mauss analyzed the ethnography of gift exchange in his classic work, *The Gift*.[13] As opposed to the West's subordination of gifts to the level of sentimentality while giving primacy to the value of the exchange of material goods as a source of wealth, the practices described in the literature included celebrations in which status was rewarded to those who expended or destroyed their most precious possessions, and to those societies whose prized possessions served only to be given away in a cycle of exchanges. Mauss discerned that every contact with difference—other families, tribes, orders of being—was caught up in the matrix of an ongoing system of exchange. He determined that any particular exchange is structured as a recip-

---

[12]Weston LaBarre, "Materials for a History of Studies of Crisis Cults: A Bibliographical Essay," *Current Anthropology*, 12 (February, 1971) pp. 3-44. There is an extensive literature devoted to this topic as LaBarre's essay will show. My own interest is expressed in an article, "Cargo Cults as Cultural Historical Phenomena," *Journal of the American Academy of Religion*, 42:3 (1976) pp. 403-414.

[13]Marcel Mauss' classic, *The Gift*, trans. by I Cunnison (New York: Norton, 1967), has been commented upon several times. The most interesting commentaries for my purpose are those of Marshall Sahlins, *Stone Age Economics*, (Chicago: Aldine Press, 1972); and Pierre Bourdieu, *Outline of a Theory of Practice*, (Cambridge: Cambridge University Press, 1977). See also my essay, "The Religious Implications of Cultural Contact," in *Significations* (Philadelphia: Fortress press, 1986).

rocal, bilateral relationship governed by the obligation to give and to receive.

The exchange is expressed in several modes: 1) it is a total social phenomenon, embracing the religious as well as the political; 2) it assumes the guise of a moral gesture as it is seen from a number of viewpoints as selfless and unmotivated by private interests; 3) it is an obligation; 4) the gift usually lacks practical value, in that it does not satisfy material needs; and 5) there is no immediate return. Because every contact occurs at, even as it presupposes, a boundary, gift exchange also attempts to regulate access to excess. As in situations of cultural contact, the boundary is ambiguous: two incompatible orders seem to exist.

Cargo cults afford a perspective of their own to this incompatibility, a perspective I have found helpful in rethinking issues of exchange, oppression, materiality, and knowledge—issues that lie at the heart of the contemporary crisis in liberal education. The situation of education in general, and especially at the level of liberal education, constitutes a crisis; and in many respects, discussions of issues in education center around some of the same dynamics as those of the cargo cult. At one level, the cargo cultist accepts the reasons and rationales of the westerners who have impinged on their culture. What is bewildering to them is that the westerners, those in positions of dominance and power, cannot understand the notion of reciprocity and the exchange of gifts—gifts of goods and gifts of knowledge. Instead of exchange, there is only domination and suppression. In this situation, alienation and objectivity go hand in hand. The empirical actualities of contact with the other culture are deemed inadmissable as the basis for *human* and cultural knowledge; knowledge gained from the contact must be deployed as objective and scientific. Under the aegis of scientific scholarship, exchange comes to be viewed in terms of contagion within the native's religious world. This posture obscures the actuality of contact. It also precludes the possibility of exploring new modalities of knowledge and new meanings of the human which those in the cargo cult believe possible through exchange.

Throughout this paper, I have placed the issue of education within the wider context of the exchanges within our culture—exchanges in the gross and conventional sense of economy, exchanges between reason and the ground of reason, and exchanges of modes of communication. If we are now experiencing a crisis in education, this crisis is felt at every level of these exchanges. There is indeed a crisis within the economic order that affects the meaning of education; we are equally experiencing a crisis of reason—reason as the conventional wisdom of our culture, as well as reason as self-conscious intellectual reflection. This crisis relates to the older, Enlightenment view of reason that understood education as a universal process in the discovery of human value. Jay Geller has explored aspects of this crisis with a discussion of the dynamics of exchange as they affected Enlightenment societies.

> Mauss' description of gift-exchange society recalls (nostalgically) the Enlightenment ideal of the public sphere or *Oeffentlichkeit*. The spirit of the gift, like universal reason, ensures the maintenance of the individual's autonomy within a relationship. Although the relationships within exchange were agonistic, the mediation of the spirit of the gift deters the two threats, domination and war, inherent in both alternative determinants that govern the interaction: private interest and state.[14]

The claims of universal reason have not protected us from war, nor provided a safeguard from state domination. The universal meaning inherent in Enlightenment reason has been an important factor in the political processes that enable us to recognize the legitimacies of all persons, ethnic groups and classes in our society. But does such a recognition, in a paradoxical sense, now contain these newly liberated ones within structures based upon the fear of war or state domination? Such reflection gives rise in a radical manner to a new problematic meaning of human knowledge in general and the specific meaning of the processes and content of knowledge as related to the institutional meaning of education.

I am not limiting the implications of the notions of cargo cult and gift exchange simply to those areas of liberal education that have to do with courses in religion. To be sure, issues of exchange will bring us to rethink how we go about teaching such courses; but they also allow us the opportunity to think through the many implications this perspective might have for the entire curriculum as it concerns given boundaries—boundaries between practical/theoretical reason, professional/non-professional, university/public arena, privileged/oppressed, undergraduate/graduate, material/ideational, etc. Such an approach also has the advantage of authentically grounding these realities and modes of thought within the institutional grasp of the university.

Religious Studies from this point of view may not simply be one of the elements in the structure of a liberal or general education curriculum. Its processes could become a defining structure for much of it. More and more, a literature is emerging that could aid us in this

---

[14]Jay Geller, "Contact of Persistent Others: the Representation of 'Woman' in Friedrich Schlegel, G. W. Hegel, and Karl Gutzkow," Ph.D. Dissertation, Duke University 1985 (unpublished) p. 12, 13. I am highly appreciative of the work of Jay Geller who wrote this dissertation under my advisorship. Not only am I indebted to the passage cited, but to the many stimulating conversations we had while he was a graduate student.

task.[15] This perspective on the meaning of a liberal education has the advantage of preserving reason as the organizing principle of the university, while equally recognizing the impediments and restraints within the clear rendering of reason within the structures of the "objective" sciences and disciplines. It is often stated that Religious Studies is an inter-disciplinary area. I should like for this to mean more than simply the addition of various approaches from various disciplines. I think that knowing how to learn and learning how to know requires that a community of scholars become a community of thought. Religious Studies, through a realization of the problematics of the study of religion itself in our time, might thus provide a basis for the rethinking of reason in the university.

---

[15]There is a growing body of literature dealing with issues of this kind. Just a few of the texts: Raymond Schwab, *The Oriental Renaissance,* trs. Gene Patterson-Black and Victor Reinking (New York: Columbia University Press, 1984); Edward Said, *Orientalism,* (New York: Pantheon Books, 1978); Johannes Fabian, *Time and the Other* (New York: Columbia University Press, 1983); Ashis Nandy, *Traditions, Tyranny and Utopias* (Delhi: Oxford University Press, 1987); Stephen Greenblatt, *Renaissance Self-Fashioning* (Chicago: The University of Chicago Press, 1980).

"Seeking an End to the Primary Text"
or
"Putting an End to the Text as Primary"
Lawrence E. Sullivan

What writing itself, in its nonphonetic moment, betrays, is life. It menaces at once the breath, the spirit, and history as the spirit's relationship with itself. It is their end, their finitude, their paralysis . . . It is to speech what China is to Europe. . . . The horizon of absolute knowledge is the effacement of writing in the logos, the retrieval of the trace in parousia . . .

—Jacques Derrida[1]

The science of writing as a new realm of linguistic operation; of writing as language, but not as vocal speech or grammatical chain; of writing as a specific signifying practice that enables us to perceive unknown regions in the vast universe of language—this science of writing has yet to be developed.

—Julia Kristeva[2]

Acquaintance with literacy in most cultures is rather recent. The religious life of Africa, Oceania, the native Americas, and large areas of Asia reminds us that the experiment with text is fairly new in human history. For the most part, the problems of meaning, understanding, communication and interpretation have been thrashed out without reference to texts and without resort to text as a primary metaphor. The word "illiterate" conjures up images of "unwitting," "unknowledgeable" and "unreflective" peoples. But the long-standing creativity of unlettered peoples—the existence of their shrewd reflections and exfoliating aesthetic life—challenges the choice of "text" as the most exemplary vehicle of intelligibility. The notion of text and

---

[1]Jacques Derrida, *Of Grammatology*, trans. Gayatri Chakravorty Spivak. (Baltimore and London: The Johns Hopkins University Press, 1974) pp. 25-26.
[2]Julia Kristeva, *Language—the Unknown: An Initiation into Linguistics*, trans. Anne M. Menke (New York: Columbia University Press, 1989) p. 30.

the overly literal metaphors about language stand out as peculiar in human history.

That we currently base our cultural investigations upon the notion of text and its metaphors is understandable in light of the dominant place of sacred texts in the history of biblically based cultures.[3] But this bias that regards scriptured expression as the primary mode of intelligibility is misguided and distracts from the issue. Religious studies in the liberal arts offers special promise in the first place because, more than any other discipline of the arts and sciences, it is prepared to examine the religious foundation of scriptural origins and the cultural limits of the privilege accorded "the text." Secondly, religious studies admits into the western scene the meanings—the cultural construals of cosmos, space, and time—of the *other* because it wrestles with the products of the imagination and interprets the process by which the imagination confronts the specific conditions of meaning in the place where that human life is rooted. Historically speaking, most humans have not centered themselves over the image of the text. Religious studies wants to come to grips with alternate construals of meaning as they are found in other cultures. The desire to achieve this curious goal impels religious studies to unfasten the bonds placed on inquiry by culture-bound notions of text and give fair hearing and sight to the imaginal expressions that lie well outside of the singular expression of writing.

We cannot try to escape the text and remain responsible interpreters of our own culture where text plays an important role. We are a literate society with values and awarenesses shaped by an important literary history. The proposal that writing or text become the primary vehicle of intelligibility has been put forward in a strong form by the French philosopher Jacques Derrida and has received support. He has developed Sigmund Freud's suggestion that the psychological processes of consciousness, perception, and awareness of existence in time might best be understood as writing—the sort of tracing left by a child who uses a stylus to press a piece of waxed paper against a dark, waxen backboard. Everything written in this way, of course, exists in a state subject to erasure. Such writing is the upwelling of hidden, unknown, alien forces that press pointedly against consciousness and leave a trace of their passing presence. Such writing preexists and conditions all other cultural forms of knowledge

---

[3] A fine example of the text-talk analysis of culture is Paul Ricoeur, "The Model of the Text: Meaningful Action Considered as Text," in *Interpretive Social Science: A Reader*, edited by P. Rabinow and W. Sullivan (Berkeley: University of California Press, 1979). Works that recast the symbolic expressions of culture into narrative or mythopoetic forms for analysis can become a long list and can be far less interesting than Ricoeur's study. By way of critique, see Edward Said, "The Text, the World, the Critic," in *Harari* (1979) pp. 164-66.

(even spoken language) and is, therefore, the best key to their meaning.

> [T]he very idea of science was born in a certain epoch of writing. . . .
> [W]riting is not only an auxiliary means in the service of science—and
> possibly its object—but first, as Husserl in particular pointed out in *The
> Origin of Geometry*, the condition of the possibility of ideal objects and
> therefore of scientific objectivity. Before being its object, writing is the
> condition of the *epistémè*.[4]

Derrida proposes a science of writing which looks for its object at the very root of scientificity (a science of the very possibility of science) and a history of writing that turns back toward the origin of historicity (a history of the possibility of history). "Before being the object of a history—of an historical science—writing opens the field of history—of historical becoming."[5]

The impulse to view all cultural expressions as a series of systems best analyzed through the structure of language precedes the French Deconstruction of the past decades, as well as the earlier linguistic breakthroughs of Jakobsen, Troubetzkoy, and de Saussure. Analysis of culture through the application of linguistic models was already a major theme for the Encyclopedists of eighteenth century France. Condillac argued that nonverbal cultural expressions, such as dance or music, were languages, in the sense that languages consist in a system of hieroglyphic signs arbitrarily attached to ideas. Denis Diderot held that the arts of music, painting, and poetry could best be analyzed as sign systems, hieroglyphic systems, strictly analogous to the sign system of language, which he derived from his comparative examination of deaf-mute signs with spoken French.[6] Voltaire, in his

---

[4]Derrida, *Of Grammatology*, p. 27. "I would wish rather to suggest that the alleged derivativeness of writing, however real and massive, was possible only on one condition: that the 'original,' 'natural,' etc. language had never existed, never been intact and untouched by writing, that it had itself always been a writing. An arche-writing whose necessity and new concept I wish to indicate and outline here; and which I continue to call writing only because it essentially communicates with the vulgar concept of writing. The latter could not have imposed itself historically except by the dissimulation of the arche-writing, by the desire for a speech displacing its other and its double and working to reduce its difference. If I persist in calling that difference writing, it is because, within the work of historical repression, writing was, by its situation, destined to signify the most formidable difference. It threatened the desire for the living speech from the closest proximity, it *breached* living speech from within and from the very beginning. And as we shall begin to see, difference cannot be thought without the *trace*." Derrida, *Of Grammatology*, p. 56.

[5]Derrida, *Of Grammatology*, p. 27.

[6]Denis Diderot, "Letter on the Deaf and Dumb for the Use of Those Who Hear and Speak," in *Diderot's Early Philosophical Works*, trans. Margaret Jourdain (Chicago: Open Court Press, 1916). For further consideration of encyclopedic

Philosophical Dictionary, believed that scrutiny of linguistic order
would reveal the well-grounded analytical order innate to human beings. Consequently, he proposed the formation of a universal ency-
clopedia which would conceptually organize all knowledge according to the framework of categories revealed in grammar.

The power of text, language, and writing holds contemporary
cultural studies in so fast a grip that, in aiming to propel modern
people beyond the current "era of humanism" toward something as
yet unknown, Julia Kristeva feels obliged to begin with language, for
"is it not indispensable to approach this unknown through language,
which is and will always remain more unknown than man, and
coextensive with his being?"[7] Thus, in *Language—the Unknown*, Kristeva sketches the history of the central linguistic question: how can
language be thought? To her credit, Kristeva makes linguistics itself
become the question, the locus of an enigma, and she concentrates on
the materiality of writing. When language is taken as the material
object of thought, the history of linguistics is portrayed as a discourse
that effectively binds philosophical thought to linguistic practice.
Kristeva concludes her initiation into the riddles marked by the very
existence of a science of linguistics, when it is employed as a model
for all cultural sciences, with a call for a more general theory of signification:

> [T]he expansion of the linguistic method to other fields of signifying
> practices . . . has the advantage of confronting this method with resisting
> objects. It shows more and more that the models found by formal lin-
> guistics are not omnivalent, and that the various modes of signification
> must be studied independent of the summit-limit reached by linguistics.
> . . . The West, reassured by the mastery it has acquired of the structures
> of language, can now confront these structures with a complex and con-
> stantly transforming reality. It can find itself face to face with all the for-
> gotten and censored things that enabled it to erect this system—a sys-
> tem that was only a refuge . . . [8]

In order to enter our own historical moment and come to grips
with the multiplicity of historical consciousnesses that increasingly
act as agents in our world, we can no longer take refuge in writing.
We must reckon with those objects that resist expansion of the linguistic methods. Becoming responsible interpreters of our own culture is the obligation of every creative citizen and a primary goal of
liberal education. To achieve this end we must seek the end of the
text. That is, we must discover the limits of the text as the prime vehi-

---

models see Lawrence E. Sullivan, "Circumscribing Knowledge: Encyclopedias in
Historical Perspective," *Journal of Religion* 70, no. 3 (July 1990).

[7]Kristeva, *Language—the Unknown*, p. vii.

[8]Kristeva, *Language—the Unknown*, p. 328-29.

cle of intelligibility and we must probe the meaning of the fact that the religious conditions of humanity lie largely beyond the sacrality of scripture (scripture in the sense of canonical scripture, but also in the sense of written narrative and interpretive terminologies derived from the study of written narrative, as well as scripture in the sense of written history).

I want to speak out against the tyranny of text and, by extension, the "linguistic turn" of the Enlightenment cultural sciences. I agree that this tropic twist has given new depth to cultural studies by showing that what humans do to speak about themselves is symbolic. That is, language is not only referential (denoting particular realities), but also self-referential, turning back on itself to refer to the nature of its own structures and processes. Language refers to the symbolic mode itself and is, therefore, a metalanguage. I recognize the contributions of this "linguistic turn," but want to complain about its exclusiveness. As Bronislaw Malinowski recognized in the mid 1930s, this concept of language is a thimble into which you cannot pour the ocean of religious conditions, as if language were the single, self-referring symbolic expression of religious experience.

For the moment, text is the dominant symbol, or domineering symbol, of reflexive human existence. It engulfs every other form of human intelligibility and intentionality. Since anything may be described—"written down"—any form of intentionality or intelligibility risks capture by the text and confinement within its structures. In that way, text bears a genetic resemblance to the notions of history of which it is a generative expression. Both text and history are accumulative and acquisitive realities.

Talk of text overly constrains the discussion of interpretation and hermeneutics. I recognize that scrutiny of texts and conflicts of textual interpretation generated much of the current hermeneutical discussion. This point is demonstrated in two different appraisals of the Protestant Reformation's involvement with literacy: Hans Frei's *Eclipse of Biblical Narrative* and Marilyn Chrisman's *Lay Culture, Learned Culture.*[9] Each author examines how the Reformation theology of translating "God's word," the political economy of printing, the growth of lay literacy, and the subsequent multiplication of non-authoritative interpretations created an interpretive maelstrom that provoked reflection on and sought authority in the *process* of interpretation and hermeneutics. This flight from magisterial authority and quest for authoritative reading has been propelled by assessments of the written word. Our own documents now push us beyond the nar-

---

[9]Hans Frei, *The Eclipse of Biblical Narrative* (New Haven, Conn.: Yale University Press, 1974); Miriam Usher Chrisman, *Lay Culture, Learned Culture: Books and Social Change in Strasbourg, 1480-1599* (New Haven, Conn.: Yale University Press, 1982).

row discussion of hermeneutics as it stems from textual interpretation.

The notion of text now stifles the attempt of religious studies to confront the full range of religious experiences and expressions—even those recorded in texts. These experiences can be considered textual, literary or linguistic only by analogy, sometimes only by stretching the metaphor of text to creative extremes. Particularly troublesome is the linguistic doctrine of the arbitrariness of the sign that undergirds much of the linguistic turn. The principle of the arbitrariness of the sign dislocates meaning. The image of text and derived notions about the structures of language or narrative overly accentuate the picture of meaning as a consensus or an agreement or a puzzling out. Using the text as a primary image of intelligibility exaggerates the view that meaning is a construction, the result of a process like sentence construction or paragraph building. This view obscures the very widespread religious notion that meaning is *a priori* given in the cultural situation through primordial appearance, revelation, or spontaneous insight. Text and the "language" derived from notions of texts are stylizations of cultural existence which make their meaning remarkable in historical terms. They do not create that meaning. The view that they do create that meaning, insofar as it is predicated on the essential arbitrariness of any single sign, mistakenly identifies sentence production with construction of a meaningful language. In actual fact, even linguistic analyses depend on a fair supply of well-formed sentences. That is, the ability to construct a grammar or a transformational grammar or an outline of deep structural processes depends on the givenness of a well-formed spoken language, which preexists the notion of constructed meaning or constructed grammar. In short, even the linguistic analysis which concludes that signs are only arbitrarily linked to their referents presupposes a meaningful world of communication from which exemplary, well-formed sentences are drawn and in which linguists themselves think and communicate their thoughts. Our notions of text and of arbitrary signs too easily skirt the *givenness* of meaning in the human situation.

Another reason to find text objectionable is that it overlooks the materiality of language and its constant proximity to material chaos.[10] Instead of calling attention to the material base of language, text-talk highlights what is intentional, sublime, intellectual, formal, and deliberate or controlled. Lost in this overly smooth, clear, and determined view is the struggle of the human imagination with the *chaos* inherent in the *matter* of speech (breath, muscles, organs, bones). The force of imagination organizes the corporeal mass of the body

---

[10]Paul Friedrich, "The Symbol and Its Relative Non-Arbitrariness," in *Language, Context, and the Imagination*, by P. Friedrich (Stanford, Calif.: Stanford University Press, 1979), pp. 1-62.

into cultural orders that reflect those imaginative efforts and processes.

The dominance of contemporary talk about "text" also obscures the performative quality of writing and reading language. By default, then, interpretation of "texts" takes refuge in notions of trope or narrative order and immerses itself in forms of rationality that derive from the text as reflected in the structure of sentence, trope, narrative, or deep grammar. Such interpretive strategies hide from the fundamental unreason of language and of printed matter (the physicality of the book, ink, and paper), an unreason that never ceases to undergird the processes of communication, understanding, and meaning which condition a particular society. The rationality we discern in text and linguistics could not account for the communication that transpires in any given cultural community and addresses itself only to a fraction of the process of human understanding.

The problems I have outlined arise because text has a certain space and time of its own, a fact that Paul Ricoeur confronts us with in *Time and Narrative*[11] and Jacques Derrida has visited on us in several works.[12] Narrative texts house meaning within particular frameworks of speech or writing. Textual dwelling places cannot accommodate the large family of religious conditions. This can be seen clearly in cultures that have transmitted forms of knowledge and structures of experience from generation to generation without ever employing text as a conveyance. Text is likewise an inadequate vehicle for transporting the full cargo of religious experiences of literate peoples, including those of our own culture.

The dominance of text and its derivative notions of language and hermeneutics have narrowed this wide range of human reflection and distorted the many modes of reflection as they are found in historical cultures. And these text-analogues and metaphors blind us to the engagements of the human spirit with various modalities of matter, a phrase that could define reflection. The book, together with the process of printing, writing, and reading it, is a material expression of a given sort, but there are other modalities of matter. Canoe making has never been a dominant metaphor in the post-Enlightenment academy. But riverain or ocean-going cultures, as numerous examples from Polynesia, Africa and Amerindia have shown, employ the

---

[11]Paul Ricoeur, *Time and Narrative,* trans. Kathleen McLaughlin and David Pellauer (Chicago: University of Chicago Press, 1985).

[12]The space and time of writing has been used to understand mystical speech and experiences, as in the examinations of the texts of Saints John of the Cross and Theresa of Avila by Michel de Certeau ("L'énonciation mystique," *Recherches de science religieuse* 64:2 (1976) pp. 183-215). See also Susan Sellers, ed., *Writing Differences: Readings from the Seminar of Hélène Cixous* (New York: St. Martin's Press, 1988).

symbols of canoe-construction and navigation as a principle vehicle of intelligibility and the main way of organizing meaning.[13]

Pottery is another way of engaging the human spirit with a distinct mode of matter. Claude Lévi-Strauss's recent book *La potière jalouse* is an example of an attempt to enter into the consciousness of the potter and the world of cultural meaning centered, through pottery, on the material involvement with clay, earth, and water.[14] Throughout the world, basket making has long been a precise way of reflecting on and participating in the cosmological process that sustains the existence of the universe. Beautiful baskets are often a symptom of wisdom gained in the seclusion of initiation where one encounters supernatural forces and spirits.[15] Similarly, weaving allows one a role in the process that knits together the cosmic forces to create a fruitful universe. Gerardo Reichel-Dolmatoff's study of the Kogi Loom of Life shows how preparing wool, spinning yarn, and weaving it into cloth organizes human beings' participatory knowledge of the cosmos. The weaver imitates the movements of the sun which each day threads its way across the earth like a shuttle that passes colorful strings of material, seminal light, through the fecund darkness of the earth. Throughout the year the sun weaves its way across the horizon, moving back and forth between the outermost points of the two solstices. The weaver's loom is kept in a solarium. The woven textiles literally incorporate the patterned movements of the sunbeams that streak through the hole in the roof at different angles during the different seasons of the year.[16]

The detail that this form of knowledge merits must be passed over in favor of noting the materiality of some other modes of reflection. House construction is one, as exemplified in Daniel de Barandiarán's studies of the Dekuana roundhouse which, as a microcosm, is oriented to the light of seasonal stars, the changing angle of the sun, and the prevailing winds that pollinate flowers and fruit trees in due season. Episodes of the life cycle and the structures of society are orchestrated through the symbolism of the house, which thus provides society with an image of its own integrity and offers individu-

---

[13]See, for instance, Johannes Wilbert, "To Become a Maker of Canoes: An Essay in Warao Enculturation," in *Enculturation in Latin America: An Anthology,* ed. Johannes Wilbert, UCLA Latin American Studies, vol. 37 (Los Angeles: UCLA Latin American Center Publications, 1976) pp. 305-58; and Johannes Wilbert, "Navigators of the Winter Sun," in *The Sea in the Pre-Columbian World,* ed. Elizabeth P. Benson (Washington, D.C.: Dumbarton Oaks Research Library and Collections, 1977) pp. 1-62.

[14]Claude Lévi-Strauss, *La potière jalouse* (Paris: Librairie Plon, 1986).

[15]Johannes Wilbert, *Warao Basketry: Form and Function* (Los Angeles: UCLA Museum of Cultural History, 1975).

[16]Gerardo Reichel-Dolmatoff, "The Loom of Life: a Kogi Principle of Integration," *Journal of Latin American Lore* 4:2 (1978), pp. 5-27.

als an image of their cultural identity.[17] Musical performance of specific instruments is generally linked to the entire mode of economic production that prepares these material instruments and coordinates their performances. The studies of John Blacking, Anthony Seeger, and Ellen Basso show that the manner in which the human body is organized while playing music can become the normative image for organizing society.[18] Society, in this view, is first and foremost a musical composition. Astronomy, as studied by Gary Urton and Anthony Aveni,[19] stands out as a profound basis for reflection on the orders of the cosmos and for reflection on the human capacity to imagine connections among the lives of stars, animals, water, mythical beings, and human societies. Reflections on the calendric order of stars and discernment of the human relationship to that order become the reflective basis of social organization and economic system. None of these material spiritualities has anything to do with a text. Of course, they could be understood as permutative linguistic codes, in the way that Lévi-Strauss analyzes them. But that is like passing light through a prism. To be sure, the prism factors light into a spectrum of various bands whose properties and relations can be plotted to "analyze light." But what is actually analyzed is the state to which light has been reduced by the instruments of explanation. There is no need to be an anti-reductionist; but one should choose one's reduc-

[17]Daniel de Barandiarán, "El habitado entre los índios yekuana," *Antropología* (Caracas) 16 (1966), pp. 3-95; and Barandiarán, *Introducción a la cosmovisión de los índios Ye-kuana-Makiritare* (Caracas: Prensas Venezolanas de Editorial Arte, 1979).

[18]John Blacking, "The Study of Man as Music-Maker," in *The Performing Arts: Music and Dance,* ed. John Blacking and Joanna W. Kealiinohomoku (The Hague: Mouton Publishers, 1979), pp. 3-16; Anthony Seeger, "What Can We Learn When They Sing? Vocal Genres of the Suya Indians of Central Brazil," *Ethnomusicology* 23:3 (September 1979) pp. 373-94; Anthony Seeger, "Porque os indios suya cantam para suas irmas," in *Arte e Sociedade,* ed. Gilberto Velho (Rio de Janeiro: Zahar, 1977) pp. 39-64; Anthony Seeger, "Oratory is Spoken, Myth is Told, and Song is Sung, But They Are All Music to My Ears," in *Native South American Discourse,* eds. Joel Sherzer and Greg Urban. (Amsterdam: Mouton de Gruyter, 1986) pp. 59-82; Ellen B. Basso, "A Musical View of the Universe: Kalapalo Myth and Ritual Performances," *Journal of American Folklore* 94:373 (1981) pp. 273-291; Ellen B. Basso, *A Musical View of the Universe: Kalapalo Myth and Ritual Performances* (Philadelphia: University of Pennsylvania Press, 1985). See also Lawrence E. Sullivan, "Sacred Music and Sacred Time," *World of Music* (Berlin) 26:3 (1984) pp. 33-52; Lawrence E. Sullivan, "La persona y la sociedad como composiciones musicales," *Cuadernos internacionales de historia psicosocial del arte* (Barcelona) 3 (1983) pp. 9-17; and Lawrence E. Sullivan, "Sound and Senses: Toward a Hermeneutics of Performance," *History of Religions* 26:1 (1986) pp. 1-33.

[19]Gary Urton, *At the Crossroads of the Earth and the Sky: An Andean Cosmology* (Austin: University of Texas Press, 1981); *Ethnoastronomy and Archaeoastronomy in the American Tropics,* eds. Gary Urton and Anthony F. Aveni, Annals of the New York Academy of Sciences, vol. 385 (New York: New York Academy of Sciences, 1982).

tions carefully. If the instruments and terms of analysis distort what one intends to study, interpretive strategy derails the course of understanding. Text is one strategy that diverts us onto a wide detour that escapes a confrontation with other modes of intelligibility. In the course of such textual excursions, text itself has remained irreducible to other cultural terms and interpretive ends.

Religious studies is a most promising place for the liberal arts to pass through and beyond the text because of its unique involvement with the sacrality of scripture and the history of scriptural interpretation. The problem of text becomes most acute in the study of religions because, in some religious traditions, text achieves its most hallowed state. At the same time, the comparative and historical study of religion makes clear that only in a few historical instances have texts been central to religious life. Even in literate culture, whose respect for writing, reading, and textual interpretation stem from the sacrality of the written word and its involvement with divine will, it remains questionable how fully the notion of culture-as-text can account for religious experience and expression.[20] Freud's over-determined examination of dreams that are not literate or textual realities, for example, opened whole new ways of understanding symbolic life. Freud's dream material was limited to middle-class neurotics from Vienna but, even so, his discoveries revolutionized our sense of our-

---

[20]In *Beyond the Written Word: Oral Aspects of Scripture in the History of Religion* (Cambridge and New York: Cambridge University Press, 1987), William A. Graham examines the oral uses of scripture, in particular of the Qur'an. "The oral character of the Qur'an is readily perceptible in almost any sector of Muslim life, today as in every previous age of Islamic history . . . This recitative function of the Qur'an has been of paramount importance especially in public ritual and private devotional life over the centuries" (p. 96). According to Graham, attending to the oral uses of scripture will lead to examination of the sensual dimension of religion, that dimension of forceful religious experience that is related neither to literacy nor to articulated discursive ideas (pp. 162-65). He looks at the Christian emphasis on written scriptural text as an oral phenomenon, where reading and copying were vocal exercises, liturgical ones at times (pp. 123 ff.). Pachomian monks, for example, practiced recitation of sacred scriptures as ascetic exercises of vocal meditation during labor. Their life was thus permeated by the living word (pp. 129-40). Martin Luther stressed the hearing of the word and the oral preaching of the word of God in a voice that would resound through the whole world (p. 149). Investigating the impact of the oral recitation of scripture on post-reformation France, Furet remarks that, "Literacy was born at the point where religion and society meet; but little by little it passed under society's sway. When scholars lost their monopoly, reading and writing very quickly became instruments of social utility and status symbols as well" (François Furet, *Reading and Writing: Literacy in France From Calvin to Jules Ferry* (Cambridge: Cambridge University Press, 1982) pp. 166-67). Regarding motives for recitation of texts, see also J. Stephen Lansing, "The Aesthetics of the Sounding of the Text," in *Symposium of the Whole: A Range of Discourse Toward an Ethnopoetics*, eds. Jerome and Diane Rothenberg (Berkeley: University of California Press, 1983) pp. 241-57.

selves and the vocabulary which the general public—including students in undergraduate classrooms—employs in evaluating its most profound experiences. This one attempt to understand another vehicle of intelligibility (heretofore reckoned as trivial unreason) altered the sense of culture and individual, and has coined new vocabulary for public use. I am suggesting that religious studies could look not only at dreams but at shadows, at flowers, at sounds, at pottery and basketry, at smells and light, at the crafts and domestic sciences, and regard them as symbolic vehicles for the full load of human experience. Where does one turn to decide what all this means, if not to the text as the primary vehicle? Religious studies has precedent for inquiring of cultural actors themselves and interpreting realities in their terms.

Weeping is one such alternative to text. Huizinga, in a study of medieval rites, once complained that there was little information about the meaning of weeping, which he saw at work in so many festivals. And that is all he could say about it. He mentions the ritual act of weeping and drops it. Later, an Italian anthropologist, named Ernesto de Martino, who pursued the comparative sociology of religion, wrote a book called *Morte e Pianto Rituale* (Death and the Ritual Act of Crying).[21] De Martino collected data on stylized weeping from classical antiquity to the early 1950s. He included funeral laments in Magna Grecia as well as weeping statues of the Virgin in modern Italy. He aimed to isolate historical continuities and morphological similarities without a lot of interpretation. The book is thought-provoking, although few scholars since de Martino have known quite what to do next with the theme of ritual weeping. I was struck by the symbolism of tears and weeping while reading an Andean history written by a native chronicler of the late 16th century. His pen name was Guaman Poma. (We know little or nothing about his life or his "real" name.) His first name, Guaman, means "eagle" which is the emblem of the upper, heavenly realm of the universe as well as the mythical animal associated with one half of society. The second name, Poma, is the word for puma, the feline associated with the earthly realm and a different social moiety. Guaman Poma penned a thousand pages of historical manuscript and three hundred

---

[21]Ernesto de Martino, *Morte e pianto rituale nel mondo antico: Dal lamento pagano al pianto di Maria* (Turin: Edizioni Scientifiche Einaudi, 1958); Wm. A. Christian, Jr., "Provoked Religious Weeping in Early Modern Spain," in *Religious Organization and Religious Experience*, ed. J. Davis (London: Academic Press, 1982) pp. 97-114. On ritual weeping, see also Laura Graham, "Three Modes of Shavante Vocal Expression: Wailing, Collective Singing, and Political Oratory," in *Native South American Discourse*, eds. Joel Sherzer and Greg Urban (Amsterdam: Mouton de Gruyter, 1986) pp. 83-118.

ethnographic drawings.[22] We are unable to reckon the toll this labor took on him when he tells us, "To write is to weep!" His one thousand pages of tears were usually attributed to the fact that he wrote an apocalyptic history of his people, calling it "The First New Chronicle" of the Indian peoples. Insofar as they thought about the matter at all, most analysts attributed his "weeping" to the fact that he was documenting a tragic disaster. He did, in fact, consider himself a reporter of the apocalypse. The social disintegration of Andean peoples, ravaged by waves of economic destitution, military oppression, epidemic devastation, and religious disorientation, signaled the end of the world. In fact, Guaman Poma intended his history to be an apocalyptic book because he looked upon writing as a species of symbolic action consonant with the eschaton. His stylized acts of writing, just as his neighbors choreographed acts of frenzied dancing, would hasten the end of time. These marks, these stylized moves of the hand-with-pen on paper were intelligible and meaningful within the new mode of existence, the New, Literate Epoch brought into being by the Conquest.[23] Guaman Poma's book is in the form of a letter to the Messiah, who was, ironically enough, the King of Spain (since the royal Inca had been beheaded). The King of Spain would be moved to tears when he opened the letter, and anyone who saw the book would be certain to weep. Many of Guaman Poma's drawings depict crowds weeping. The stars and heavenly beings would pour down torrents of tears and the earth would well up in flood. A deluge would destroy the world and end time.

Guaman Poma's notion of the effectiveness of weeping springs from Inca concepts of what it means to weep. They arise from images of the first destruction of the world, sometime after it was first created. The dancing stars of the Milky Way and the sacrificed animal constellations (for example, Mother Llama and her crying child, Baby Llama) whose tears stream profusely from their bright eyes, appeared on the horizon for the first time at the beginning of the deluge, the

---

[22]Felipe Guaman Poma de Ayala [Waman Puma], *El Primer nueva corónica y buen gobierno*, eds. John V. Murra and Rolena Adorno, trans. Jorge L. Urioste (Mexico City: Siglo Veintiuno, 1981).

[23]Guaman Poma's view of writing as an effective sign of the conquest is taken up in Juan M. Ossio, "Guaman Poma: Nueva coronica o carta al rey. Un intento de aproximación a las categorias del pensamiento del mundo andino," in his *Ideología mesiánica del mundo andino*, pp. 155-213; and Ossio, "The Idea of History in Felipe Guaman Poma de Ayala," Xerographic Copy of Thesis for Degree of Bachelor of Letters. Oxford University, 1970. See also Frank L. Salomon, "Chronicles of the Impossible: Notes on Three Peruvian Indigenous Historians," in *From Oral to Written Expression: Native Andean Chronicles of the Early Colonial Period*, ed. Rolena Adorno, Foreign and Comparative Studies, Latin American Series, no. 4 (Syracuse: Syracuse University Press, 1982) pp. 9-40.

first rainy season that initiated a New Age.[24] This is not just literary metaphor. Perhaps one could call it metonym. Whatever be the tropic tag we apply, the symbolism of weeping is coinvolved here with the material reality of flooding rainwaters and a new quality of time. When he says, "To write is to weep," Guaman Poma uses the efficacious power of weeping to understand what writing might be and what the quality of time is, for which writing stands as a symptom. Guaman Poma's approach turns our notion of text on its head because he uses other vehicles of intelligibility, in this case ritual weeping, to circumscribe the limits of scripture and to find out where the boundaries of text as a vehicle of meaning might be. As teachers of religious studies, such alternative significant realities are available to us in abundant supply and, as cultural resources, we should make clear their power, logic, and coherence to our students.

Another example combines two other vehicles of meaning as alternatives that could prevent us from overemphasizing text as the primary metaphor of intelligibility. One is sound, the other is shadow. These are combined in studies of the Boróro and Krahó Indians of Brazil by Manuela Carneiro da Cunha, Renate Brigitte Viertler, and Jon Christopher Crocker.[25] The Boróro are the people that Lévi-Strauss visited and writes about so often. Viertler, Crocker and Carneiro de Cunha show that every Boróro and Krahó individual has at least two souls, one of which is the shadow. This shadow-soul concept occurs very frequently in cultural systems around the world. We all have shadows; shadows are singled out as carriers of meaning and bearers of a uniqueness that constitutes the individual.

The Bororó and Krahó illuminate the process by which the structure of the shadow and of sound organizes society. The shadow (seen more clearly in dreams and visions) and the sonic element that is involved with the sound of one's voice and the sound of one's name are

---

[24]See the discussion of underlying Inca beliefs concerning the stars, the calendar, the rains, and weeping in R. T. Zuidema, "Catachillay: The Role of the Pleiades and of the Southern Cross and alpha and beta Centauri in the Calendar of the Incas," in *Ethnoastronomy and Archaeoastronomy in the American Tropics*, eds. Anthony F. Aveni and Gary Urton, Annals of the New York Academy of Sciences, vol. 385 (New York: New York Academy of Sciences, 1982) pp. 203-29.

[25]Manuela Carneiro da Cunha, *Os mortos e os outros: Uma análise do sistema funerário e da noção de pessoa entre os índios krahó* (São Paulo: Editora Hucitec, 1978); Manuela Carneiro da Cunha, "De amigos formais e pessoa: de companheiros, espelhos, e identidades," *Boletim do Museu Nacional.* N. S. Antropologia, no. 32 (1979), pp. 31-39; Renate Brigitte Viertler, "A noção de pessoa entre os Bororo," *Boletim do Museu Nacional.* N. S. Antropologia, no. 32 (1979), pp. 20-30; Jon Christopher Crocker, *Vital Souls: Bororo Cosmology, Natural Symbolism, and Shamanism* (Tucson: University of Arizona Press, 1985). See also Roberto da Matta, *A Divided World: Apinaye Social Structure,* trans. Alan Campbell (Cambridge: Harvard University Press, 1982).

unique to each individual personality. When one traces the symbolic history of these two elements that are nestled in each individual, one sees to what extent they are "full symbolic facts" (playing on Marcel Mauss's notion of "the total social fact"). They offer access to social organization, political life, economic order, and cultural system, but as these realities are perceived by the cultural actors themselves. By not looking upon Boróro or Krahó cultures as texts one "reads" and by looking on society, politics and economics as species of the movements of shadow and sound, one beholds cultural order through the eyes of the people who embody and sustain it through their own understanding of it.

Let me make some general, illustrative remarks. In these groups, each individual has a name, but naming patterns differ for men and women. When a man marries, he marries out of his house, whereas a woman stays in her natal home; the man marries into the wife's father's house. When a young man moves to the woman's house to marry, he changes his name. Actually, men change their names rather frequently. They receive new names for hunting, when they kill certain animals for the first time, at initiation, at the moment when they receive a penis sheath or hair tube, and when they die. Men move from place to place in their lifetime and take on new names rather frequently. Names are, in fact, the places where heroic actions unfolded in mythic times. Women take names which are theirs for a lifetime and are derived from people who lived two generations before them and whose bones have now turned to powder. Women stay in the same residence throughout their lifetime. Over the course of many generations, women's names rotate, generation by generation, from one household to another, in circular fashion. There is a certain rhythm to this rotation of women's names, a lurching beat that advances only after long pauses. Men physically move in a diametric motion that cuts across the circle during their own life time. This circle and its radii represent the physical layout of the village.[26] The names people assume are the names of mythic heroes who performed extraordinary events at memorable places in mythic geography, as

---

[26]See the discussion of village form in da Matta, *A Divided World,* and also in Claude Lévi-Strauss, *Tristes Tropiques* (New York: Atheneum, 1974) pp. 220 ff. "The circular arrangement of the huts around the men's house is so important a factor in their social and religious life that the Salesian missionaries in the Rio des Garcas region were quick to realize that the surest way to convert the Bororo was to make them abandon their village in favour of one with the houses set out in parallel rows. Once they had been deprived of their bearings and were without the plan which acted as a confirmation of the native lore, the Indians soon lost any feeling for tradition; it was as if their social and religious systems . . . were too complex to exist without the pattern which was embodied in the plan of the village and of which their awareness was constantly being refreshed by their everyday activities" (ibid., p. 221).

recounted in the serial episodes of epic. The hero's name actually derives from the place where important mythic events unfolded. The layout of this enormous circular village (in former days housing more than a thousand people but now containing 100 to 400) reflects the order achieved in heroic actions, for the different houses represent the loci where the names of heroes descend from mythic time to the present day. The physical layout of the village is a static but summary representation of the achievements of mythic reality, which is projected through time, in a more dynamic and polyrhythmic way, through the lives of men and women. What men do in space in the rather short period of their own lifetime, women as corporate groups (lineages through which names descend over multiple generations) accomplish in opposite, but complementary fashion. This is as sophisticated a spatiotemporal calculus as the projection of a mathematical set across multiple topologies of space-time, a project which undermined Boolean algebra and quantitative logic and inspired the mathematician Saunders Mac Lane. The shadow and sound (name and voice), which are elementary structures of Boróro and Krahó order, do not derive from or inhere in a text. They reside in the matter of the human body. The name lodges in the marrow of the long bones of the leg. When a man dies, his bones, the container of his name, are transported back to his maternal home. The shadow is resident in the flesh until it putrefies. When flesh decomposes, the shadow (seen heretofore as a dream image in the form of an animal) transmigrates to take up residence in some other fleshly form, such as an animal, or is stored in the silent darkness of a mortuary gourd.

Obviously the views of the Boróro and Krahó pass beyond the Frazerian or Tylorian sense of shadow and souls. E. B. Tylor had lengthy discussions of shadows and souls in *Primitive Culture*,[27] but his concern was simply to discover that people have these ideas all over the world. He had neither the ethnographic details nor the hermeneutic sense to sift carefully through the applications of soul symbolism and sort out the subtle differences. We need not return to a time of such loose and nongenerative comparisons that only recognize apparent similarities. The imagery of shadow and sound would delineate interesting and different constructions of social reality and open up new critical understandings of social existence far from the "world of the text." These nontextual orders break the ice for a new hermeneutics of culture.

Boróro or Krahó name, voice, and shadow complete the physical construction of the human body. The sonic structure of bone marrow

---

[27]Edward Burnett Tylor, *Religion in Primitive Culture* (Gloucester: Peter Smith, 1970). More contemporary treatments of the notions of soul in religious traditions across the globe may be found in Lawrence E. Sullivan, ed., *Death, Afterlife and the Soul* (New York: Macmillan Publishing, 1989).

and the shadows inherent in the flesh lead to consideration of the whole material involvement of human individuals (their bone and their flesh) in the construction of social reality "on the ground" and in the images that any individual employs to reflect upon social reality as an historical and long-term existence. One recognizes oneself in the process: you are *there*. There is a sense of your agency, and also a sense of the way in which you have been subjected to this history that is your own. These are important issues to unearth in front of an audience of maturing young adults, for they illustrate how one gains a critical grasp of one's culture and history and how one evaluates one's place in it.

Besides weeping, shadow, and sound, a nontextual basis for reflecting on the human spirit's engagement with the world is the image of the body itself. A striking example of this is the study of the Belgian scholar René DeVisch, *Se recréer femme*, where he examines the body as a set of materially-based and ordered understandings that recreate culture.[28] Along quite different lines, Eduardo Viveiros de Castro, in his studies of the ritual construction of the person among the Yawalapiti, looks on the body as a container that self-consciously carries on a series of exchanges of fluids between itself and the outside world.[29] The internal items given off to the outside world in culturally defined ways include: sweat, urine, feces, blood, food, saliva, milk, semen, breath (controlled as speech) and so on. Viveiros de Castro emphasizes two moments to this micro-economy of exchanges effecting the human body. One process is fabrication. This is a negative process of alienation and increasing self-awareness. One denies oneself the eating and excreting habits of animals (or uncultured humans). Heightened symbolic control over bodily intake and output is especially noticeable during the critical moments of life passages. Basically, socially recognized moments of passage are possible because the body is an instrument riddled with passages (mouth, anus, ears, vagina, eyes). Throughout the process of individual acculturation, cultures puzzle themselves together in distinctive ways. At critical junctures of the life cycle (initiation, birth, death, marriage) special care is taken of one's ingestions and excretions and these ordered processes of care are the recognizably cultural patterns of table manners, sexual mores, bathroom postures and hygiene, observance of private spaces for sex, birth, initiation, and eating. One gives off fluids in culturally governed ways. Learning to control these fluids in the manner prescribed by your culture and becoming aware

---

[28]René Devisch, *Se recréer femme: Manipulation sémantique d'une situation d'infecondité chez les Yaka du Zaire* (Berlin: Dietrich Reimer Verlag, 1984).

[29]Eduardo B. Viveiros de Castro, "A Fabric\ação do corpo na sociedade xinguana," *Boletim do Museu Nacional*, N. S. Anthropologia, no. 32 (May, 1979) pp. 40-49.

of that self-control (the imposition of conscious form on matter) provokes individual growth and acculturation. That is the heart of initiation. One not only does not urinate, eat or have sex wherever and whenever one wishes, but one discovers cultural reasons for the abstentions. Through the acts of control and the reflections on its meaning, one becomes aware of *oneself* as the *person* governing urination, emissions of semen, or milk, or menstrual blood, or whatever fluid is controlled in a prescribed cultural manner. By regulating the micro-economic exchanges of the body and by denying to the individual the other possible ways of controlling these fluids (ways characteristic of animals or other cultural varieties of humans), an individual is "fabricated" by society. Fabrication is a negative process because it alienates nonhuman possibilities from human self-awareness and practice. Culture is reproduced while the individual is being fabricated. Each culture has its notions about what a human being is.

The cycle of life passages fabricates a person because the body itself is an instrument of passages. The body has openings and appendages that penetrate those openings. The mouth, the anus, the ears, the vagina, the penis, the nipples of the breast exhibit rhythms and periodicities which can be coordinated culturally. Learning how to coordinate them is a negative process that defines distinct cultures. The controlled micro-economy of symbolic exchange during initiation and other life passages pares down the options to reveal the quintessentials of being human, the image of the wise person, and the normative or ideal humanizing process. In this view, language is one of the controlled excretions of the body. The mouth excretes air in a way that is temporally coordinated with the movements of the material body—lungs, teeth, tongue, lips, saliva—and coordinated as well with movements to express cultural purpose and historical understanding. Language is thus a distinctive instrument of human culture, but it is not the only or all-embracing one. Speech is one form of critical excretion.

Viveiros de Castro does not think that the ritual construction of the person is only a negative process. There is a second, more positive process called metamorphosis. Once one has fabricated a critical and self-aware practice of one's difference from other cultures and from animals, cultures intentionally set in motion the process of metamorphosis wherein one reappropriates, though self-consciously, the behaviors and timings that were said to belong to other kinds of beings. One lives beyond the norm, deliberately and symbolically extending experience by acting like a foreigner or animal during a festival dance or dressing and eating like a god or mythic hero. The process of metamorphosis cuts against the process of fabrication, but self-consciously. Human consciousness transcends its limited bounds and expands its horizons.

There is no need to defend this approach to make my point. I am simply suggesting that religious studies has many ways of coming at culture. Table manners, bathroom etiquette, private property, arts and crafts, sexual mores, sound, shadow, and speech itself can lead to full and stimulating accounts without passing through textual metaphor or linguistic orders derived from texts. And these alternatives open to a hermeneutics, to a fully critical appraisal of the process of interpretation.

By discovering the limits of text as the governing or domineering image in literate cultures—biblical, in the wide sense—we can set language in context and see it as a *species* of symbolic performance. This better allows us to grasp what is distinctive about language and literacy as a cultural style of human existence in time. My purpose in discovering an end to the primacy of text is not simply to disparage text. I wish to understand text, because it is one of the great motivating realities in our own cultural existence. I wish to examine the cultural and cognitive ends of a text-based existence. I am suggesting ways in which religious studies can come to grips with that. Text and language need not create meaning, especially where meaning in the religious tradition is often a given or revealed reality. But texts can be stylizations that make meaning remarkable and give it specific historical forms and terms, just as dance, music, and bathroom etiquette do. I entitled this reflection "Seeking an End to the Text" in order to underline the need to find or bring an end to an overly literary approach to the religious condition, because religious life has thrived without the written word. If there exists an intrinsic relationship between religiosity and literacy, it is not literacy that is the all-embracing set that includes religious expression, but the other way around. Seeking an end to the text means dealing with the forms of religious reflection that lie beyond the margins of the text and beyond the materiality of language. By discovering those realities at the borders, or by probing those obstinate objects in the center of our vision which resist complete assimilation to text-metaphors, we can move toward a better grasp of the singularity of text: not only the *terminus a quo* of the text, the point at which text ends, but also the *terminus ad quem*, the end *towards* which language and text impel us. We can also evaluate in a more critical way—continuing the pun here—the interpretive terminology generated in interpreting text.[30] We can come to terms with

---

[30] "[O]ne cannot assign a place to linguistics, much less make a science of signification, without a theory of social history as the interaction of various signifying practices. Then the true value of the thinking that sees every realm organized as a language can be appreciated. Only then can the place of language, as well as that of meaning and the sign, find their exact coordinates" (Kristeva, *Language—the Unknown*, p. 328).

the peculiarity of textual terminology and we can scrutinize its relative appropriateness and adequacy for understanding the religious condition of being human.

PART II: KNOWLEDGE, POWER AND THE CULTIVATION OF VALUES

RETHINKING THE HUMANITIES FOR THE 1990S: REDRESSING THE BALANCE OF POWER[1]

George W. Pickering

It seems almost certain that no one will refer to the 1990s, as almost everyone does to the 1890s, as the "gay nineties." Too much has both happened and failed to happen in the last hundred years for that. The very word "gay" has lost its innocence. The celebration of wealth has revealed its dark side. Industry and technology have lost their apparent autonomy. The sciences have become more powerful in the culture at large, but less intelligible and therefore more frightening to the average citizen. The "American Moment" in world history has come and gone, and the "restructuring" of international relations is under way for the second or third time in this century. The simple harmonies of Strauss waltzes and the regular cadences of Souza marches have given way to polyphonic dissonance in popular as well as "classical" music.

And there it is. Even to speak that sentence, we have to put the word "classical" in quotation marks. The whole standard for what should count as "classical" has not only ceased to be self-evident; it has become a "battlefront" where the smoke is so thick that culture, politics and religion have become virtually indistinguishable. This is not all bad news.

When I was a boy at the Boston Latin School, we got a "classical" education. That meant we learned Latin and other European languages, studied history and math and became immersed in the uses of our own language. For all the adaptations which had been made over the centuries, we were still relying on the Renaissance concept of "classical." This was still the case when I got to Bates College in the mid-1950s.

[1]I want to thank The Atlanta University Center, the Southern Education Foundation, and the Andrew W. Mellon Foundation for their support in the preparation of this paper and for the invitation to participate in their consultation, "Re-thinking the Humanities for the 21st Century," October 12-13, 1989.

I have no desire to see the Renaissance expelled from the academy; but the whole pressure of the mind in the twentieth century has been to broaden the notion of "the classical" it has long defined. We have wanted a Renaissance of our own. For some portion of this century, many believed that it was happening under the aegis of "Progress." No one can believe that anymore. The Renaissance of the twentieth century, if there is to be one, will depend on two things: the recovery of the Enlightenment, not as a frozen ideal for a settled universe, but as a space/time station, a spiritual starting point for the exploration and renovation of an unfinished one; and the broadening of the canon to include other cultures and other voices within our own. That is, our goal cannot be a repristination of the Renaissance, but a recovery its spirit. If we may take Erasmus as our guide, being true to the spirit of the Renaissance is the only profound way to be true to it at all, the spirit of overcoming provincialism, sectarianism, and dogmatism in order to provide an education which not only informs the mind, but liberates the human spirit as well.

There are today, however, articulate and well-financed voices urging us to return to a more restrictive version of the Renaissance as an alternative to recovering the Enlightenment in our thinking about the humanities, voices endeavoring to shrink the canon in the name of wisdom. The name of Allan Bloom comes readily to mind in this context. His message is that the ancients were right, that the life of reason really is only for the few, that it is irrational to believe otherwise; this being the case, the recovery of the humanities requires turning its curriculum into a fraternity in the nearly literal, colloquial sense of that word. The Enlightenment with its egalitarian appeals was a mistake for politics and for "philosophy"; the time has come to rectify that mistake and regain the aristocratic grounds that true humanists know is their only salvation. Professor Bloom does not shrink back from the political conclusions which his argument implies: since irrational claims to equality are the ruin of philosophy (which is his code word for the humanities generally), and since these same claims are a threat to American power, philosophy should not be too proud to make the alliances necessary for its own well-being. It should come to aid of American power in its battle with their common enemy: egalitarian ideals. That is the way Allan Bloom wants to rethink the humanities for the 1990s.

It is not the way I want to rethink the humanities for the 1990s, but credit should be given where it is due. Bloom put his finger on the central issue for the humanities in our culture and all others: what to make of the Enlightenment claims for universal and equal rights. As Bloom would have it, these claims were just a "noble lie" and have now outlived their usefulness; indeed, they have become dangerous as both "philosophers" and American statesmen can see. "For the first time in four hundred years, it seems possible and imperative to begin all over again, to try to figure out what Plato was talking about, because it might be the best thing available," writes Bloom with reference to the Republic.[2] In this, he at least put his finger on the intrinsically political character of rethinking the humanities. It is not a simple question of how we shall present the past. It is basically a question of how we do in fact present the sense of what is humanly possible and desirable, the possible reach of the human spirit and the institutions that have been and may be needed to support that reach.

In Professor Bloom's world this is a settled question because, as he would have it and have it taught, "[In] antiquity all philosophers had the same practical politics, inasmuch as none believed it feasible or salutary to change the relations between rich and poor in a fundamental or permanently progressive way."[3] In his tradition, this is what the humanities have always understood and taught; and in his future, it will have to be understood by the populace as well, even if it takes the full use of American power to teach that lesson.

Bloom's reading of antiquity is not all that unusual. When Ernst Troeltsch did his study of the social teaching of the Christian Churches in 1911, he came to much the same conclusion. His thoughts are worth recalling:

> A religious doctrine like that of Christian monotheism, which takes religion out of the sphere of existing conditions and the existing order and turns it purely into an ethical religion of redemption, will possess and reveal the radicalism of an ethical and universal ideal in face of all existing conditions. But, on the other hand, just because it is a religious faith which believes that the whole world and its order is being guided by God, in spite of devils and demons, just because it means submission to the Will of God who predestines and allows all kinds of human differences to exist, it can never be a principle of revolution. So far it will always have a conservative trait of adaption and submission towards the existing social order and social institutions, the conditions of power and their variations. A theoretic revolutionary tendency will only be possible in the sphere of abstract rationalism which, from the point of view of the individual and his generally reasonable point of view, restores the rational element, and only recognizes the Divine element in the universality of reason, but not in the irrational course of things which cannot be controlled by the individual. Therefore modern rationalism alone

---

[2]Allan Bloom, *The Closing of the American Mind: How Higher Education Has Failed Democracy and Impoverished the Souls of Today's Students* (New York: Simon and Schuster, 1987) p. 310.

[3]Bloom, p. 289.

provides the sphere for a revolutionary principle in theory and practice
which will construct Society according to the claims of Reason.[4]

Ancient religion, like ancient philosophy, did not think of recon-
structing society and its politics along *any* sort of egalitarian lines, no
more in Augustine's *City of God* than in Plato's *Republic*. On this,
Bloom and Troeltsch agree. For Troeltsch, however, egalitarianism
defined the new task of reason which the Enlightenment ushered in.
For Bloom, it is time to say that this move towards egalitarian ideals
was a mistake. We cannot teach the humanities in the 1990s without
taking sides on this issue.

By "the Enlightenment," I have in mind that cluster of ideas
which asserted that reason had a constructive and progressive role to
play in human affairs, that everyone would be better off politically
and materially if new roles for reason could be institutionalized, and
that the key to this revolution lay in affirming the basic and fundamental equality of human beings as creatures with rights, inalienable
rights—not just as creatures with negotiable interests; and that securing those rights provides the substance of justice—not the whole of it,
but the indispensable bedrock of it, the absence of which was
grounds for altering or abolishing governments. It was a vision that
the grounds for civility were also the grounds for revolution if they
were sufficiently violated. It was actually Thomas Jefferson who put
the matter this way, even though he is commonly left out of
generalizations about the "Enlightenment."

We cannot turn our backs on the delivery of power, authority and
dignity into human hands which was represented in the Enlightenment, any more than we can avert our eyes from the murderous potential which was and is part of that delivery. The American Enlightenment, at least, left us more than a collection of philosophical tracts;
it left a legacy of constitutionalism and rights-regarding institutions
for us to work with and to work on. What we have learned from the
Enlightenment—and, to some extent, because of it—is to be aware of
the social consequences of universals. The role of reason in human affairs remains the great hope, and one of the deep mysteries, of the
human condition. Certainly we have to get over what James Luther
Adams called "the immaculate conception of ideas," the notion of
pure autonomous reason unaffected by the context in which it must
operate, and unmindful of the social and political consequences
which must inevitably follow in the wake of its logics.

Consider what happened to Darwin in the nineteenth century. No
sooner had he proposed his law of natural selection and genetic vari-

---

[4]Ernst Troeltsch, *The Social Teaching of the Christian Churches,* Olive Wyon trans.,
with an introduction by H. Richard Niebuhr, Harper Torchbooks, The Cloister
Library (New York: Harper and Brothers, 1960) p. 85.

ation as a possible universal for explaining the biological evolution of species (a proposition which could not be fully demonstrated even in its intended sphere of application until Watson and Crick cracked the genetic code in the 1950s), no sooner was Darwin off the press than his universal was taken to be the explanation of social life generally— the survival of the fittest—and turned into a justification for racism, poverty, powerlessness, inequality and the idea that democracy was an *unnatural* idea. Modern science, it seemed, had formed an alliance with ancient wisdom: freedom was for the few who could make it to the top of the heap, whatever it was a heap of.

It was the Enlightenment that put the issue of human rights at the top of the political agenda; and it is only in situations where some lively connection with the ideas of the Enlightenment has been maintained, that rights have had any place at all on either the political or the intellectual agenda. Admittedly, the phrase "some lively connection" is vague, though deliberately so given the manifold forms of the historical connection with the Enlightenment to which it refers. Whitehead said that the story of the modern world is the story of Steam and Democracy, the story of brute force and civilized purpose in their many-layered encounters with each other, their diverse compromises with each other, their endless struggle with each other.

The understanding, the analysis, and the evaluation of that story, the ways in which it rose out of materials provided by older traditions, the ways in which it transformed and transfigured those older cultures, the themes which it incorporated and the themes which it left behind, the incredible chain of global consequences which it set in motion and which have not yet played themselves out, the transformations and transfigurations which it has undergone as it has touched and been touched by the diverse cultures, the new energies that have been released and the institutions that have been altered or invented to accommodate those new energies, all this is the task of the humanities. Taken as a whole, "the humanities" have to survey the human enterprise both descriptively and normatively with a view to showing students what ideas people have lived with and lived by, what forms human communities have taken, what purposes have been pursued and to what effect, and where we are now, that is, what ideas and what forms of community and range of purposes are available to us, and what the current arguments are about and why they matter.

It is clear that we cannot do this on a "value-free" basis. I see no problem in that because it is clear to me that it has never been done on a value-free basis. We are, after all, *professors*. We profess something. And our students need to know what that is, whether we are purporting to teach them the structure of a good sentence or the structure of a good society. By virtue of our power, we have our academic freedom in the classroom. As a practical matter, once we enter the classroom our courses are about whatever we say they are about. Everyone is counting on us to make judicious, professionally informed, culturally productive and educationally relevant decisions on that score. Maybe we do, maybe we do not; but *we* do it. It is imperative, therefore, that we organize our instruction in such a way as to promote the academic freedom of our students. That is our contribution to enhancing their freedom as citizens and as private persons.

We achieve this end partly by classroom strategies, and partly by asserting and demonstrating the intellectual claims of the humanities. I have some thoughts about the first, though I believe the second is really at the heart of the matter. Teachers have to employ classroom strategies that fit their general personalities. A University of Michigan study of teaching styles and teaching effectiveness, researched by McKeachie and Newcomb in the 1950s, stands as a monument to common sense.[5] They found that the teaching style which is most effective was the one with which the teacher felt most at home. Period. So the issue of classroom pedagogy is one which each teacher must work out individually, though not without being as well-informed as possible about alternative strategies and the range of available options.

There is a point, however, where classroom strategy and the substance of the humanities must be consonant with each other. That is the issue of judgement. Making judgements about human activities is what we do in the humanities. We teach the judgements that others have made about the human condition and its prospects. We need, therefore, to teach students what is involved in making judgements of their own, providing some reasonable standards for that, including enough diversity in the materials we present so that they are not required to adopt our judgements in order to pass the course. Pedagogically, this is the challenge of the humanities; but it will degenerate into *mindless* relativism unless it be joined with the intellectual claims of the humanities. It comes down, then, to a question of just what claims the humanities make in culture, in society, and therefore in the university. I need not rehearse the bad time we have had these past thirty years in articulating these claims whether we consider the intellectual, the cultural or—indeed, especially—the administrative claims of the humanities.

It is all about power, what we teach and why we teach and whom we teach. My thesis from here on out is that when we lose track of

---

[5]W. J. McKeachie, "Procedures and Techniques of Teaching: A Survey of Experimental Studies," in Nevitt Sanford, ed., *The American College: A Psychological and Social Interpretation of the Higher Learning* (New York and London: John Wiley and Sons, Inc., 1962) pp. 312-64.

that, we lose track of everything. Education is for the empowerment of the students, to help them in their efforts to make a living and to have a life of their own. When they come to see us, they know that they have to make a living; but they have much less clear ideas about what is involved in having a life of their own. How best to do that seems to most of them "a matter of opinion," not a matter of alternative virtues and values. Indeed, virtues and values of all sorts seem to them to be mostly, or merely, a matter of opinion; and, once this great truth has been spoken, they do not have much of an idea where to take the conversation from there. It appears to them to be a way to stop a discussion, not a way to begin an inquiry. Most of the students I am referring to here are between eighteen and twenty-two years old. As we see more and more students over thirty in our classrooms, we begin to deal with people who know in some existential way that having a life of your own is a problematic proposition, and that making a living does not automatically solve that question and may, in fact, complicate it. Either way, it is hard for students to see what on earth the humanities might have to do with either making a living or having a life of your own.

Even though they do not know much science, they do know what a science is as a career option. Even though they do not know much about business, they are aware that "business" is full of career options. It is the same with engineering, architecture, education and the other professions—medicine, dentistry, law, ministry and their allied career options. But what about the humanities? What does that lead to? Maybe a handful of students want to be writers. Another handful think of academic careers. The rest take humanities courses because they have to: the course is in the core curriculum, or law schools want it.

If they look beyond themselves to the society at large, what do they see? They see that in a world where everything is supposed to pay its own way and do a little better than that, the humanities are a charity case. Where others get contracts, the humanities get grants, really small ones by contemporary financial standards. The message is clear that the humanities are more or less luxuries—not, it is true, very expensive ones, but luxuries nonetheless that get funded after the big ticket items have been secured. "Culture" is for people who have some extra time and money. I remember Robert Frost lecturing at Ann Arbor in 1961. He remarked how he was always being invited to universities, libraries and museums to read his poems, not to Rotary Clubs, engineering societies and business meetings. He said he was really tired of men who would come up to him and say, "My wife just loves your poetry." He had taken to responding, "What's the matter with you? Can't you read?" If our students look beyond themselves to the society at large, this is what they see, or something just like it.

If they look around campus, the picture is not much different. Psychology and communications do well because business is interested in them. Economics, when it is still included in the humanities, does well for the same reasons. Departmental budgets and faculty rewards seem to follow the same drift. The administrative class which has emerged on campus as an independent force over the past thirty years has about the same values and perspectives as in-coming freshmen. As a result, we find these values and perspectives—sometimes dignified with references to a "market orientation"—communicated in their policies and practices. In my experience, this is not a phenomenon of the "Reagan years." Its emergence preceded that era by about a decade.

After the first ten years of teaching at a university, I sat down to record my reflections; and as I reread them yet another ten years later, I can see that it had been a long, hard decade, the 1970s. "Had I not read Albee and Pinter in the 1960s," I wrote, "I wouldn't have had a clue to higher education in the 1970s." It seemed to me that sophistry was the reigning theory in higher education, a two-variable scheme, power and opinion, under which the higher purposes and the deeper meanings of education were being betrayed. Apparently on the idea that it is better to tell the truth than to live a lie, I wrote the following: "Forget this old stuff about Arts and Sciences, Business, Engineering, and the like, hopelessly nineteenth-century stuff anyway, all based on the idea that there are actually things to be known, when in fact there are just different kinds of opinions, some of which you can get paid for holding, some of which are psychically satisfying, some of which are interpersonally attractive. We should just get on with it. Clean up the university. Reorganize again. Have a Division of Financially Rewarding Opinions, a Division of Psychically Rewarding Opinions, a Division of Interpersonally Rewarding Opinions, and (let's be liberals about this) a Division of Utterly Optional Opinions. That is where the humanities end up anyway." There is an unmistakable tone of feeling abused and sorry for oneself in those reflections; and I quote them with some embarrassment only because I believe they reflect a mood which everyone associated with the humanities over these past thirty years can recognize and remember. That is the mood we get into, and that is the shape that our world assumes, when we lose track of the fact that our subject matter is power, and that both our students and our culture are deprived of important resources when we do forget that.

In rethinking the humanities for the 1990s, we need to pay attention to the internal need for renewal in the humanities as well as the external and environmental impediments on which we so self-servingly love to dwell. Earlier on, I stressed the Enlightenment notion of human rights and the practical uses of reason as a context for this renewal; but we still have to look at the issue of broadening the canon in that context as well. And I will say, as an opening salvo on this topic, that the use of predigested textbooks, written at a high school level, complete with study guides for the teachers no less than the students, is a more scandalous betrayal of the humanities and of our students than all the acts of administrative terrorism that we have lived through these past twenty years. The use of these books is self-inflicted trivialization.

The use of these textbooks, which is apparently very widespread given the mass marketing of them, is a sure sign that we are lost, not only in our concept of higher education, but in our concept of education generally. It has to mean that we are thinking of education as simply the presentation and retention of information. Learning some information and remembering some of it is surely part of what education is about; but it can never be what education itself is about, or even basically about. The National Endowment for the Humanities keeps releasing surveys showing what high school and college graduates have forgotten, if they ever knew; and that is supposed to stand not only as evidence of our poor education process, but also as an indication of how to improve it. We should run schools where students remember the information they have heard or read. This is called "getting tough," having standards.

It is not surprising that the President and the Governors could meet at the University of Virginia in September 1989 to discuss the problems of education and not come up with a single new idea on the subject. Students should be able to read, write, do math, and think. Schools should have to meet tough standards on these counts—or else. Kids should start earlier, work harder, stay longer in school. Something bad should happen to teachers and principals if their students keep failing. None of this should cost any more money than we now spend on the schools that we do not like. So much for ideas, not to mention new ideas. These are tired old slogans. Do we want better schools? Then let's talk about renegotiating the implied contract between the schools and the business community. The old one, the one that sustained both public and private schools for a century, from the 1840s to the 1950s, has broken down. During those years, elementary and secondary schools did reasonably well in preparing students to make a living. To be sure, they never did that well for blacks. Absorbing them into the business system on an equal basis with everyone else was not part of the compact. Making it part of the new compact is sociologically and morally the single most pressing item on the national agenda. Making the schools work for those children is the key to making them work better for everyone.

Real education is a transfer of power; and the society has to stand behind that transfer of power, or else it will not take place no matter how good the teachers and principals and professors may be. Plato stressed the two-fold character of power, the power to influence and the power to be influenced. So did John Locke. That is not the issue on which ancients and moderns part company. Once this two-fold character of power is admitted, however, we are faced with the dilemma posed by Aristotle in his *Ethics and Politics*, namely, that no sharp distinction can be made between our ethics and our epistemology, or between education and politics: to get a good society, we need a good system of education; but to get a good system of education, we need a good society. The defects in the one are an accurate indicator of the defects in the other, not the sort of thing contemporary presidents and governors like to talk about.

We cannot expect to improve our education while avoiding the moral dimension of the question; and having said that, we are back to the intellectual, cultural and administrative claims of the humanities. All education aims at enhancing the agency of the students, increasing their capacity to act as individuals and in association with others. We do this by introducing them to the disciplined study of "the powers that be": in nature, in history, in bodies of knowledge, in organizations, in language, custom, critical analysis and creative imagination. But education is a promise on the part of the society that if students will learn these things, that is to say, if they will develop some of these powers and make them their own, then we will do everything in our power to make room for them.

This means that the education we offer has to be morally competent and it has to be an education into moral competence. In the final analysis, the actual worth of an education depends on the virtues it promotes; and make no mistake about it, *all* education promotes some virtues. They may be high or low, they may be relevant or irrelevant to either making a living or having a life of your own; but it is the task of the humanities to examine these questions. When the humanities are weak, such questions are not pursued with their full intellectual seriousness; and their absence makes for the stuff that predigested textbooks are made of.

In rethinking the humanities for the 1990s, therefore, we must begin by taking stock of what virtues we are in fact promoting in our classrooms, in the encounter of students with materials, and in the encounter of students with us. Are we promoting the active or the passive virtues? The passive ones are: be obedient, don't cheat, keep quiet, stay to yourself, don't forget what you've been told, work hard and then you can get to tell other people what to do. Actually, these would be better termed "passive-aggressive virtues." Active virtues are more complex and capacitating: the capacity for association involves the virtue of sociability; the capacity for taking initiatives involves the virtue of personal responsibility; the capacity for giving and withholding consent involves the virtuous arts of persuasion; the capacity for making judgements involves the virtue of conscience; the capacity for purposeful interaction involves the virtue of political responsibility; the capacity to reason involves the virtue of intellectual responsibility. All I am saying here is that we have to think about this question of the virtues that we are actually promoting in our direct teaching.

Then we have also the question of virtues by which others have lived, the reasons they have found for doing it, and the ways they have found to express themselves—that is, the virtues encountered in the subject matter of the humanities. Here I think we must rely on primary sources and actual studies as much as possible, so that our students can see what it looks like when people are really trying to make sense of things; they also allow our students to see that even those who have made momentous contributions may still have serious weaknesses of their own. Until very recently, we do not find writers making the effort to be gender inclusive in their language. In fact, given our history, it is a wonder that the Humanities were not called the study of Man. Students need to see the habitual sexism even in otherwise excellent thinkers in order to understand why gender-inclusive language is an important issue. In order to see the virtues of others, we no not need to be blind to their vices, nor indeed to our own.

This is one important step in expanding the canon; but another important step is listening to new voices, the voices that criticize the western canon, and the voices that come out of other histories entirely. Here we need to listen very carefully, because these voices test our powers of judgement in new ways. They speak from new metaphors.

The spread of Religious Studies Departments and the internal development of religious studies as a field of inquiry has been one of the very important forces in the curriculum for expanding the canon; but it also brings us face to face with the central and abiding issues of the humanities. *We cannot give up our own metaphors and we cannot be dismissive of others.* At this point, the word "comparative" becomes a crucial and problematic term. We cannot help but be comparative in our presentation of the abiding and deep diversities which have always characterized humankind. Neither, however, can we avoid the fact that "comparative" is a word that implies judgement. This is an issue which is inherent in all humanistic inquires. The good thing about religious studies is that it is one field in which this issue cannot be buried. Alternative religious orientations offer and assert alternative comparative standards, and the study of them gives us an opportunity to see those standards in operation, as historic and live options.

Religions are the poetry of power, the complex metaphorical structures in which metaphysical claims are ultimately made and lived by. They represent apprehensions of what the ultimate powers are with which we have to deal in having "a life of our own," as individuals, as communities, as humanity. Religions bring us face to face with what William James called the *reality* of the unseen. Power, after all, is invisible. It is experienced; but it is not "empirical" in the usual sense of the word. Its presence has to be expressed symbolically and metaphorically. This is the stubborn fact that we are up against in religious studies; and therein lies the revelatory power of religious studies for the rest of the humanities, if I may put it that way. I am not arguing for theology as the queen of the sciences, but I am saying that religious studies goes to the heart of the humanities and lays open the profound issues with which we must all deal. All disciplines deal with metaphors of power which have metaphysical claims deeply embedded in those metaphorical structures. The metaphoric structures of the sciences, the roles of organization, concepts, research, evidence and "results" within those structures is an important field of inquiry in its own right; it is also important because it might make science more intelligible to the citizens of this scientific culture in which we find ourselves. The same is true of business, engineering and the professions. Acknowledging the metaphoric structures of disparate disciplines and bringing to light their conjunctions in culture and society are neglected tasks in the humanities.

Instead of treating these enterprises as competitors for student attention and feeding off the ironies of their pretenses, we should try to produce courses and a literature which can help to assess them as humanistic endeavors, in need of being judged by their actual ambiguous achievements and not just by their idealistic theories. We do this for religion; we can do it for the other power centers as well. This is an expansion of the canon which I hope some of us involved with the humanities in the 1990s will help to produce. There is no reason why the critical task of the humanities cannot also be a constructive task that not only extends our knowledge, but our self-understanding as well.

There is much work for the humanities to do in the decade ahead: defending human rights as a rational idea, exploring the conditions under which they can be secured, expanding the canon, exploring the diverse metaphoric structures which are meeting and mingling around the globe as we speak; and in the midst of all this, helping as best we can to increase the power of our students to have a decent life of their own.

CONFIDENCE AND CRITICISM: RELIGIOUS STUDIES AND THE PUBLIC PURPOSES OF LIBERAL EDUCATION

Robin W. Lovin

Much ink has been spent of late documenting the self-centeredness and privatization that characterize American life today.[1] Peter Berger describes the deterioration of the "mediating structures" that once provided communities on a human scale between the isolated individual and the impersonal state. Christopher Lasch speaks of a "culture of narcissism" that absorbs persons in an infinitely regressive search for self-awareness and fulfillment. Robert Bellah and his colleagues suggest that Americans at the end of the twentieth century lack even a language in which to express their commitment to values and causes larger than their own satisfaction.[2] Even those whose reading in social analysis extends no further than the Sunday papers are aware of the "Yuppie's" fierce competitiveness and consumerism, and of the "New Age" religious movements which seem to fulfill Ernst Troeltsch's prediction that the characteristic religion of the modernity would be an individualized mysticism without social structures.[3] We are increasingly clear that as a society, we do not know how to explain what it is that binds us to one another, or why it is that we ought to do something to preserve those social ties and pass them on to future generations. Beyond all the particular issues of taxes, trade, arms control, or abortion, there is a growing doubt about our capacity to make public choices about any of them.

As if that general malaise were not enough, those who study and teach in higher education, and especially in the liberal arts, seem to be

---

[1]The author is grateful to the faculty of Lafayette College and to the Association for General and Liberal Studies for opportunities to present and discuss earlier versions of this essay.

[2]Peter Berger, *Facing Up to Modernity* (New York: Basic Books, 1977); Christopher Lasch, *The Culture of Narcissism* (New York: Norton, 1978); Robert Bellah, *et. al.*, *Habits of the Heart* (Berkeley: University of California Press, 1985).

[3]Ernst Troeltsch, *The Social Teachings of the Christian Churches* (Chicago: University of Chicago Press, 1976), pp. 797-802. [First published, 1911.]

experiencing their own crisis of purpose. There is a continuing debate about what liberal arts students ought to know, which students are most likely to benefit from this type of education, and how its goals cohere with the relentless emphasis on career preparation that dominates many institutions. Allan Bloom has sparked the widest discussion of these issues,[4] but most of the readers of this essay will have more specific and vivid memories of this controversy in their own experiences.

That these two crises, the crisis in public life and the crisis in liberal education, should occur simultaneously should be no surprise to those who understand the historic connections between liberal education and public life. The root idea of a liberal education, after all, is not a curriculum heavy on French, philosophy, and English literature, rather than, say, mechanical engineering or accounting procedures. The root idea of a liberal education is preparation for the *public* choices that must be made in a free society. The idea of liberal education is that above and beyond what you have to know to manage your own affairs, there is what you have to know to help shape the life of society as a whole wisely. At a time when we are confused about how those public choices are to be made and whether they are even possible, liberal education inevitably begins to be problematic, too. If public choices are impossible, or if public life is not worth the effort, then liberal education as preparation for that life seems pointless.

It is that intrinsic connection between public life and the problems of liberal education that I want to focus on in this essay, in the hope that a clearer understanding of the public purposes of liberal education may suggest new ideas about the study of religion as a part of that education. My aim, then, is to identify a distinctive role that religious studies might play in a renewal of thinking about public life that needs to happen in the society at large.

One way to formulate liberal education's contribution to public life is to say that it should provide both *confidence* and *criticism*. Liberal education should build in its students a certain security about their mastery of the achievements of human civilization. One of the things that prepares liberally educated men and women for participation in public life is the sense that they understand, in depth, the issues about which they are called to make choices, and that the things they have learned and the values they have adopted in the course of their education are adequate to these challenges. When someone with a liberal education confronts a group at the school board who want to censor the books in the high school library, she needs to know enough about the traditions and values of human cultures to come up

---

[4]Allan Bloom, *The Closing of the American Mind* (New York: Simon and Schuster, 1987).

with a less parochial view of what is acceptable, and she needs to know enough about the traditions of free speech and constitutional protections to take on the issue with confidence that she can come up with a better answer. Building that confidence in the resources one brings to public life is part of what liberal education is about.

There is, however, also a critical side to liberal education, without which confidence quickly degenerates into arrogance. Liberal education is about developing an awareness of one's own limitations. Liberal education includes learning how statements of noble ideals sometimes mask rather crude assertions of self-interest, learning that problems are never as simple as they first seem, and that the real motives for a person's actions and choices are often hidden, even from the person who acts and chooses. Since Socrates, liberal education has measured its success in part not by the confidence it builds, but by the way it undermines confidence in easy and self-serving answers.

What I want to suggest, then, is that our uncertainty about how to prepare persons to make public choices is reflected in our inability to strike a working balance between confidence and criticism in liberal education. We cannot get along with an idea of liberal education that relies only on confidence *or* criticism, but we cannot appreciate the difficulties in striking the balance without some historical perspective on how the problem as we now have it emerged. The changing place of religion in liberal education reflects the unstable equilibrium between confidence and criticism, and the possibility of striking a new balance between them requires, among other things, a reassessment of the place of religious studies in the liberal arts curriculum.

II.

Sometime during the nineteenth century, and probably before rather than after the middle of it, an observer of colleges and universities in the United States could have concluded that liberal education and *confidence* were intimately related. In most schools, the highest purposes of education were acknowledged to be moral, and the mark of an educated man was a character shaped to fit the requirements of a civil society composed of free and equal individuals.[5] For most undergraduates, liberal education culminated in a course on moral philosophy, taught by the college president, which summarized and rendered explicit the moral foundations of the entire curriculum.[6]

---

[5]See, for example, the popular textbook by Francis Wayland, *The Elements of Moral Science* (Cambridge, Mass.: Belknap Press of Harvard University Press, 1963), pp. 174-181, 306-23. [First published, 1835.]

[6]D. H. Meyer, *The Instructed Conscience: The Shaping of the American National Ethic* (Philadelphia: University of Pennsylvania Press, 1972); Wilson Smith, *Pro-*

These courses frankly served the social purpose of instilling standards and expectations that matched the needs of the society, but
they were not without critical standards. Far from encouraging rote
conformity or passive acceptance of tradition, the aim of education
was to provide a rational system that would overcome oppressive,
inegalitarian customs and provide a logically compelling argument
for Enlightenment morals. Kant's "categorical imperative" suggests
the key idea of this critical method. It requires, in one of its formulations, that any proposed action be tested against the question, "Could
I will this action as a universal law?"[7] That is, could I consistently
propose not only that I do this, or that members of my group, or my
social class, or citizens of my nation do it, but that every rational being similarly situated should do it? It is a test that, taken seriously,
would rule out a great many traditional social practices and irrational
preferences for one's own good above that of other persons.

Kant's categorical imperative has become the paradigm of a critical principle, but in Britain and America, the standard most often
employed was the utilitarian principle first suggested by the Scottish
moralists of the eighteenth century and elaborated by Jeremy Bentham and John Stuart Mill. The principle of utility requires that
courses of action be evaluated in terms of whether "the tendency
which it has to augment the happiness of the community is greater
than any which it has to diminish it."[8] Proponents of utilitarianism
were convinced that this test would rule out a great many familiar
social discriminations, especially those that excluded talented people
in favor of persons who were entitled to positions by birth and the
discriminations that kept women out of education and positions of
leadership. For Bentham, especially, "custom" and "tradition" were
negative terms, almost as bad as what he called "superstition," by
which he meant especially religious standards of conduct that do not
conform to the principle of utility.[9]

Nevertheless, those who adapted the utilitarian ideas of Bentham
and Mill to the requirements of collegiate education found the principle of promoting the greatest happiness of the greatest number
broadly consistent with the requirements of customary morality and
the teachings of Christianity. William Paley, the Anglican theologian
whose *Principles of Moral and Political Philosophy* remained an important text through most of the nineteenth century, offered a defense of

---

fessors and Public Ethics: Studies of Northern Moral Philosophers Before the Civil War
(Ithaca: Cornell University Press, 1956).

[7]Immanuel Kant, *Groundwork of the Metaphysics of Morals*, trans. H. J. Paton
(New York: Harper Torchbooks, 1964), p. 88. [First published, 1785.]

[8]Jeremy Bentham, *The Principles of Morals and Legislation* (New York: Hafner
Publishing Company, 1948), p. 3. [First published, 1789.]

[9]Ibid., p. 59.

a broad range of English social and legal practices in utilitarian terms, while suggesting moderate reforms in property law and criminal punishments according to the same principles.[10] Francis Wayland, whose *Elements of Moral Science* largely supplanted Paley's work in the United States, was less explicitly utilitarian, but no less certain of the rational and moral foundations of his New England society. Equally important, customary practices that were inconsistent with that way of life—most notably Southern slavery—stood morally condemned and could not be defended rationally.[11] For all of these writers, the aim was not a moral or social revolution, but a demonstration that the key elements of an enlightened, democratic version of Christian morality would pass the critical test. Critical thinking about morality was not an alternative to conformity to the highest social standards. It would provide an additional reason for following the customary code.

That idea of education placed a high value on the moral themes of Protestant Christianity, but it left no specific place for the study of religion in the curriculum. Students were generally required to participate in some form of public worship, and few professors felt our contemporary scruples about the introduction of explicitly religious ideas into discussions of law, literature, or history. Nevertheless, precisely because the study of moral philosophy explicated moral laws that carried the universal sanction of reason and corresponded perfectly to the requirements of religion, there was no need to study religious thought independently. Writers of moral philosophy textbooks regularly insist that revealed religion is an important reinforcement to the truths of rational morality. Perhaps, given the limitations of human understanding and our tendency to accept weak arguments against uncomfortable demands, revelation is even *necessary* for an adequate grasp of moral truth,[12] but moral and metaphysical studies specifically under the aspect of religious teaching were not essential to a liberal education. That curriculum could be reserved for the denominational theological seminaries, which were also growing rapidly during this period.

Scant attention is paid to non-Christian religious ideas in the textbooks of moral philosophy, unless one counts the references to the religion of ancient Israel. Knowledge of other traditions and their scriptures was not well-developed at this time, of course, and even the more advanced treatments of them tended to be mere extensions of the project of rational natural theology. Other religions were called as witnesses to the universal truths best expressed in Christianity, or

---

[10]William Paley, *The Principles of Moral and Political Philosophy* (Houston: St. Thomas Press, 1977). [First published, 1785.]

[11]Wayland, pp. 188-98.

[12]Wayland, pp. 122-25.

alternatively, demonstrated to be inferior to Christianity in their grasp of these rational requirements.[13]

Confidence in the links between reason, religion, and prevailing moral standards was not so easily sustained in the face of further developments in critical thinking. The works of Marx, and later of Freud, not only demanded an evaluation of social values and practices against a universal, rational standard. They also called into question the objectivity of the evaluator.

It is one thing to test the standards and values of society against a utilitarian standard when you are confident that your education and wide experience of life give you insight into what the greatest good really is. It is another thing to confront the possibility that your estimate of the greatest good may be nothing but a report of your own preferences, distorted to conform to the interests of an economic and social elite that controls the education. Once that possibility is raised, William Paley's argument for the social value of an established church appears a transparent rationalization for his own position, and even Francis Wayland's attack on slavery elicits the observation that this passion is most easily sustained by New Englanders who have nothing to lose by abolition.

There is a place for the study of religion in this context, but it is subordinated to the critical project as surely as the earlier developments in critical thinking subordinated it to the apologetic purposes of natural theology. Now the point is not to demonstrate that one's own faith is different from the contingent loyalties and irrational superstitions of others, but precisely to show that it is no different. Christian festivals, to use Durkheim's famous example, serve the same social purposes as the civic observances of a secular Republic. All faiths in a Freudian perspective arise from the same primitive fears and needs.[14]

What has happened to liberal education in the course of the development of modern critical inquiry, then, is an almost complete reversal of its role in relationship to social values. Where education once shaped those values in each new generation, preparing them for the choices they would have to make as members of a free society,

---

[13]One might also employ comparative studies as a tool in Christian polemics, demonstrating, for example, that the ideas of one's theological opponents bore more resemblance to the errors of non-Christian religions than to (one's own) Christian truth. These patterns of argument, all of which subordinate a real investigation of other religions to a rational exposition and defense of Christian teaching, were well-established by the end of the eighteenth century. See David Pailin, *Attitudes to Other Religions: Comparative Religion in Seventeenth and Eighteenth Century Britain* (Manchester: Manchester University Press, 1984).

[14]Emile Durkheim, *Elementary Forms of the Religious Life* (New York: Free Press, 1965), p. 475. Sigmund Freud, *Civilization and Its Discontents*, ed. James Strachey (New York: W. W. Norton, 1962).

education—especially higher education—now assumes that the values are given. They are formed in some other realm of experience, in the family, in the church or synagogue, in the music, movies, and heroes of popular culture.

The proper role of education, then, is to develop critical distance and an appropriate sociological and psychological understanding of why people hold the values that they do. The contribution that education makes to freedom is not to shape the values of a free people, but to put some limits on their commitments. Education is a remedy for ideological rigidity. Given enough of it, people become quite flexible in the social arrangements they will accept, less prone to demand that things be the way they think they ought to be, and more susceptible to persuasion in terms of the requirements of social harmony.

III.

We cannot eliminate these critical theories from our thinking, any more than we could solve the problems of modern agriculture by going back to horse-drawn plows and pitchforks. The point is not nostalgia for a precritical age, but a recognition that now that these various forms of critical reflection have been securely incorporated into the thinking of educated men and women, the educators have a new task of thinking more clearly about the limits of that critical thinking, and about the ways that an appropriate confidence in institutions, loyalties, and commitments might once more figure in what it means to be an educated person.

One reason why this task urgently demands our attention is that the critical approach to education simply assumes that our students *do have* uncritical loyalties and commitments in which they need to be shaken. While that assumption may have made sense in the early decades of the twentieth century, it is no longer clear that it fits the social reality of American education today. To be sure, we still see in every first-year class those students who have never questioned the faith and loyalties into which they were born. We even see every year a few second-semester seniors who have managed to get seven-eighths of the way to a degree with their original commitments unscathed. We know enough about education and the processes of critical thinking to know what we need to do for them.

We are, however, unprepared for a new type of student who arrives without values and who is skeptical of all value claims. These students lack values, not because they have been prematurely exposed to the acids of criticism that were supposed to be applied in measured doses during their collegiate years, but because they had no values or commitments beyond the self from the beginning. Such students are often very able. They do well in their classes, but one senses that in fact they do not want a liberal education. They want skills that will enable them to exploit the opportunities for self-advancement. They want credentials.

To reach such students, a liberal education must do more than teach them critical skills. These students probably display more cynicism than critical subtlety, but they are not likely to gain subtlety merely by exposure to more criticism. What they need to prepare them for public tasks is precisely that confidence in values and commitments that the critical skills seem largely to have eclipsed.

The need for confidence is increasingly recognized, both in religious circles and among moral philosophers. Alasdair MacIntyre, in *After Virtue*, pointed to the strange way that moral language loses meaning when it is deprived of its place in a shared tradition. In his recent *Whose Justice? Which Rationality?*, he tries to demonstrate that the important discussions in the history of philosophy arise from shared questions held to be important *within* a tradition or a community, not from a critical inquiry imposed from outside. "There is no standing ground, no place for enquiry, no way to engage in the practices of advancing, evaluating, accepting, and rejecting reasoned argument apart from that which is provided by some particular tradition or other."[15] So too, Iris Murdoch and Philippa Foot call for the development of an ethics of virtue, which would place more emphasis on how we become certain sorts of persons in relation to others than on critical standards for the evaluation of particular moral acts.[16]

It is hardly surprising that scholars and teachers in religious ethics and religious studies have welcomed these developments into their own writings and into their syllabi.[17] Not only do the new views offer important reasons for studying traditions and communities as part of an understanding of the moral life; religious traditions and their scriptures, especially, are filled with saints and heroes whose ways of living seem worthy of study and emulation, even if we cannot draw direct lines from the exemplary lives to contemporary moral decisions.[18]

---

[15]Alasdair MacIntyre, *Whose Justice? Which Rationality?* (Notre Dame, Ind.: University of Notre Dame Press, 1988), p. 350. See also his *After Virtue*, 2nd. ed. (Notre Dame, Ind.: University of Notre Dame Press, 1984).

[16]Iris Murdoch, *The Sovereignty of Good* (New York: Schocken, 1971); Philippa Foot, *Virtues and Vices* (Berkeley: University of California Press, 1978).

[17]Gilbert Meilaender, *The Theory and Practice of Virtue* (Notre Dame, Ind.: University of Notre Dame Press, 1984); Stanley Hauerwas, *A Community of Character* (Notre Dame, Ind.: University of Notre Dame Press, 1981).

[18]See, for example, John S. Hawley, ed., *Saints and Virtues* (Berkeley: University of California Press, 1988).

While this recent academic interest in traditions and ways of life calls the long-prevailing emphasis on criticism into question, it is not clear whether it represents a renewal of what I have been calling confidence, or the final defeat of that confidence. The new academic search for confidence is very often accompanied by a kind of diffidence about the importance of ideals beyond one's own cultural or religious community. We recover the importance of a particular notion of virtue and the human good, but with no claims that what we discover in that inquiry is relevant to anyone else. The point seems to be that we must seek whatever moral objectivity we can establish between those who share a way of life with us, because outside of those boundaries there is nothing but the trackless waste of relativism.

In the wider culture, however, the recovery of traditional values and ways of life is not usually so hesitant. We see an explosion of institutions that actively seek new recruits for their ways of life, or that seek aggressively to impose the symbols and values of their tradition on society as a whole. So we have the growth of evangelical Christian schools and youth organizations (and parallel developments in Judaism). We have alternative television networks, and Christian entertainers, and books and periodicals that speak to those who seek a more clearly defined environment in which to explore their traditions and develop their own identities.

These developments are often rather remote from the schools of liberal education, and from the experience of those who teach in them, but those interested in the study of religion, especially, should give some thought to the reasons why these alternative institutions grow. The alternative schools, religious television, and perhaps even the businesses that advertise themselves as Christian house painters or Christian cleaning ladies, reflect a fear that one can find an identity in society and meaning in one's own life only by fleeing the public forum for a community of faith that offers its own explanations of everything, without the inconvenience of a critical perspective that might call it into question.

Though the tension between confidence and criticism may be initially posed as a philosophical problem, we now find ourselves in a situation in which the tension is expressed sociologically. Confidence and criticism, both of which are essential to a free society, have become located in two quite different sets of institutions. Where criticism is fully developed, confidence is eroded, and we are left with the modest comfort that inasmuch as no one believes anything anyway, at least we will not be troubled by fanatics. Where confidence once more takes hold, it creates communities that try to sustain their own comprehensive frameworks of meaning and service in which critical questions are not likely to be raised.

For historical reasons which I have briefly reviewed, events have largely associated institutions of higher education with the task of criticism. As a result, the institutions of liberal education play little role in the new search for confidence, and they may be unable to perform their important role of training persons for a public life that involves both confidence and criticism.

IV.

Religious studies has a potentially important role to play in moving us beyond this impasse. Religious studies introduces students to a wide range of the ways that cultures and traditions have dealt with the recurrent puzzles of human life. Birth, death, sacrifice and self-fulfillment, commitment, betrayal, and ultimate reality are the themes of these courses, and those who study them well gain both a wider idea of human possibilities and new perspectives on the way they had previously learned to think about them.

The educational aim at present cannot, however, be reduced to the simple, critical objective of demonstrating that one's own faith is no different from all the others. The crude relativism which ensues from that "discovery" may serve some useful purpose in shaking too-secure confidences, but for those who have advanced any distance into the project that is higher education today, relativism is itself is apt to be an article of faith.[19]

"Cheap relativism" is subject to a variety of objections. Philosophers are wont to remind us that, logically, it is self-refuting.[20] However, the most effective answer to such relativism is probably experiential, rather than logical. Thoughtful acquaintance with a variety of cultures and traditions yields a critical perspective that is altogether more complex. Clifford Geertz has recently stated the case for a non-relativist position that nonetheless gives substantial weight to

---

[19]Bloom, *The Closing of the American Mind*, pp. 25-26. In the current literature, Bloom makes this point most dramatically, because he treats the relativism of collegiate youth as a settled opinion, fraught with social consequences and subject to change only by massive educational reform. Other observers have viewed this relativism with less alarm, because they regard it as a necessary stage in psychosocial development, providing a starting point for mature convictions, independently held. On this literature, see Sharon Parks, *The Critical Years: The Young Adult's Search for a Faith to Live By* (San Francisco: Harper and Row, 1986). Whether or not one shares Bloom's alarm over the situation, there is little disputing his conclusion that an education that aims at *inducing* relativism has chosen for itself a ridiculously easy goal.

[20]Because propositions like "A belief is true only for the persons or groups who hold it" make claims to state a truth which is independent of the beliefs of those who hold it.

the influence of local cultures on our more settled opinions. As Geertz
puts it:

> Though this is not precisely the most comfortable position, nor even a
> wholly coherent one, it is, I think, the only one that can be effectively de-
> fended. The differences *do* go far deeper than an easy men-are-men hu-
> manism permits us to see, and the similarities *are* far too substantial for
> an easy other-beasts, other-mores relativism to dissolve.[21]

As Geertz notes, this perspective needs theoretical refinement,
and there are a number of competing theories to explain how it is
possible to maintain an idea of moral (or religious) truth while acknowledging the realities of cultural diversity. Each instructor will no
doubt have his or her own favorite among these theories. Happily,
pedagogical success is not a matter of securing unanimous consent to,
or even unanimous understanding of, the theory. The educational
aim is rather to develop a style of critical thinking that allows some
confidence in the results of criticism, and that does not limit those results to the notion that everything can be criticized.

One way to do that is to see liberal arts education generally as the
context for the articulation of one's interests and values within the
broadest range of human possibilities. Beliefs are justified, in this context, when persons who hold them can explain what they think in relation to a wide range of alternatives, offer understandable reasons
for the particular choices they have made, and show that their
thought is clear and general enough to accommodate new possibilities that may be presented.[22]

By articulation, of course, I do not mean just the techniques of
clear speaking and writing, though these are basic to all subjects in
liberal education. I am referring to a larger set of educational processes in which persons become aware of their interests, beliefs, and
values and learn to express them in ways that other people can un-

---

[21]Clifford Geertz, *Local Knowledge* (New York: Basic Books, 1983), p. 41.

[22]Much is packed into this concept of 'articulation' which requires further
development. I have attempted a somewhat more extensive statement of it in
"The School and the Articulation of Values," *American Journal of Education*, 96
(February, 1988), pp. 143-61. Two points, particularly, should be noted with respect to religious studies. First, to give one's reasons for a comprehensive religious or moral choice does not necessarily mean to offer a foundational justification that refutes all the alternatives. Among the reasons could be a self-conscious
awareness of the importance of a tradition or ritual in forming one's own identity
or moral sensitivities, or a limited claim that in one's own social and cultural context, this tradition provides the best way to express some important value. Second, showing that one can accommodate new possibilities *may* mean arguing for
the stability of one's beliefs in the face of any likely challenges, but it may also
include a specification of what new information or new circumstances would
lead to a change in these beliefs.

derstand. A classroom or course in which articulation is the aim of education will be quite different from one which has the comprehensive critical objectives we discussed earlier. In the critical context, the expression of one's own commitments is discouraged among the students and rigorously forbidden to the instructor. "Value neutrality" and "methodological atheism" in academic inquiry rest on the assumption that moral values and religious beliefs are the contingent products of one's own upbringing and cannot be taken seriously as claims on another person's understanding.[23]

Articulation, by contrast, does take values and beliefs seriously, but insists that if you want me to understand the world on your terms, rather than just performing a critical reduction of those values and beliefs, *you* must take the primary responsibility for stating those terms so that I can understand them. To do that, you must know clearly what you believe, and how it relates to and differs from what I apparently believe. The context of liberal education should be one in which that kind of articulation is both modelled by the faculty and elicited from the students.

Because articulation involves relating one's own beliefs to the ideas of others, it is than bringing a preexisting set of beliefs to expression. It may mean providing a student with a larger system of ideas in which to understand a particular concern, or introducing the student to the traditions of ritual and reflection by which others provide a context of meaning for practices and beliefs which the student initially finds bizarre or repulsive. Religious studies of sacrifice and the worldviews in which sacrificial rituals are embedded provide paradigm examples for an understanding of other peoples and traditions which is prerequisite for an articulate statement of one's own.

Other forms of articulation may require deeper knowledge of Western traditions. A student who has trouble reconciling her objections to war and militarism with her sympathies for revolutionary struggles and interventions to protect human rights needs to know the religious and philosophical traditions of "just war" to provide a larger historical perspective and a more articulate statement of the issues which concern her.

Religious studies also suggest the possibility that values and beliefs important to today's students may find aids to articulation in religious traditions of times and places other than in Western traditions with which they have most direct experience. Those who are troubled by the materialism of contemporary culture and the emphasis on ac-

---

[23]The classic statement of value neutrality in education comes from Max Weber's essay on "Science as a Vocation." See Hans Gerth and C. Wright Mills, eds., *From Max Weber* (New York: Oxford University Press, 1958), pp. 129-56. On "methodological atheism," see Peter Berger, *The Sacred Canopy* (Garden City: Doubleday, 1969), p. 100.

quisition and consumption in modern life need to know some of the variety of ways in which the world's religions have understood the uses and dangers of possessions. Students who are committed to environmental protection need to know the economics and the biology behind the problems they tackle, but they also need to explore the ways of relating human life to a larger ecology that are suggested in African and Native American spiritualities.

Articulation, then, includes training in the skills of public expression, but it also involves linking present, existential concerns to larger traditions of reflection and discourse. In this process, the professor's role is not restricted to a "value-free" analysis, but neither is the professor simply an apologist or evangelist for his or her own position. The requirements of the educator's role are rather that one be broadly aware of the traditions, values, and discussions that are available, and that one be willing to help the student explore those that seem closest to his or her own concerns, whether or not the professor finds them convincing. This does not imply indifference to the students' choices or an uncritical affirmation of whatever prejudices they arrive with at the beginning. The requirement is simply that we recognize that the range of intellectually acceptable positions is wider than the set of positions we ourselves hold. The constraint that the teaching task imposes on us is that we deal with that wider set, rather than the narrower one, when we are trying to help students articulate their own values and beliefs.

V.

Higher education today must recognize, alongside the critical agenda that has been incorporated into the liberal arts curriculum, an important task of building the confidence that is necessary for participation in decision-making in a free society. This confidence comes from an awareness that one's ideas have been tested and clarified in a discussion that was truly open to other possibilities. What we want is not the dogmatic insistence that some ideas and values are exempt from criticism, but the confidence that what one thinks has been critically tested, and has survived.

What survives, of course, will also be changed. If liberal education lasts a lifetime, then the values and beliefs of educated men and women should be constantly retested and always subject to revision. People who hold their convictions in that way are equipped to enter into public discussions with the awareness that their choices are important, that the options are *not* all equal or indifferent. Others will find it all too easy to transform a pluralistic society into an arena of competing interest groups, each trying to insure its own share of the goods and none taking an interest in the good of the whole. There are signs that our society is in fact moving in that factional direction, and though liberal education is a very large and important factor in our national life, it would be too much to claim that liberal education alone can prevent this fragmentation from happening.

The connection between liberal education and the skills of public life is an old and intimate one; and, despite the crises of purpose that today afflict many of its institutions, liberal education has a secure place in the future of any free society. The first step in reclaiming that historic role, however, is to realize how far we have departed from it. If we can create in our courses and classrooms an articulate discussion that begins to show what is possible for society as a whole, then we may proceed not only with new confidence in the future of liberal education, but new hope that its values and purposes may eventually be realized beyond the campus gates as well as within them.

EDUCATION AND THE INTELLECTUAL VIRTUES

Lee H. Yearley

The purpose of education, when defined most generally, is to develop all those human excellences, or virtues, a culture thinks are important. Typical American institutions of higher education, however, neither have the time nor possess the ethos to develop ethical virtues like courage or generosity. Indeed, it would be self-deceiving, probably self-serving, and possibly silly to believe that such institutions can fundamentally change the ethical dispositions that have been formed by the powerful forces of family, early schooling, and culture. Ingrained dispositions can be changed; traditional institutions for religious cultivation, such as monasteries, show this. But four years in a normal university or college bear little resemblance to those situations. Recognizing these limitations can lead teachers to think little significant cultivation of virtue is possible, and that they must therefore do something else, such as develop technical skills or impart information.

I will argue, however, that we can develop virtues or excellences, but that these are intellectual not ethical virtues. (Indeed, I think that higher education is one of the few places—I am sometimes tempted to say only place—in our society where the training of such excellences occurs.) These intellectual virtues are valuable in themselves. Moreover, they can affect the ethical virtues in extremely significant ways. To guide students through Christian, Confucian, and Taoist ideas about benevolence, for example, is to help develop in them intellectual virtues. Those virtues are precious additions to the self; they enable people to flourish in new and important ways. Furthermore, these virtues inform the exercise of ethical dispositions. I cannot train students to feel pleasure when they behave benevolently toward people, and pain when they do not. But I can help develop those intellectual dispositions that guide the exercise of their virtuous disposition.[1]

Defending a claim like this involves me in tangling with some oversized issues. Many of these issues revolve around the different conceptions of the self that underlie different ideals of education. Especially important is one modern conception of human beings that influences many in the country at large and in higher education in particular. Proponents of this conception (which we will examine later) believe that calculating or procedural rationality is the most important human faculty, and that its development is the major goal of higher education. This conception provides, I think, a remarkably impoverished basis for thinking about education, especially when religion is the subject matter. Yet this conception is so powerful that even to talk with it, and therefore to use its assumptions, is to surrender much of what is most important before the discussion begins. Given this, I think we must start from an alternative model of the self if we are to think productively about the study of religion. I will sketch out here such a model, one that rests on the idea of human virtues.

To couch a discussion of education in terms of virtues may seem odd or even dangerous. The word "virtue" has an archaic ring for many today. Moreover, it often is associated with problematic perfections, like extreme scrupulosity, and it has figured prominently in some extreme, wide-ranging criticisms of the whole fabric of American society. Nevertheless, an approach relying on ideas about virtue provides us, I think, with illuminating ways to conceptualize our experience. It helps us overcome roadblocks to productive thinking about what can occur in teaching about religion, and allows us to see more clearly what actually does happen. That is, virtue theory provides us with concepts, such as the conception of dispositions, and analyses, such as how reason informs emotions, that enable us to think in a more fruitful way about the processes involved in teaching religion.

An added advantage of thinking in terms of virtues is that it allows us to connect more easily with one tradition in the study of religion which those doing comparative or non-Western studies often find foreign. Most such people define themselves in terms of some version of the "science of religions" that grew up in 19th century Europe. But another tradition, exemplified by J. H. Newman's *Idea of a University*, connects the study of religion to the cultivation of the intellectual virtues. Certain of this tradition's presumptions or conclusions may not always fit easily within the comparative study of reli-

---

[1] For an example of how these ideas affect the teaching of an actual course, see my piece in the Harvard volume: "Bourgeois Relativism and the Comparative Study of the Self."

gion. But this tradition is an important part of the history of religious studies, and it contains a full discussion of issues about the normative sides of education and of religion, even if only in the limited context of debates about the truthfulness of Christianity's claims.

Consider, for example, the late Victorian debate about the "ethics of belief," which arose largely from the claims made by this tradition. The debate centered on the degree to which one should be morally constrained from believing things one could not validate by generally acceptable means. One side argued that people ought not believe more than normal thought allows. The other side argued that an ethical or religious failure occurs when people refuse to move beyond the normal senses of the reasonable: unbelief is a sin, just as faith is a virtue. That debate continues today and underlies many disagreements about the role of theology in religious studies and of religious studies in higher education. It is, I think, a debate about what intellectual virtues are and thus about what human beings are, especially human beings in their religious dimension. Focusing on the idea of virtue allows us, then, to connect comparative studies in religion to a prominent strand in modern Western religious thought, and to a debate that constitutes part of that strand.

More important, focusing on the idea of virtue allows us to think more productively about how we teach religion. Let us now turn to that subject. I begin by examining three elements in the model of the self that virtue theory employs; I also describe briefly, for purposes of contrast, the model of rational selfhood that underlies much of higher education. After a succinct depiction of what is probably the most influential Western depiction of the character of intellectual virtues, I will conclude with a consideration of three specific topics. The first concerns how practical intellectual virtues can, in fact, affect the living of life. The second discusses needed changes in the traditional idea of intellectual virtues, especially when comparative religions is the subject. The third deals with the idea that virtues are magnetic, and uses it to analyze the problem of achieving intellectual balance when we teach about religion.

The Understanding of Dispositions, Practical Reason, and Emotions in Virtue Theory, and a Brief Description of the Modern Ideal of a Rational Agent

My main business is to explicate three features in the model of the self on which virtue theory rests. Describing briefly a contrasting model, that of an ideal rational agent, is useful however, especially because it influences so many in education. In this model, which it is easy to caricature, ideal people freely choose reasons for action after surveying those ordinary facts to which everyone has access. Highly self-conscious and self-contained, ideal people's actions arise from an independent will rather than from a substantial self constituted by dispositions. Their actions reflect some more or less complete version of an intelligently applied decision theory. That is, ideal people will choose those acts that most effectively, and at least cost, attain all or most desired goals. Choice, then, rests basically on assessing probabilities and weighing preference interests.

Reason's most important characteristic is understood to be its ability to calculate and weigh. People rarely need to reflect on the general goals they seek (the ends to which the means are calculated) because present desires or the demands of institutional roles provide them with acceptable goals. Moreover, emotions are treated as arational forces that reason controls. When people deliberate, reason controls the emotions to ensure that they do not make people give more weight to an element in a decision than cool reflection would allow. When people act, reason controls the emotions by forcing them to follow reason's judgment. In this view, then, ideal people are free, detached, rational, and self-aware. Their natural attachments are understandable and controllable, their motives unambivalent, and their fantasies conquerable. Such people belong to communities or traditions only because they chose to belong. Moreover, they have little attachment to traditional religious ideas and actions, believing them to be suspect at best and potentially dangerous at worst.

This picture presents, I think, a modern spiritual ideal. Recognizing the spiritual character of this ideal is necessary if we are to explain its grip on people and its contrast with other religious ideals. A human can attain perfection when she disengages herself from the world and the normal self's vagaries by objectifying them and being able to use them. She manifests the new freedom, dignity, and power that clear-headed planning can produce. That ability to be disengaged and to plan enables her, then, to rise above the merely human.

Virtue theories rest on a very different model of a human person. The self is substantial, is constituted by dispositions and thus by communities and traditions. Moreover, reason makes judgments about both specific situations and general goals, and it influences the form of emotions. This model rests, then, on important (and controversial) claims about the character of *dispositions, practical reason, emotions,* and the relationships among the three. Claims about these three phenomena are, for our purposes, the basic conceptual building blocks of virtue theory. As they underlie our later analyses, we need to examine the character of each, illustrating our theoretical account with examples from teaching about religion.[2]

---

[2]I will not even attempt here to provide either the references or the analyses that can, I think, support the more technical aspects of my claims. Considerations

Dispositions are real additions to the self that fundamentally change what a person is likely to do. A disposition signifies less than an actuality, in the sense that no act is occurring. But it signifies more than just a potentiality, what something could do or be, because the presence of appropriate circumstances and judgments make it very likely that a particular kind of action will occur. That is, the notion of dispositions functions as the middle term in a basic conceptual framework that contains two other terms: capacities or potentialities, and actions or actualities. A potentiality signifies what something can do or be; an actuality signifies what something is or is doing; and a disposition signifies what something is likely to do.

Higher education can produce intellectual dispositions, or virtues, even if it cannot produce ethical dispositions. If I am a normal human, for example, I have the capacity to learn to identify specious arguments within different systems of religious thought. (What is a specious argument in a Buddhist system may not, of course, be one within a Christian system.) I also have the capacity to identify subtle features of different ritual systems and to identify when an act has religious import. (Again, what counts as a religious act or a subtle feature in one religion may not in another.) Learning to identify these elements involves acquiring a disposition, and therefore demands more than just memorizing or even studying material, although that also usually occurs.

Once I do learn to identify such arguments or features, I have more than a simple capacity because even if I am not now utilizing the disposition, I can actualize it if an appropriate situation arises. That action involves, however, a rational choice. I may, for various reasons, decide not to actualize my disposition. I would decide against such actualization, for example, if the student presenting the specious argument is timid and trying for the first time to express a deeply held, though rather innocent, position. Similarly, if a student asks a probing question about a ritual and I do not at this point in a course want to unravel the full complexity of a ritual system, I will not actualize my disposition.

The *practical reason* that guides my activation of dispositions involves situational appreciation: a recognition of the salient character-

---

about genre and limitations on space are the major reasons, but I also have two forthcoming pieces that provide further analyses and bibliographic references; see my "Recent Work on Virtue," *Religious Studies Review*, 16:1 (1990), pp. 1-9; and my *Mencius and Aquinas: Theories of Virtue and Conceptions of Courage* (Albany: State University of New York Press), forthcoming in 1990 in the series, F. Reynolds and D. Tracy, eds., *Towards a Comparative Philosophy of Religions*.

I also will speak as if only one theory utilizes the idea of virtue, although I realize that different kinds of such theories exist; either Wang Yang-ming or Hume, for example, differs from much of what is presented here—see the pieces noted above.

istics, the pertinent concerns, in a situation. It rests on an adequate specification, an appropriate description, of what is to be heeded, realized, or safeguarded in any circumstance. When I teach, my practical reasoning produces all the delicate judgments I make about what is pertinent and needed in the situations I face, and therefore in what I should say or do. When I try to induce this kind of reasoning in others, it involves (as we shall see later) a variety of actions that show students when and why they are perceiving and reasoning well and badly.

All these specific judgments are guided, moreover, by my picture of the general goods that I want to realize. I aim to help students reach those goods that appear, for example, when people can approach religious phenomena with sensitivity and understand religious arguments with critical sympathy. My picture of just how those goods inform a fully flourishing life may be difficult to specify clearly. But that picture underlies all of my specific judgments, and it is one on which I continue to reflect as I teach.

These ways of thinking about the character of practical reason and dispositions underlie the "cognitive" or "interpretative" view of the *emotions* contained within virtue theory. Emotions are thought of as more or less intelligent ways of conceiving a situation dominated by, or involving, a strong feeling. Emotions are, then, formed in large part by the beliefs from which they operate. I believe that something is dangerous (whether that something be a tiger or an authoritative female), and thus I feel fear. Emotions also involve physiological changes, such as an increased pulse rate, and desire, conceived here mainly as the source of an inclination to act. But the interpretative elements in emotions are crucial because people are inclined to give and respond to certain descriptions of situations. Almost all emotions, then, involve some judgments about the import or significance of the objects to which they relate. This import explains why something matters and thus provides the cognitive basis for the feeling. It is, for example, what allows me to say that I felt embarrassment mistakenly when I recognized that other people's laughter, which had induced my embarrassment, was directed at someone else's witticism not my own clumsy behavior.

Recognizing the role of practical reason and dispositions in the production of emotions is important if we are to understand what can occur when we teach about religion. We cannot, of course, easily change people's beliefs and dispositions. But we can over time modify them in ways that allow people to entertain beliefs that have emotional impact. For example, once students begin to appreciate a Taoist position, such as Chuang Tzu's, you can ask them to imagine how they and Chuang Tzu would react emotionally if a large earthquake occurred. Their own fear arises from beliefs about the significance of human beings, but they can begin to "feel" what a Taoist perspective would involve—or learn the valuable lesson that they are unable even to entertain the beliefs that would allow them to so feel.

Virtue theory portrays emotions, practical reason, and dispositions in ways that enable us to think more productively about how best to teach about religion. We will use these conceptions when we consider our three specific topics. Now, however, we need to examine the traditional Western account of the intellectual virtues, note difficulties in it, and reconstruct parts of it. (A civilization like China's presents a quite different picture of intellectual virtues, but we will—ironically, given our general subject—examine only Western ideas: the song finitude produces can often be discordant.)

The Content of and Problems in the Traditional Western Idea of Intellectual Virtues, and an Account of How Practical Intellectual Virtues Can Affect Life

Different views about the character and number of the intellectual virtues have, of course, operated in the West; but I will concentrate on what is probably the West's most influential picture, that found in the Aristotelian tradition. After a brief outline of this tradition's account, I will examine why most today find some of its significant features problematic. I then argue that we can, however, utilize other features of the account by combining them with the three ideas in virtue theory we just examined. That reconstruction enables us to analyze our first specific topic: the direct effect of practical intellectual virtues on the way in which we perceive, feel, and live.

Proponents of the Aristotelian tradition divide the the intellectual virtues into two kinds: theoretical or contemplative virtues, and deliberative or practical virtues. In most classical formulations, the former deal with the unchanging, produce "truth," and are marked by a certain passivity or receptiveness. The latter, in contrast, deal with judgments about the changing world, aim to produce a product, either an act or artifact, and usually involve some evident activity.

Further distinctions are made within each realm. Within the theoretical, three powers are distinguished: the ability to grasp immediately the truth of some idea, such as that humans are mortal; the ability to deduce conclusions from premises, to gain new knowledge from knowledge already possessed, such as that I am mortal; and the ability to use these two powers in harmonious concert. (Many people do not, of course, think mortality is the last word in human affairs, but the point here is that they must think it is the first word—that it provides the context for thinking—if any other words are to have meaning.) The practical or deliberative virtues divide into excellences

of doing and making: the former—discussed earlier as practical reason—guide judgments about, and actions in, the world; the latter
guide judgments that aim to create a product. (The distinction between doing and making resembles the distinction between virtues
and skills, and therefore helps us answer questions, as we will see,
about education's goals.) The line between the two can be sinuous,
even more sinuous than Aristotelians have thought. But the paradigm
cases are my thinking about and deciding to be stern with a recalci-
trant child, and my thinking about and deciding to make a chair from
the planks of wood that confront me.[3]

Christian additions to this picture are many, but most crucial is
the addition of the theological virtues of faith, hope, and charity.
Aristotle articulates only five exercises of the theoretical intellectual
powers. The first three are assents that rest on self-evidence, reasons,
or a harmonious combination of the two. Beneath these, for Aristotle,
are the states of doubt, manifested in withholding assent, and of
opinion, manifested in tentative assent that allows for the possibility
of error. Christian thinkers add faith to this picture, an unquestioning
assent where neither compelling reasons nor self-evidence are present. Moreover, they see this assent as resting on love and hope, and
they think the resultant state also affects practical action. The permu-
tations that flow out from these changes are many and varied,
whether in the hands of old masters, such as Aquinas, or more recent
masters, such as Newman. But they all lead to striking reformulations
of the idea of knowing, including a blurring of the distinction between the theoretical and the practical realms. Christian thinkers, for
example, will often focus either on how certain levels of understanding involve trust and unformalizable kinds of sensitivity, or on how
love—or even hope—produces contacts with religious realities that
can be reached in no other way.

For many in the past, and for some today, the actualization of the
theoretical intellectual virtues represents the purest form of knowledge, the goal of education, and the highest flourishing of humanity.
(One reading of Allan Bloom's *The Closing of the American Mind* is that
he embraces this ideal, and is willing to live with the many disturbing
consequences that follow from it.) This claim rests on the idea that

---

[3]The Greek and Latin terms for the five are as follows, with the order following
their presentation in the text: *nous/intellectus; episteme/scientia; sophia/sapientia;
phronesis/intellectus practicus; techne/ars.* These distinctions reflect a faculty psychology, but statements can always be reformulated as statements about what
human beings as possessors of such powers do or can do. Also note that
"thinking about," as used here, does not refer to a little bit of conscious thought
followed by a little bit of action. Rather, it refers to the ability to give some account of what you have done and why you have done it.

such actualization allows humans to contact the "really real," and thereby to exercise the highest, the most divine capacity they have.

Many today are far less sure than were people in this tradition either that immutable truths exist or that our knowledge can reflect or correspond to them. Moreover, almost all agree that identifiable characteristics differentiate scientific and humanistic inquiry, despite the more skeptical results of the history or philosophy of science. With science, a remarkable convergence of belief occurs among those who are qualified to judge; its history of changes in ideas leads us to speak cogently of development; and the ability to use something "out there" to produce and test results characterizes its inquiries. None of these three marks is as clearly evident in humanistic (or practical) inquiry and action.[4]

Nevertheless, however attenuated we may think links with the truly real are, some humanistic activities do share the family of characteristics associated with the theoretical virtues, and they do represent an important kind of human excellence. These activities usually represent most clearly those intellectual pleasures, those fulfilling satisfactions, that are a significant part of the love of learning we enjoy and hope to inculcate. Such pleasure is defined not as a feeling, but as a participation in an activity that can be characterized by effortless attention, the miraculously quick passage of time, and the utilization of high, subtle, and self-validating dispositions. Through such pleasure we participate in something that helps us transcend our egoistic concerns, that lifts us beyond ourselves and puts us in touch with the other or more than human. These pleasures are among the most alluring and most characteristic aspects of any significant intellectual work. Despite that, the intellectual virtues most intimately involved with the humanities are often closer to the practical than the theoretical intellectual virtues.

The practical intellectual virtues are, however, extremely important, far more significant than many traditional thinkers realized. Their importance arises from the way in which they can affect directly how life is lived, the first of our three specific topics. As we discussed when analyzing virtue theory, practical reason forms the emotions and thus creates new dispositions. Reason does not simply command or control emotions, and receive its goals from them, as is the case in the model of the modern rational agent. Rather, in virtue theory, practical reason alters the emotions either indirectly or directly. Reason alters the emotions *indirectly* when it leads a person to undertake a process of self-cultivation in order to change, by training

---

[4]For an example of the kind of position on this issue that I find persuasive (but not because I am an expert), see Bernard Williams, *Ethics and the Limits of Philosophy* (Cambridge: Harvard University Press 1985), pp. 132-155. That book also contains an excellent, and critical, treatment of the Western virtue tradition.

over time, specific emotional reactions. Such indirect alteration often occurs in the process of extended self-cultivation found in, say, monasteries. Yet, as noted above, contemporary educational institutions cannot foster such changes.

Reason, however, also *directly* alters emotions either almost immediately or over a fairly long period of time. The exact character of the reflections that generate these changes is often difficult to articulate or even to trace. The reflective process usually is not explicit, and it often relies on necessarily vague pictures of the world's character and a human being's ideal way of life. Nevertheless, direct alteration of the emotions by reason does occur. When I was younger, for example, I may have reacted with intense emotional perturbation whenever anyone, even dull-minded or odious people, failed to show respect for me. I may also have had deep enough emotional reactions to the idea of being poor that I would never consider taking a job, however worthwhile, that would leave me in poverty. Those emotional reactions can simply cease to exist as my reflections on what I think is valuable both become clearer and inform more completely my overall perspective. After I have rationally come to understand that poverty is not a mark of disgrace or a state that destroys the ability to live well, I no longer have the same emotional reaction to my possible poverty. After I have grown to realize that only good people's judgments on me tell me anything of importance about myself, I no longer react with emotion to the judgments of dull or bad people. The rational realization of such things literally changes the valence, the form, and the import of the relevant emotions. I become *incapable* of feeling a certain sort of perturbation because of what my reason tells me. Reflection presents me with a different view of the world and of human ideals, and that literally changes the form of my emotional reaction.

Simple lived experience brings many of these changes. Nevertheless, our monumental inability to process experience in ways other than those we acquired when we grew up (a topic on which Freud may have no master) means we desperately need to be given new ways to structure our experience and powerful new pictures of what the world is like. We all resemble the sailor who has traversed the globe, yet understands virtually nothing.

Formal, higher education is what often either produces these changes or, more usually, accelerates them and gives us new ways to understand them. We see, for example, how and why love fails and turns to hate, or shifts to debilitating jealousy or even to skillful cruelty. Such education provides us, as the medievals were fond of saying, with the shoulders of those giants on whom we can stand to see. A Mencius or Aquinas can often show us things we can never show ourselves. When I study Aquinas on avarice or the vow of poverty, I see the range of deformations involved in the fear of my own possible poverty. When I study Mencius on the role of other people's evaluations and the sources of true respect, I understand the deep difficulties in my desire to find esteem in the wrong places.

Formal education can, then, develop practical intellectual virtues that affect the way life is lived. That this can occur is one important reason why education in the humanities, and perhaps especially about religions, is often best seen simply as a keeping alive of crucial insights about life and approaches to it. These might be lost if we did not use our wit and training to present them in ways that will engage contemporary listeners. The loss would be great one.

Let us now turn to examine our second topic: the need to add other virtues to the traditional list of intellectual virtues and therefore to rethink some features of that traditional framework. Both changes arise from the distinctive senses of finitude and of multiple kinds of human flourishing that arise from comparative studies in religion. Both changes will also affect the way life is lived, as they involve practical intellectual virtues.

New Intellectual Virtues That Accompany the Comparative Study of Religion

Some of what we do in teaching comparative religion resembles traditional theoretical inquiries: for example, the explication of a religion's symbol system or the philosophical analysis of the rationale for seeing the self as insubstantial in Buddhism. But a number of the virtues we manifest, aspire to, and attempt to cultivate in our students fit uneasily into the old vision. When I compare Buddhist and Christian views of the self, I often aim not at a truth about how things are, but at a truth about how a culture or tradition thought things were. Indeed, I usually face two apparently very different, or even contradictory, but powerful pictures of the truth on this and other subjects. Similarly, my study of a symbol or ritual system leads me not to abiding truths but, at best, to local truths.

Hesitations to use comparative inquiries to make claims about the world's constitution, or at least about how humans must perceive the world, can arise from unbecoming timidity, intellectual failures of nerve, or an oversensitivity to context. Many such hesitations, however, arise from a healthy respect both for the diversity of religions and for the complexities involved in doing comparisons that are accurate and textured. We desperately do need, I think, to face more directly than we often do the normative implications that much of our work contains. Nevertheless, if comprehensive, exceptionless statements are what the older notion of theoretical intellectual virtues demands, we cannot explain or defend many of our activities in terms of the development of those virtues.[5]

Significant aspects of our teaching, however, can be defended on the grounds that it develops intellectual virtues that enable our students to understand and deal with people who manifest integral views of life that differ from their own. (Such virtues are, of course, of growing importance in a national and international world where contacts among diverse peoples continue to increase.) Certain of the virtues needed are only versions of ones with which we are familiar. We need, for example, to reconstitute virtues such as appreciative toleration, and make them considerably more prominent parts of our picture of a virtuous person than they often have been in the past. Other, sparer virtues, which we probably need only at specific times, are more clearly new. The character of these virtues can often only be expressed in such oxymoronic pairs as steadfast doubt and willed tentativeness. Still other intellectual virtues are both more central and more distinctively modern. They also display important features of the new kind of spiritual and intellectual disciplines which we must embody, and about which we must teach.

An especially illuminating example of these kinds of virtue is what I will call spiritual regret. Spiritual regret arises when we understand both that different but legitimate ideals of religious flourishing exist, and that conflicts among them are deep enough that no single person can even come close to exhibiting all of them. Each of us must be a limited specialist in the human good. Moreover, the specializations available to us will usually be determined by forces beyond our control. Spiritual regret arises, then, when we face confrontations, and thus choices, that fit between the notional and the real. A notional confrontation occurs when I ask myself if I can imagine, without ceasing to be me, incarnating the excellences of a T'ang dynasty Buddhist monk. A real confrontation occurs when I ask myself what I can say to my child's desire to move into a Tibetan monastery in New Jersey. To be tempted by a religious excellence and yet to understand that you cannot, and should not, pursue it is at the heart of spiritual regret.[6]

---

[5]I discuss at length the issue of the normative implications of comparative studies in my book *Mencius and Aquinas;* see especially chapter one, section five; chapter three, sections eight and nine; and chapter five, sections three and six.

[6]For the distinction between notional and real confrontations, see B. Williams *Ethics,* pp. 160-167; he never discusses confrontations that fail to fit easily into either category. A helpful analysis of philosophical issues related to the general topic occurs in Stuart Hampshire, *Morality and Conflict* (Cambridge: Harvard University Press 1983), pp. 20-26, 32-43, 127-169. I develop various features of the idea of spiritual regret in a forthcoming piece in a volume edited by G. Outka and J. Reeder, "Conflicts Among Ideals of Human Flourishing."

Spiritual regret does not resemble other regrets. It arises neither from my recognition that I did something I should not have done, nor from my doing something I know to be virtuous even though it causes results I abhor. Nor is it the kind of regret (although it resembles one kind of nostalgia) that can arise from my having lost full engagement with my tradition. Spiritual regret results from being grasped by powerful and accessible religious ideals, at the same time that one is learning another lesson in the hard curriculum that human diversity and our finitude press on us.

Recognizing that we all walk lopsided to the grave is sobering. The better part of us realizes, however, that in many important areas a "no shopping" principle operates. We cannot pick and choose among ideals of religious flourishing as we pick and choose among food or clothes. Our inability to shop is most clear, I think, in those painfully illuminating moments when we deeply appreciate a religious ideal, say a meditative achievement, which we know is an unacceptable option for us.

This understanding, although sobering, ought also to produce a kind of joy. The joy arises from our recognition that a plethora of religious goods are present in the world, and that they have the form they do because no single person can possess them all. Indeed, understanding my inability to actualize many religious states produces sadness only if I think I am the sole locus of value in the world, the only being worth considering. This posture displays an intellectual vice that is also a spiritual deformation, just as spiritual regret displays an intellectual virtue that is also an instance of spiritual flourishing.

The example of spiritual regret illustrates well, then, those new intellectual virtues that arise from and accompany the comparative study of religion. These virtues must be added to those contained in the traditional list, just as we saw earlier how practical intellectual virtues need to be highlighted, and their importance rethought, in a way that they were not in the traditional formulation. Let us turn now to our third topic and examine a situation where the general idea of intellectual virtues illuminates well a crucial issue in teaching about religion. The issue is the attainment of proper intellectual balance.

Magnetic, Expanding Virtues and the Problem of Intellectual Balance

One characteristic of virtues is especially important with intellectual virtues: their magnetic quality, and the tendency to expansionism and excess it generates. This aspect of virtues arises because the exercise of virtues relies on practical reason's ability to pick out and attend to a situation's most salient characteristics. In some situations, the relevant factors are clear enough that the appropriateness of a virtue's exercise can hardly be questioned. In other situations, however, the virtuous person may focus the salient features in a way that both is inappropriate and makes almost inevitable the exercise of the virtuous disposition.[7]

Indeed, part of the built-in dynamic of virtuous dispositions is to look for situations in which they can be exercised. My courage leads me to see difficulty and temptation which I must courageously confront, when a more appropriate response would be either to find an imaginative compromise or to view the situation with ironic detachment. Virtues are, then, "magnetizing," in that they attract situations in which they can be exercised; they are "expansionistic," in that they tend to exceed their appropriate areas and move into realms where they do not belong. The possessor of a virtue either gravitates toward situations that will elicit it, or, more important, creates situations in which the virtue can be given full play.

The magnetic, expansionistic quality of virtues affects deeply the more academic of the intellectual virtues. These academic intellectual virtues create the very worlds I see when I teach. When faced with a religious phenomenon, for example, I may either see a world of unconsciously distressed people seeking illegitimate consolations, or see a world of religiously attuned people attempting to discern those traces of the sacred that lie in their world. The tendency to create a world that elicits those academic intellectual virtues I possess is a constant temptation. If I am particularly adept, for instance, at taking apparently meaningless behavior and showing its symbolic significations—its religious flavor—I may well find such significations everywhere I look.

A similar phenomenon occurs when the issue is not simply the application of a particular intellectual approach, but the application of any sophisticated intellectual approach at all. To possess and value refined intellectual virtues, to gain identity and self-satisfaction from them, is also to be prone to use them when they are inappropriate. Relatively harmless, if common, cases occur in situations such as family gatherings or meetings with old friends. The virtues needed there are usually social virtues such as amiability, controlled humor, and secure unassertiveness. The intellectual virtue of analytic acuity may quickly turn a genial conversation into an embarrassing silence or a one-sided disquisition. More serious instances of improper expansion, all too familiar to those who teach religion, occur when we face situations where intellectual virtues of a more academic sort encounter mysteries or sufferings that yield uneasily (if at all) to such

---

[7]My general analysis of this topic is indebted to Amelie O. Rorty, *Mind in Action, Essays in the Philosophy of Mind* (Boston: Beacon Press, 1988), pp. 299-329.

analysis. The expansion of many intellectual virtues into those situations may simply strike an off-key note. But they may also do serious harm by causing real and unproductive pain, or destroying mute pity or joy, or rending the delicate fabric of a situation.

In noting these aberrations, I am not counseling that we become uncritical appreciators of religious phenomena. Indeed, I think we should normally, and even boldly, exercise intellectual virtues even when their critical edge generates discomfort for us and for others. The hesitancy to exercise such virtues has many roots, but a major one is the virtual disappearance in our culture of the idea that educated people who are not scientists can be experts on something other than the facts. We need to recognize that other people's lives and decisions may be greatly improved by our applying academic virtues. Moreover, such virtues are an intimate part of what an academic is. The failure to present them to people is a failure to present one's self, and that may induce, or manifest, a significant disregard for either one's self or others.

The key question in all these situations is deciding exactly when certain virtues are or are not appropriate. Answering it well often underlies the excellence, or even adequacy, of our teaching. Although no book of rules contains the answer, it is clear that intellectual virtues must be located within a system of checks and balances. (Put in traditional terms, the question is that of the connectedness or unity of virtues.)

When we teach about religious phenomena, the expansionistic, even addictive, aspects of one intellectual virtue—the propensity to seek clear explanations—must be counterbalanced by another virtue—the propensity to realize the complexity of lived situations. Similarly, the disposition to seek reductive explanations of religious phenomena needs to be checked by the disposition to recognize the possible existence of higher, even sacred forces; the disposition to pursue symbolic significations in religious behavior needs to be countered by the disposition to recognize routinized, or simply selfish, behavior. The ability to exercise such checks and balances is what we mean, I think, by phrases like a "well-schooled mind" or even "depth or quality of mind." But giving an abstract account of the desired state is difficult.

Even more difficult, and more relevant here, is understanding how we cultivate the desired state in students. This education seems to occur, in large part, through a variety of small and relatively easily performed actions. In such activities, we help students to see, for example, the falseness, difficulty, or incompleteness of an interpretation or argument. We also lead them to see the possible productiveness of another approach or a different set of questions. Moreover, we also function as models in the way in which we handle not only material, but also people and situations. Much of what we teach is the way we teach it. Indeed, we can often teach more by the way in which we teach than by the material we teach. That way of teaching usually includes dispositional responses of which we are only vaguely aware, especially as regards their impact on students: for example, the passion we do and do not show, the approach we take to perplexity and disagreement, the larger religious questions we seek out or from which we turn away.

Our ability to help students in this crucial area is limited. We can never induce a coherent set of checks and balances in each student, even if we work closely with a person for a long time. In fact, we often seem most easily able to produce two deformed states, states that manifest an excess and deficiency of what we aim to produce. One deformation is that kind of brittle intellectuality in which a person counters any interpretation with some other interpretation, any argument with some other argument, in an on going game that yields neither conclusions nor insights. This kind of flexibility of mind serves neither the person nor the subject. Knowledge of different approaches and arguments, and a flexibility of mind in applying them, is a very important check to the expansionistic tendencies of the intellectual virtues. But an unwillingness to give some final accounting of what is thought to be true represents a significant deformation of both character and material. This remains so whether the person doing that accounting claims to have found a single truth or claims only that a variety of conflicting perspectives exist.

The other deformation is the narrow specialist. Such a person lives not by checks among and balances of intellectual virtues, but by a honing of the expansionistic, magnetizing qualities of a single intellectual virtue or closely related set of them. The pursuit of a specific technique or the utilization of a particular approach characterizes the intellectual activities of such people. (The more aware of them may fight the expansionist tendencies of these virtues, but the result is that they have little to say about many things of great importance within even their own subject.) This deformation is more the speciality of graduate or professional education than of undergraduate education. But undergraduate education often either paves the way for it, or does little to impede or ameliorate it.

Moreover, in the case of religion, both of these deformations also fail to meet one of the more pressing needs we face: the full intellectual engagement of students who are religiously committed. By adopting one of these two deformations, those students can often become expert at doing exercises that involve the analysis of religious material and yet remain untouched by the meaning of those exercises. To use the traditional distinction, they acquire a skill but not a virtue, and their intellectual activity touches nothing fundamental about their character.

These two deformations and the implications of the problems they present were probably best painted, and on a properly large canvas, by Plato. The dialogues abound with clever and quick witted "relativists" who think they can destroy any conclusion by the application of various arguments or interpretations. (Plato's conclusions about the difficulties with such people are usually quite chastening: they do not care enough about what they ought to care about, and it is unclear how anyone can ever lead them to care as they should.) The problem of "specialization" also haunts Plato's work. The dialogues have a number of conventionally committed people whose narrow focus allows them never to question their commitments.

Plato's ideal is a just balance of various virtues within each person's life. But he also recognizes that the best that may be accomplished is nothing more than a balance of specialized people within a community. In his more somber moments, he thinks that unbalanced virtues, nurtured by specialization and always moving to expansionistic excess, may be all we can hope for from most individuals. (Many departments, of course, are built on just such an ideal, as are many liberal visions of society.) We must remember however, again with Plato, that what he called "the memory of justice," a state where each receives its due, should be the ideal that both guides and haunts us, even if it is not always realized in either an individual or a community.

Pipe dreams about what is possible can, but ought not, give solace. Nevertheless, I do think that education can often realize more than just these two deformations. Moreover, religious studies, especially in its comparative dimension, is particularly well-situated, if only by happy chance, to attempt to realize that ideal. The combination of subject matter, of a tradition of using different disciplines, and of a concern for various human goods that is displayed by many of our teachers gives us special possibilities and responsibilities. We must, however, recognize both what we should seek and what we must fear. Hopefully, this analysis begins to show the significance of the idea of intellectual virtues in contributing to those recognitions.

PART III: RELIGIOUS STUDIES AND THE QUESTION OF VALUES

THE LEGAL STATUS OF RELIGIOUS STUDIES PROGRAMS IN PUBLIC HIGHER EDUCATION

W. Royce Clark

> Freedom to differ is not limited to things that do not matter much. That would be a mere shadow of freedom. The test of its substance is the right to differ as to things that touch the heart of the existing order.[1]

No freedom in the Bill of Rights has been accorded greater status in the history of America than the freedom to differ religiously. At the same time, there is little that "touch[es] the heart of the existing order" more than the complex and highly charged issues of religion and law. An inherent tension surfaces when a nation nobly attempts to preserve an existing order that grants, as one of the primary rights of all citizens, the prerogative to believe and practice the religion of their choice. During the past few years, the Supreme Court has encountered that tension in attempting the adjudicate the two religion clauses of the First Amendment. Freedom to differ is guaranteed by the "free exercise" clause; religious freedom is also protected by the clause forbidding the government's "establishment" of religion. Yet neither clause can be interpreted so broadly as to allow a violation of other guaranteed rights, or to negate otherwise legitimate state interests such as the health and safety of its citizens. If the government offers too much protection under the "Free Exercise" clause, it may well be guilty of violating the "Establishment" clause; if it is too stringent in its ruling against any establishment, it may well infringe upon an individual's free exercise. In the balance lies the legality of religion and religious studies in the public school system.

For the past quarter of a century, religious studies in public higher education has appeared to be firmly established as constitutional. Significantly, however, the Supreme Court has not directly ruled on religious studies in public higher education. The closest the

---

[1] *West Virginia State Board of Education* v. *Barnette*, 319 U.S. 624, 642 (1943).

lower federal courts have come was with a decision that an English department at a Washington State University could offer a class in "The Bible as Literature," so long as it was taught critically and not by a "theologian." The Supreme Court refused to hear the case; that is, it denied certiorari.[2] Despite the restricted context of this case, there was strong dissent that saw even the critical approach to the Bible—the alleged "teaching about"—quite disconcerting, if not indoctrinating, to many students' faith.[3]

This kind of dissent raises questions concerning the degree to which, as Lovin discusses with his contribution to this volume, a liberal education can cultivate either "criticism" or "confidence" without working to the detriment of the students. Some would oppose even a balance of criticism and confidence, persuaded that any critical method or pluralistic content produces relativism which dissolves religious faith. Chief Justice Rehnquist came close to expressing this sentiment in his dissent in *Thomas* v. *Review Board*,[4] when he indicated that loss of a student's faith occurs in secular public education when it has no reference to religion or to absolutes:

> There can be little doubt that to the extent secular education provides answers to important moral questions without reference to religion or teaches that there are no answers, a person in one sense sacrifices his religious belief by attending secular schools.[5]

This fear, echoed in the recent criticism of public higher education by educators themselves, simply confirms to many citizens that higher education's pluralistic approach remains inimical not only to religious belief, but to the basic moral sensitivity so vital to citizenship.[6] We thus find evidently valid legal concern now stemming from

---

[2]*Calvary Bible Presbyterian Church* v. *Board of Regents*, 436 P.2d 189 (1967). The Supreme Court's denial of cert. does not constitute the Court's "final" decision as asserted by David Fellman, "Religion, State, and Public Universities," in *Religion and the State*, ed. James E. Wood (Waco, Texas: Baylor University Press, 1985) p. 312.

[3]Ibid. at 195-6.

[4]450 U.S. 707 (1981).

[5]Ibid., note 2 at 724. His basic criticism is that the "tension" now felt between the two clauses conflicts with the Founding Fathers' understanding. He insists that they could not possibly have foreseen 1) the evolution of the welfare state of the twentieth century, nor 2) the "incorporation" of the First Amendment via the Fourteenth to make it applicable to separate states, nor 3) the unnecessarily expansive interpretation the Court would give to each of the clauses until they collided with each other (ibid. at 720-22).

[6]Clearly the most prominent example in recent years is to be found with Allan Bloom's *The Closing of the American Mind* (New York: Simon and Schuster, 1987). Against Bloom, it can be argued that it is not pluralism nor dissent that produces relativism; rather, the cheap relativism he so vigorously argues against is propa-

arenas beyond the more familiar domain of having secular objections raised against the dissemination of particular religious ideas.

As a recent innovation, religious studies in public higher education is therefore supported by mixed signals and varied justifications which often conflict with one another. The presence of religious studies has time and again been deemed essential to a complete education. But its place in the curriculum has been defined by the "teaching *about* religion," which some are coming to claim is but a pseudonym for "secular humanism." As we shall discuss with this paper, the legal community recognizes the vulnerability of traditional justifications to such claims. Moreover, this vulnerability is only heightened by the fact that the Court's decisions are generally based on its judgment of whether the content under dispute is "religious," although the Court has yet to provide a general definition of "religion" by which one could distinguish religious from nonreligious content. The Court has also insisted that public education must not only help students learn to be critical, but it must inculcate values in our students that they will need to be responsible citizens of this country. Yet, in employing the standards or "tests" it has devised to validate a given practice as constitutional, the Court has refused to allow such value-inculcation to be associated with anything that even appears to be religious.

Given this situation and the recent willingness to litigate that characterizes parties at both extremes of the religious continuum in America today, it might be overly optimistic to expect litigation regarding the two religion clauses to avoid these broader ideological issues and to confine itself within mere property disputes among churches, issues such as abortion, or concerns of merely the public elementary and secondary schools. It may well be time, therefore, for those involved in religious studies programs to acquaint themselves with the inherent problems of such programs in higher education. To do otherwise is simply to wait for this litigation to occur, or to allow a state attorney general's opinions to affect a disbanding of their programs for fear of litigation.[7] Since the many scholars of this project have attempted to define what religious studies involves and how it

---

gated more by indifference, mental laziness, or a refusal to take a position seriously enough to dissent or differ with others.

[7]Witness the disbanding of Bible Chairs at the Universities of Texas subsequent to the 1987 Attorney General's opinion regarding the constitutionality of such chairs in view of the monetary support they received by supporting denominations. The impact of this opinion was felt beyond the demise of the Chairs themselves, as it severely inhibited efforts to "develop a serious program in religious studies" on the Austin campus. This situation was discussed by Howard Miller in delivering a paper, entitled "The Church-State Context for Religious Studies Programs in Public Institutions of Higher Education," at the 1989 Berkeley Workshop on "Religious Studies and Liberal Education."

relates to the liberal arts, it is appropriate to try to clarify whether such studies in public universities are, indeed, constitutional; and if so, under what conditions.

Determining the constitutionality of religious studies programs in higher education leads in the first instance to the landmark decisions of *Schempp* and *Edwards*. Although these cases dealt with public education at the primary and secondary levels, their arguments brought the Court to consider the role of religious studies in more general terms. Upon reviewing these two decisions, we will turn to the "tests" the Supreme Court has devised for determining constitutionality under the Establishment and Free Exercise clauses. Reviewing the various ways these "tests" have been applied will allow for reflection concerning the import they might have if the legality of religious studies is ever ruled on by the Court. Finally, we will turn to questions of "value inculcation" in public education, and to the bearing these issues have on the definition of religion which the Court adopted in deciding *United States* v. *Seeger*.[8] This discussion will suggest that we may do well to reconsider—or perhaps give up altogether—the phrase "teaching *about* religion" which continues to be favored as a defence for Religious Studies Programs in public universities.

I. *Religious Studies and* Abington School District *v.* Schempp[9]

At the turn of the century, the curricula of parochial schools and religiously affiliated colleges were free from any governmental restrictions, as these schools received no public funds. This has since changed to a degree by the Court bestowing benefits in its "accommodative" mode. In some cases the Court has thus had to wrestle with methods of providing for parochial education what it considered as benefits, state protection, or funds to which all citizens were entitled, without thereby illegally establishing religion. On several occasions in recent years, the presupposed common "interest of the state" has surprisingly won out in the high court over what certain religious people took for granted to be their protected religious interests—interests they had presupposed would be "accommodated" by the Court and government. On the other hand, since the religion clauses of the First Amendment were applied not just to federal law, but to state law by their "incorporation" in 1940 and 1947, states are no longer free to forge their own way. They, and the educational programs they support, must also hold to the standards and "tests" by which the Supreme Court determines violations

---

[8]*United States* v. *Seeger*, 380 U.S. 163 (1965).
[9]374 U.S. 203 (1963).

of the Establishment clause. Included in this, of course, are religious studies programs at publicly funded universities.

The profile of religious studies programs in higher education dramatically changed with the ruling in *Schempp*. To be sure, such programs were already in existence. The first to be established at a university with no connection to any church was at Boston University in 1873. The religious studies impetus, propelled primarily by the "history of religions" approach, produced ferment for a couple of decades at the turn of the century, 1890 to 1910, but did not sustain very significant growth until after World War II. The majority of religious studies programs, however, were established after 1950, and especially since the *Schempp* decision of 1963.[10] This decision found unconstitutional the practice of opening the public elementary and secondary school day with prayer and a reading from the Bible.

Of significance to higher education, however, was not the ruling but a dicta which distinguished between teaching "religion" or "of religion" and teaching objectively "about religion." "Dicta" are statements made by the court which were not necessary to the decision and therefore are not binding and have no precedential value.[11] Nor do dicta represent an advisory opinion (which the Court is not allowed to give, although the *Schempp* dicta have often been interpreted as such by professors of religious studies and some legal scholars.)[12] Instead, the dicta were in this instance offered more as a

---

[10]Claude Welch, *Religion in the Undergraduate Curriculum: an Analysis and Interpretation* (Washington D.C., 1972) p. 50.

[11]As the Court refused even to consider the possibility that the Bible reading was simply secular moral instruction rather than a religious devotion, since it was accompanied by a prayer, the dicta in Schempp are probably "obiter dictum" rather than "judicial dictum," though some might argue the latter merely on the basis of the counsel's oral argument. For the brief and oral arguments, see *Landmark Briefs and Arguments of the Supreme Court of the United States: Constitutional Law*, ed. Philip Kurland and Gerhard Casper (Washington, D.C.: University Publications of America, 1975) p. 682.

[12]As Chief Justice Rehnquist reminded the Court not long ago, "This Court is without power to give advisory opinions." *Larson* v. *Valente*, 456 U.S. 228 (1984) (dissenting), quoting Hayburn's Case, 2 Dall. 409 (1792). Yet some interpreters have treated this dicta in *Schempp* as if it were an advisory opinion. For example, see Niels C. Nielsen Jr., "The Advancement of Religion versus Teaching About Religion in the Public Schools," and David Fellman, "Religion, the State, and the Public University," both in *Religion, the State and Education*, ed. James E. Wood Jr. (Waco, Texas: Baylor University Press, 1984); Robert C. Casad, "On Teaching Religion at the State University" *Kansas Law Review* 12 (1964) pp. 405, 409; Robert Michaelson, "The Supreme Court and Religion in Public Higher Education," *Journal of Public Law* 13 (1964) pp. 343, 345; Ron Flowers, "The Teaching of Religion in Higher Education: The Perspective of the State University," *Journal of Church and State* 10 (1968) pp. 219, 220; Wilbur G. Katz, "Religious Studies in State Universities," *Wisconsin Law Review* (1966) pp. 297, 299-300, 303-4; John J. McGo-

palliative to protect the Court from the charge of being hostile to religion.

Moreover, the "tests" the Court has devised to determine constitutionality under the Establishment and Free Exercise clauses have become much more refined since *Schempp*. Significantly, they are "tests" which indicate the problems inherent to the very idea of religious studies in public education, and the Court has yet to clarify how the dicta of Schempp might be related to its "tests."

Further, it must be noted that during the period of growth in religious studies sparked by the *Schempp* case, the Court has ruled unconstitutional every contested case of religious practice or expression on the premises of public elementary and secondary schools. This, despite the fact that the expressed intent in some cases was only to inculcate the desired democratic values and basic morality.[13] On the level of curriculum, appeals to *Schempp* objectivity have also been unconvincing in most public elementary and secondary cases brought into the lower federal courts, despite the proponent's argument that they were only teaching "about religion" pursuant to the *Schempp* dicta.[14] Likewise, appeals to the mere inculcation of nonsectarian

---

nagle Jr., "Teaching about Religion in the Public College and University: A Legal and Educational Analysis, *American University Law Review* 20 (1970) p. 74.

[13]The *Edwards* decision of 1987 struck down a statute requiring "creation science" to be taught wherever evolution was taught. *Grand Rapids School District v. Ball*, 473 U.S. 373 (1985), invalidated a statute authorizing the use of religious school teachers in the public schools. *Wallace* v. *Jaffree*, 472 U.S. 38 (1985), found illegal establishment in the statute requiring a moment of silence for prayer, since related statues made evident its religious purpose. *Stone* v. *Graham*, 449 U.S. 39 (1980), held illegal a statute requiring posting of plaques of the Ten Commandments in classrooms, since the content of the commandments contained some explicitly religious material. *Epperson* v. *Arkansas*, 393 U.S. 97 (1968), invalidated a statute that forbade the teaching of evolution, since informing this prohibition was only the religious purpose of propagating a fundamentalist interpretation of the biblical creation narrative. *Schempp* (1963) struck down voluntary daily devotional Bible reading and recitation of the Lord's Prayer, despite its alleged purpose of inculcating morals and good citizenship. *Engel* v. *Vitale*, 370 U.S. 421 (1962), invalidated the daily reading of a prayer composed by the state. *Illinois* ex rel. *McCollum* v. *Board of Education*, 333 U.S. 203 (1948), overturned a "release time" program in which religious teachers provided sectarian instruction on the campuses of public schools.

[14]*Crockett* v. *Sorenson*, 568 F. Supp. 431 (1983), found illegal the claim of objective academic study in voluntary Bible classes on the grounds that forty years earlier there had been the purpose of indoctrination. *Hall* v. *Board of School Commissioners of Conecuh County*, 656 F.2d 999 (1981), found prayers and a class in "Bible as Literature" to be an unconstitutional establishment because of the narrowness of the sources and approach of the Baptist minister. *Malnak* v. *Yogi*, 592 F.2d 197 (1979), found an academic class in TM at a public high school to be illegal because it required *puja* off campus and assigned metaphysical attributes to Guru Dev. *Wiley* v. *Franklin*, 468 F. Supp. 133 (1979) ruled against Bible classes

moral values in both *Schempp* and *Stone* were ineffective in preventing the Supreme Court from ruling practices or symbols unconstitutional because of their form, content or function. Moreover, in higher education, religious studies professors in state universities have come to recognize the beguilingly simple distinction between the teaching "of religion" and the teaching "about religion" to be riddled with inherent philosophical and pedagogical difficulties.[15] As discussed by articles in this volume, many professors perceive epistemological and pluralistic problems which preclude any possibility of a pure state of critical objectivity. All the same, the *Schempp* dicta continue to be interpreted by many as a litmus test for the constitutionality of religious studies departments across the country. In the process, it has forced these departments into a rather impossible defensive posture of sustaining pure objectivity in teaching, a requirement not imposed on any other discipline in the university.

In light of the significance yet attributed to the phrase "teaching *about* religion," we will do well to consider the legal ambiguities to which it gives rise in the context of the *Schempp* ruling. As noted above, the Court in this case struck down voluntary Bible reading and recitation of the Lord's prayer in public elementary and high schools as an unconstitutional establishment. To try to defuse the public outrage which the Court had encountered following its prior decision of *Engel* v. *Vitale*, Justice Clark quoted Justice Douglas' famous line: "We are a religious people whose institutions presuppose

---

supported by the argument that they were taught from an objective literary and historical viewpoint, as objectivity was not found sufficient to offset illegal religious purpose by *McCollum* standards. *Wiley* v. *Franklin*, 497 F. Supp. 390 (1980), approved Chattanooga's Bible study courses on the basis of their secular approach, but determined those of Hamilton County to be "impermissively religious in nature." Voluntary Bible reading and mass non-denominational prayers were found illegal in Pennsylvania and Alabama because they did not provide the objective study of the Bible mentioned in *Schempp*. See *Mangold* v. *Albert Gallatin Area School District*, 438 F.2d 1193 (1971) and *Alabama Civil Liberties Union* v. *Wallace*, 331 f. Supp. 966 (1971). With *Vaughn* v. *Reed*, 313 F. Supp. 431 (1970), the Court found illegal establishment despite the teachers' assertion that they were teaching only "about religion" per *Schempp*. These cases indicate that on curriculum issues, *McCollum* has been more dispositive than has *Schempp*.

[15]For extreme views, compare Allan A. Andrews, "Meditation as a Resource for Teaching at a State University: an Application of the Phenomenological Method," *The Council on the Study of Religion Bulletin* 16:2 (1985) pp. 40-41; Robert N. Minor and Robert D. Baird, "Teaching About Religion at the State University: Taking the Issue Seriously and Strictly," *CSR Bulletin* 14:2 (1983) pp. 70-72; Julia B. Mitchell and David B. Annis, "Teaching About Religion at the State University: A Reply," *Bulletin* 14:4 (1983) pp. 113-14; Philip B. Riley, "Teaching About Religion at the Religiously-Affiliated University: Taking the Issue Seriously and Strictly" *CSR Bulletin* 14:5 (1983) pp. 145-46.

a Supreme Being."[16] The Court acknowledged the depth and significance of both the religious character of the nation, as well as the nation's legal protection of religious freedom for all. Rather than refer to the "wall of separation" between religion and government, it defensively articulated the government's stance as one of "wholesome neutrality" toward religion.[17] The government can neither aid any one religion, nor all religions.[18] The establishment clause denies "that the states can undertake or sustain [religions] in any form or degree,"[19] even if it were to "treat them all equally."[20] It cannot force one "to profess a belief or disbelief in any religion," whether such belief is nontheistic or involves an acceptance of the existence of God.[21]

Although the Court determined illegality in the *Schempp* case on Establishment grounds, the decision was ambiguous enough that many have thought it to have been resolved by Free Exercise criteria. The Court insisted that while both clauses protect religious freedom, they do it in quite different ways. The Free Exercise clause necessitates coercion in order to be violated; significantly, however, the Establishment clause has never required such. The Court held that the illegal "establishment" occurred because religion was connected to mandatory education: "When the power, prestige and financial support of government is placed behind a particular religious belief, the indirect coercive pressure upon religious minorities to conform to the prevailing officially approved religion is plain."[22]

As part of the *Schempp* Court's conciliatory tone, it went beyond the issue at hand and offered its dicta on the subject of teaching religion legally:

> In addition, it might well be said that one's education is not complete without a study of comparative religion or the history of religion and its relationship to the advancement of civilization. It certainly may be said that the Bible is worthy of study for its literary and historic qualities. Nothing we have said here indicates that such study of the Bible or of religion, when presented objectively as a part of a secular program of

---

[16]*Schempp* at 213, citing to *Zorach v. Clauson*, 343 U.S. 306, note 38 at 313 (1952).
[17]Ibid. at 222.
[18]Ibid. at 216-17, citing *Everson, McCollum, McGowan* and *Torcaso*.
[19]Ibid. at 218, citing Justice Rutledge in *Everson* at 52.
[20]Ibid. at 219, citing Justice Frankfurter in *McCollum* at 227.
[21]Ibid. at 220, citing Justice Black for the Court in *Torcaso v. Watkins*, 367 U.S. 488, 495 (1961).
[22]Ibid. at 221, citing to *Engel v. Vitale*, at 430-31. The Court was caught between the mandatory nature of elementary education, but the voluntary nature of either public or private, and the mandatory nature of the curriculum but the voluntary nature of the morning scripture reading. That is, the Schempp's daughter could absent herself from the classroom for that period of time, but her father protested that such actions placed her in a suspicious light as an outsider, so he could not

education, may not be effected consistently with the First Amendment. But the exercises here do not fall into those categories.[23]

But this dicta and that by Justice Brennan and Justice Goldberg is much more limited and ambiguous than it appears on the surface. It is somewhat debatable that either Justice Clark (writing for the Court) or Justice Goldberg (concurring) were referring to religious studies classes or a department of religious studies. Even Justice Brennan, who granted more concessions than the Court, spoke only of "teaching about the Holy Scriptures or about the differences between religious sects in classes in literature or history." He further noted that "whether or not the Bible is involved, it would be impossible to teach meaningfully many subjects in the social sciences or the humanities without some mention of religion." He then qualified even this by saying,

> There is no occasion now to go further and anticipate problems we cannot judge with the material now before us. . . . If it should sometime hereafter be shown that in fact religion can play no part in the teaching of a given subject without resurrecting the ghost of the practices we strike down today, it will then be time enough to consider questions we must now defer.[24]

It is true that the Court, as we will discuss below, has subsequently concerned itself with classes in comparative religions, ethics, and even theology. The *Schempp* dicta, however, simply conceded that within the secular study of our culture, whether in history or literature classes, references might have to be made to the scriptures or religion to make the subject intelligible; and the Court averred that even the Bible itself could be appreciated in this connection for its literary and historical qualities.

Instead of clarifying its meaning, the Court negatively emphasized that, "Surely the place of the Bible as an instrument of religion cannot be gainsaid" (a fact it felt was admitted by the State's rule that alternative versions should be used without comment, which assured the court that it constituted forbidden religious practice). The Court insisted that, "None of these factors is consistent with the contention that the Bible is here used either as an instrument for nonreligious moral inspiration or as a reference for the teaching of secular subjects."[25]

---

advise her to absent herself. So coercion was inseparable from the facts, though a rather subtle coercion.

[23]Ibid. at 225.

[24]Ibid. at 300, emphasis added.

[25]Ibid. at 222.

Because the Bible is a religious instrument, Justice Brennan (concurring) expressed some doubt as to whether the Christian scriptures could be used in the public school classroom at all without violating the Constitution. On the issue of method, as he noted, a reading without comment is the only way to avoid possible sectarian influence. Significantly, however, much of the Bible cannot be understood without comment, and the absence of comment makes it appear to the Court as an unconstitutional devotional as here. He further warned that the Bible's contents are "inherently sectarian," and to many people, any public reading of the scriptures is itself sacrilegious. He was not only convinced that in the case at hand no alleged secular moral purpose mitigated the illegal purpose; he was further persuaded that a public reading of the scriptures could be used neither to promote some tenuous "common core" of theology or religion (to avoid sectarianism) nor to inculcate moral standards as the appellants had argued. This conclusion derived from his position that the state may not employ religious means to accomplish secular ends which could be met by nonreligious means or materials.[26]

Justice Goldberg noted in a separate concurring opinion in *Schempp* (though perhaps less influenced by religious pluralism than Justice Brennan), that the First Amendment might even require the government to "take cognizance of the existence of religion" and its significant connection to "many of our legal, political and personal values," so that public schools could teach "*about* religion" without violating the Establishment clause, even as military chaplains do not create an illegal establishment of religion.[27]

Three of the four times the Supreme Court has since utilized that bit of dicta from *Schempp*, it has done so in the same way: it has referred to a hypothetical possibility of teaching "about religion" to offset the general negative holding of the case.[28] However, the ambi-

---

[26]This formulation, which remains Brennan's test and not the Court's, may not be as forbidding as it sounds, since it may be that significant interest of the general populace cannot be met by merely nonreligious means or materials. In any case, the strictness of his position on elementary and secondary schools stands in stark contrast t · his willingness in *Edwards* to allow state universities to teach not only courses in religion but in theology!

[27]*Schempp* at 306.

[28]One case was *Edwards*, which is discussed next. Another case was *Epperson*, in which the Court found unconstitutional the prohibition of the teaching of evolution while insisting that "the study of religions and of the Bible from a literary and historic viewpoint, presented objectively as part of a secular program of education, need not collide with the First Amendment's prohibition." Another reference to the dicta was in *Lynch* v. *Donnelly*, 465 U.S. 668, 679-80 (1984). Here, the citation's purpose was to argue that the first prong of the *Lemon* "test" need not be construed as requiring as "exclusively secular purpose." Chief Justice Burger, writing for the Court, insisted that if "exclusively secular" were the re-

guity and negative strictures thereby imposed—even on the positive hypothesis of teaching "about religion" constitutionally—have since become apparent. This is especially true with the Court's ruling in *Stone v. Graham* which involved privately funded plaques of the Ten Commandments which were to be placed on walls of the public schools. An inscription at the bottom of each plaque would read: "The secular application of the Ten Commandments is clearly seen in its adoption as the fundamental legal code of Western Civilization and the Common Law of the United States." The placement of these plaques was found to be an unconstitutional establishment, despite the fact that the plaques' accompanying inscription seemed to correspond with Justice Goldberg's dicta in *Schempp* cited above: religious references or symbols would be constitutional provided they were shown to be connected to "many of our legal, political and personal values." The inscription's educational value was denied, as the plaques were distinguished from an "integrated curriculum" in which "the Bible may constitutionally be used in an appropriate study of history, civilization, ethics, comparative religion, or the like."[29] The Court's paraphrase of Justice Clark's statement in *Schempp* added a reference to "ethics" and "the like." This addition made the *Stone* decision appear all the more incongruous, as the *Stone* court reiterated *Schempp*'s rejection of the legitimacy of trying to inculcate values through such an instrument of religion. The sheer appearance of the Ten Commandments, which in the Court's eyes were strictly religious rather than ethical or civil (such as the command to have only one God, to keep the Sabbath day, etc.), disqualified the plaques.

Evidently, Justice Goldberg's dictum was not reliable: once legal, political, or personal values are associated with religious ideas or symbols, the latter are understood to taint the study or reference with unconstitutionality. We cannot know whether the taint would have been "cured" if the classrooms were at public universities rather than public elementary schools. But to date, the *Schempp* dicta's hypothetical possibility of teaching "about religion" legally remains just that—hypothetical. Despite appellants' arguments of objectivity and secular purpose, ultimately the *content* of the first few of the Ten Commandments proved fatal to *Stone*'s claims for legality, even as it was the

---

quirement, then that would invalidate much of the conduct and legislation the Court has in the past found constitutional (ibid., note 6 at 681). He distinguished *Lynch* from *Stone* by honing the "purpose" idea further to suggest that *Stone* disqualified itself simply by presenting a purely religious purpose rather than being integrated into a secular education or framework (ibid. at 679-81).

[29] *Stone* at 42.

content, or the different versions of the Bible allowed in *Schempp*, that was the Court's clue to its unconstitutional religious purpose.[30]

II. *Religious Studies and* Edwards v. Aguillard[31]

The Supreme Court has provided quite different support to the legal status of religious studies in public universities with footnote dicta in the more recent case of *Edwards* v. *Aguillard* (1987)—a case in which the Court struck down the Louisiana statute requiring the teaching of "creation science" wherever evolution was taught in public schools. Significantly, however, it did so on grounds totally different than the dicta of *Schempp*. It argued that the constitutional issue was determined on the basis of the greater age and maturity of college students in comparison with those in elementary and secondary schools.

With both its brief and oral argument before the Court, the state attempted to disassociate itself from the earlier evolution case of *Epperson* v. *Arkansas* (1968) in which the Court had ruled illegal a state statute which precluded any teacher in a state-supported school or university from teaching "the theory or doctrine that mankind ascended or descended from a lower order of animals." In *Edwards*, the state insisted that its statute proposed only more science in the classroom, and thus more academic freedom; it was not attempting to bring religion into the classroom, and certainly not a study of the book of Genesis. The *Edwards* Court responded that because of the mandatory nature of elementary and secondary schools, and students' susceptibility to influence either by their teachers or peer pressure, it often had to protect this atmosphere by invalidating statutes which advanced religion, even if that required rejecting the state's "sham" secular purpose.[32]

It is rather significant that the *Edwards* Court never alluded to the objective method set forth in the *Schempp* dicta. The reason is clear: the state couched its argument in terms of providing more science, thus more academic freedom; that is, the claim that to hear only one unproven theory (evolution) was to be deprived of real objectivity or

---

[30]*Schempp* had to be disqualified on religious purpose via the content or else on Free Exercise grounds of making the students feel like outsiders since the situation allowed students to voluntarily exempt themselves from any exposure to the reading. That is, the method of presentation could have applied only to those who elected to be exposed to the reading; other criteria had to be used when the voluntary nature was emphasized. This is the reason the case sounded like it was resolving the issue from the Establishment side, although it probably achieved more from the Free Exercise approach.

[31]482 U.S. 578 (1987).

[32]*Edwards* at 584.

academic freedom. The state was claiming that "creation-science" was no more religious, or unprovable, than evolution. This was totally discounted by the Court.[33] All the Court could argue was that the state had an illegal religious purpose—behind its "sham" purpose. This conclusion of the Court was based on its observation that the only interest the schools had in teaching "creation-science" was to offset the teaching of evolution where that happened to be offered. The bill's legislative sponsor had stated, "My preference would be that neither [creationism nor evolution] be taught." The Court saw the bill as an infringement on academic freedom since it was simply trying to eliminate the teaching of evolution by granting professional protection and financial benefits only for those teaching "creation-science" but not to those teaching evolution.[34] The state thus intended to eliminate curriculum material objectionable to one particular religious group. This purpose clearly disqualified the statute, given the "tests" the Court employs to determine constitutionality. But the Court's refusal to accept the simultaneous teaching of alternative theories as indicative of academic freedom simply reveals the inadequacy of *Schempp*'s assumption that objectivity is both possible, as well as testable and enforceable.

In the oral argument of *Edwards*, both appellants and appellees were pressed by the Court on the question of whether religious studies in public universities would be constitutional.[35] Despite the extremely marginal significance of this question, it found its way into the Court's opinion in a footnote written by Justice Brennan for the Court, and in a footnote of Justice Powell's concurring opinion. In the first, Justice Brennan, writing for the Court in order to illustrate the idea of "undue influence" or the susceptibility of elementary and secondary school children, contrasted this susceptibility with the greater age or maturity of "college students who voluntarily enroll in courses. 'This distinction warrants a difference in constitutional results.'"[36] In the same footnote, Justice Brennan cited to *Widmar* v. *Vincent* and wrote, "The Court has not questioned the authority of

---

[33]*Edwards* at 587-89.

[34]Ibid. at 587-89.

[35]*Landmark Briefs*, p. 174; *Edwards* at 667-69, 689-90.

[36]*Edwards*, note 5 at 584. But he cited not to the Court's holding in *Schempp*, nor even to the Court's dicta which conceded the possible legitimacy of references to religion in history and literature classes, but rather to his own dicta in *Schempp* where he provided lengthy concurring opinion. *Schempp* did not distinguish constitutionality of religious studies classes upon any age difference. In referring to *Schempp*, therefore, he was referring not to Court precedent, but merely to the private opinion he had expressed in that case as he tried to square the holdings of *Hamilton* (compulsory military training at state university not being a violation of Free Exercise), with *Barnette* (compulsory flag salute in public elementary and secondary schools deemed a violation of Free Exercise).

state college and universities to offer courses on religion and theology." [37] Significantly, however, *Widmar v. Vincent* did not involve a university offering religious studies courses; rather, it dealt with the question of whether the university should grant a student religious group equal access to facilities as it did to other clubs. The case was decided narrowly: since the university had created a forum by allowing different groups to have access to the facilities, it could not constitutionally exclude certain groups the right of free speech merely because they were religious groups. Such exclusion would be a violation of the "content-neutral" requirement of state regulation of speech[38]; but the idea of what is allowable in an "open forum" was not relevant to the decision in *Edwards,* since it was not an open forum.

Along with Justice Brennan, however, Justice Powell joined by Justice O'Conner also cited to *Widmar* in a later concurring opinion in *Edwards.* He noted the Court's concession in *Schempp* that the Bible "may constitutionally be used in an appropriate study of history, civilization, ethics, comparative religion, or the like."[39] To show that courses in "comparative religion" are "constitutionally appropriate," he noted that state-sponsored universities in Louisiana offer a variety of religious studies courses in their curriculum.[40] He averred that the constitutionality can be determined by the difference in maturity between elementary and secondary students and college-age students. But he too confused the issue by citing to *Widmar v. Vincent,* to a note that accentuates how *disanalogous* these cases are, since *Widmar* expressed the Court's acceptance of the fact that given the circumstances, there was no danger of any reasonable inference by students that the student group in question was supported by the University.[41]

In considering the legal defence provided religious studies by the emphasis given age in the *Edwards* case, we must recognize that the ages of university students varies greatly today, with many students having not yet reached legal maturity. Age and maturity are certainly important in the philosophy of education; but it is not clear how these issues will stand up to challenge if they become the primary legal test. Although university students are generally older and more mature than high school students, there are many exceptions. One has to question whether there is any basis to assume that students could suddenly come to understand state-sponsored religious studies pro-

---

[37]Justice Powell, 454 U.S. 263, 271 (1981); and Justice Stevens concurring in judgment, ibid. at 281.

[38]*Widmar,* at 277. This allowed the group to proselytize and worship in the facility.

[39]*Edwards* at 608.

[40]Ibid., note 7 at 607.

[41]Ibid. citing to *Widmar,* note 14 at 274.

grams in terms of the state's "neutrality" toward religion, whereas the previous year, when they were yet in high school, they would have discerned such study as the state's endorsement of religion.[42] University students may not be any less susceptible to peer pressure than they were in high school; moreover, the desire to emulate their professors may be more powerful in college than before due to a newly discovered respect for teachers.

Of course, public higher education is itself not mandatory. But as Justice Brennan so aptly noted in his concurring opinion in *Schempp*, neither is public elementary and secondary education. Moreover, the college degree today might be considered the functional equivalent of a high school diploma at the time of *Schempp* or shortly before. It has certainly become a necessary "rite of passage" for those who want to enjoy fully the economic and social benefits of American society. It would thus be unwise, if not elitist, for the Court to minimize the necessity of a college education in today's society. In turn, financial reasons often force students to state universities. And parents' concern for their children's faith, emphasized so strongly by the Court in *Edwards*, is probably no less for their college-age students than it was during their high school years.

Were the Supreme Court ever to rule on the legality of religious studies programs in public universities, considerable attention would be focused on these issues of age as raised by *Edwards*, as well the issues of method as addressed in *Schempp*. Two other sets of issues, however, would also prove of primary import in structuring the case. The first involves the "tests" or standards which the Court has devised to determine legality in cases pertaining to the religion clauses, and the use made of these "tests" in decisions tangentially related to religion in public education. The second set of issues involves the Court's definition of "religion" and the relation of this problem of definition to questions concerning the legal parameters for an "inculcation of values" whose importance to education the Court has repeatedly recognized. It is to the broader ramifications of these latter issues that we now turn.

III. The Tests for Constitutionality of the Religion Clauses

As we examine the Court's "tests" for constitutionality in this section, it will become even more obvious that religious studies programs founded merely on the assumption of college students' maturity or the objectivity of college classes may collapse before an illegal

---

[42]The unconstitutional taint would not be alleviated by offering courses in several religions, since the Court has plainly forbidden aid to all religions or religion in general.

religious purpose, effect or entanglement of government and religion, or before an unjustified burden on some student's "free exercise." Moreover, the specific *content* at issue may be used by the Court to overrule any alleged secular purposes as we have noted above.

If a real case or controversy arises, the Court would likely utilize its present formulation of its two "tests," despite occasional disclaimers of their validity. As the Court noted in *Edwards*, the *Lemon* test has been applied in all cases except one since its adoption in 1971.[43] In addition to applying the "tests," the Court would likely focus on cases that dealt with a professed curriculum rather than mere symbols or worship; that is, the focus would be on cases most analogous such as *McCollum, Epperson, Stone,* and *Edwards* rather than *Schempp*.

The test for constitutionality under the Establishment clause requires a law to satisfy each of the following: 1) it must have a secular rather than religious purpose, a purpose which neither endorses nor disapproves of religion[44]; 2) it must have a primary secular effect, one that neither advances nor inhibits religion,[45] though it simultaneously could have an incidentally religious effect[46]; and 3) it must not produce an "excessive entanglement" between government and religious institutions.[47] To determine whether involvement rises to

---

[43]The only exception was in *Marsh* v. *Chambers*, 463 U.S. 783 (1983). The Court justified this single exception by the fact that a prayer by a chaplain of the Nebraska legislature had a long-standing historical acceptance, disanalogous from anything involving public schools, since they were nonexistent at the time the Constitution was adopted. See citations of *Edwards*, note 4 at 583. This argument has been correctly recognized as one which puts religious minorities always at a disadvantage, which surely was what the First Amendment was trying to combat.

[44]*Edwards* at 583, 585. The actual *Schempp* formulation of the test was not this refined (at 222). The Court has not resolved the issue of whether the purpose requirement is an "either/or," nor whether it matters which is stronger, though Justice O'Conner's emphasis on "function" in her concurring opinion with *Lynch* v. *Donnelly*, 465 U.S. 668 (1984), seems partially to resolve this.

[45]*Edwards* at 583.

[46]In *Lynch*, the Court argued that any benefit Christianity received from this was as incidental as in the Sunday closing case of *McGowan* v. *Maryland*, 66 U.S. 420 (1961).

[47]*Edwards* at 583. The standard test for the Establishment clause became more definitive in *Lemon* v. *Kurtzman*, 403 U.S. 602 (1971). As an example of the Court's utilization of *Schempp* simply to document the "wall of separation," see *Meek* v. *Pittenger*, 421 U.S. 349, 358 (1975); *Committee for Public Edducation* v. *Nyquist*, 413 U.S. 756, 773 (1973); *Board of Education* v. *Allen*, 392 U.S. 236, 243 (1968); *Beer* v. *United States*, 425 U.S. 130, n.4 at 148-49 (1975). In addition to this, at least Justice Brennan continues to cite in his concurring opinions his own three-fold division of the forbidden alliance that he first delineated in his concurring opinion in *Schempp*, at 295: "What the framers meant to foreclose, and what our decisions under the Establishment Clause have forbidden, are those involvements of reli-

the level of such entanglement, the Court would ask whether or not some form of continual monitoring by the state would be necessary. In this, it would also scrutinize four factors: 1) the nature of the religious institution; 2) the nature of the aid; 3) the type of continuing relationship that is created[48]; and 4) whether the issue is "politically divisive."[49]

Although the question of religious studies programs in state universities would probably involve the Establishment clause, Free Exercise issues might also be raised. As noted above, freedom of belief is absolute; but freedom of religious practice cannot be.[50] Therefore, a "balancing test" is necessary. One's right to Free Exercise of religion will be violated where a law places an undue burden on that exercise,[51] unless the state proves it has compelling secular interest in the law and no reasonable alternatives that are less restrictive exist.[52]

Where the challenged law restricts speech in a "public forum," the case may be decided on the free speech clause rather than the re-

---

gious with secular institutions which a) serve the essentially religious activities of religious institutions; b) employ the organs of government for essentially religious purposes; or c) use essentially religious means to serve governmental ends, where secular means would suffice" (*Lemon* at 642-43). See also *Hunt* v. *McNair*, 493 U.S. 734 (1973); *Walz* v. *Tax Commission*, 397 U.S. 664, 680-81 (1970). These obviously are not identical with the *Lemon* test, and as of yet have not been adopted by the Court.

[48]*Lemon* at 615-21.

[49]Ibid. at 621-25. There is, however, a real question as to the status of this fourth element; and even when it is utilized, its definition seems fairly arbitrary. For example, in *Lynch* at 668, 684-85, the Court emphasized that "political divisiveness alone" cannot invalidate "otherwise permissible conduct." Further, it warned that "political divisiveness" cannot be claimed by the very act of commencing the lawsuit. In *Meek*, at 367, the Court found "auxiliary services" such as remedial instruction, guidance counseling, etc. were obviously unconstitutional "entanglements" because of the potential there for fostering religion and because of the potential for "political divisiveness." Yet, ironically, as noted by dissenting Justice Brennan, the Court failed even to mention the test of "political divisiveness" as it approved funding for textbooks for the same schools (ibid. at 473-83; compare 459-62).

[50]*Braunfeld* v. *Brown*, 366 U.S. 599, 603 (1961). See also *Cantwell* v. *Connecticut*, 310 U.S. 269, 303-4 (1939): "Thus the Amendment embraces two concepts—freedom to believe and freedom to act. The first is absolute but, in the nature of things, the second cannot be. Conduct remains subject to regulation for the protection of society." However, in *Wisconsin* v. *Yoder*, 406 U.S. 205 (1972), the Court acknowledged that in the Amish context, "belief and action cannot be neatly confined in logic-tight compartments" (at 220). The Court has further admitted that ascertaining what makes either belief or action "religious" is a "difficult and delicate task," and beliefs "need not be acceptable, logical, consistent, or comprehensible to others in order to merit First Amendment protection" (*Thomas* at 714).

[51]*Thomas* at 717; *McDaniel* v. *Paty*, 435 U.S. 618 (1978); *Yoder* at 220.

[52]*Thomas* at 718.

ligion clauses. In this case, if the disputed law is not "content neutral," the state must again prove its compelling interests.[53] If the law is content neutral, it can be a valid time, place, and manner regulation by meeting the "middle" level of review, that is, by serving as a "substantial state interest" or "significant government interest."[54] But if it is content neutral and places only an "indirect" or "minimal" burden on religious speech, it evidently may be satisfied by a "legitimate state interest" which may be the lowest form of review—the rational basis test.[55]

Without detailing each of the recent tangential cases, we can suggest from their holdings and from the way the "tests" were formulated certain factors by which religious studies in public higher education might be challenged. These challenges might be made despite the apparent distinction the Court draws regarding the ages and susceptibility of primary and elementary school students versus those in college, and despite any claims of pure objectivity in teaching. Litigants might allege that a religious studies program has a religious purpose simply by virtue of its having an independent, separate identity. That is, if the historical, literary, philosophical and anthropological concerns of religious studies programs are already addressed by other academic disciplines, a litigant may conclude that a justification for such programs lies with their uniqueness which served some "religious" purpose (even if this purpose was not blatantly to indoctrinate or proselytize). In discussing *Schempp*, we will remember, the Court simply suggested that references might have to be made to religion in order to understand the history or literature of a given culture. Likewise, the decision concerning the class at Washington State University involved a class in English, rather than Religious Studies.

The class or program might also be challenged as an illegal "establishment" merely because it utilizes sacred scriptures which, in Justice Brennan's words, can constitute worship to some and blasphemy, sacrilegiousness or idolatry to others, thereby creating the primary conflict over purpose and a political divisiveness the Establishment clause was intended to preclude.[56] Or it could be enjoined as

---

[53]*Widmar* v. *Vincent*, 454 U.S. 263, 269-70 (1981). But recent lower federal court cases of elementary and secondary schools reveal the fact that although the Court views lower education as not being a public or even limited public forum, the precise factors which determine this are not yet agreed on.

[54]*Heffron* v. *International Society for Krishna Consciousness*, 452 U.S. 640, 648-49 (1981).

[55]*Widmar* at 288-89 (Justice White dissenting). This position is not clearly that of the Court's, but the cases that have been brought under both the "religion" and "speech" clauses of the First Amendment have presented tremendous confusion.

[56]*Schempp* at 224: "Surely the place of the Bible as an instrument of religion cannot be gainsaid, and the State's recognition of the pervading religious character of the ceremony is evident from the rule's specific permission of the alterna-

illegal for having either as a purpose or primary effect that of emphasizing metaphysical ideas or schemes more than commonly held cultural values, and thereby promoting primarily intangible items that have been religiously devisive.[57] It might even be challenged as

---

tive use of the Catholic Douay version as well as the recent amendment permitting nonattendance at the exercises. None of these factors is consistent with the contention that the Bible is here used either as an instrument for nonreligious moral inspiration or as a reference for the teaching of secular subjects." Also, see Justice Brennan (concurring): "Any version of the Bible is inherently sectarian, else there would be no need to offer a system of rotation or alternation of versions in the first place, that is, to allow different sectarian versions to be used on different days" (at 282). "But," he continued, "this still leaves out certain minorities' scriptures, and ultimately treats scriptures in a way either religious or sacrilegious to the adherents of the religion" (at 283-84). This criticism is part of his position against "religious" means being used to accomplish secular ends. Religious prayers and Bible readings in public schools always had primarily a religious purpose, unlike the Sabbath closing laws, and therefore cannot be accepted now as having simply a secular purpose. Finally, Justice Brennan is also convinced that the essence of particular religions cannot be boiled down to a "common core" that could be accepted by all and thus be propagated in the public schools (at 286-87). It is not clear whether he feels this way about higher education, since he accentuated the distinction between *Barnette* and *Hamilton* v. *Regents of the University of California*, 293 U.S. 245 (1934) by virtue of the elementary school involving compelled attendance, whereas university attendance is strictly voluntary (at 252-53). He insisted that the founding Fathers' more tolerant view of the place of Christian prayer and scriptures in government can be normative only in very limited ways today since the religious situation has become so much more pluralistic (at 240-41).

[57]See *Stone*. The Court here claimed the Ten Commandment plaques were not integrated into the curriculum since there were no comments by faculty on the plaques as a part of their teaching. The real problem, however, seems to be not whether comments are allowed, but whether the symbol, commented on or not, points primarily to something metaphysical rather than a mere historical fact. Thus the test is neither students' age nor objective method, but rather the content, and more precisely as we show later, the way the content functions. *Lynch* pointed further to the historical/metaphysical distinction, but this was clarified more definitively in *Allegheny County* v. *American Civil Liberties Union Greater Pittsburgh Chapter*, 57 U.S.L.W. 5045 (July 3, 1989). The Court found a crèche displayed in the court House with a prominently situated angel and sign reading, "Gloria in Excelsis Deo," unconstitutional since no secular symbols accompanied the angel other than little trees. But in the same city, a sizeable menorah displayed at the front of the City County building beside a Christmas tree with an accompanying sign about freedom, was found to be legal. The Court utilized Justice O'Connor's concurring opinion in *Lynch* to clarify what an illegal government "endorsement" is, which suggested, *inter alia*, that the test comes down to "what viewers may fairly understand to be the purpose of the display," from its total context—that is, whether they would interpret it as being a religion endorsed by the government (at 5051). This corresponds precisely to our emphasis at the conclusion of this paper on the "function," rather than the content of the symbols or behavior examined.

an illegal establishment if it could be shown that the content of the class was determined by the religious affiliation or training of the religious studies professors or churches to which they belonged, a scenario in which the state would give endorsement to one or more particular religion.[58] Illegality might also be charged if the program's primary effects benefitted any or all religions more than they benefitted nonreligious people or nonreligious institutions.[59] Or, if the legislative purpose had the intent of propagating any or all religions in the sense of influencing students to embrace any or all of these, as opposed to nonreligious views of reality, it could be struck down.[60] Opponents could also argue that the situation required monitoring to prevent possible indoctrination, and should therefore be found illegal.[61] A credible case of illegal establishment might also be generated

---

[58]This was a chief problem in *McCollum*. Using state machinery to give authority to those teaching the classes would violate the principle of *McCollum*. University classes which counted as part of the general education requirements would be more susceptible to negative judgment than pure electives, especially if it could be shown that there were insufficient course selection in the distribution so that some students actually had to take a religious studies course rather than something else. On the other hand, pure electives and the nonmandatory nature of college education might alleviate a bit of the illegality of the situation present in *McCollum*.

[59]The problems with the "incidental" religious effect are: 1) that it collapses into an examination of the purpose, since "incidental" denotes that which was not primarily intended; and 2) it is not clear which kinds of "effects" or benefits to religious people or groups can be regarded as general enough of the citizenry that they are not "religious" effects. The Court has eschewed making quantitative measurements of effect, even when it was argued that 96% of the effect of benefit went to the "religious" majority (see *Mueller*).

[60]On the Court's disposition toward legislative intent, there are cases in which the Court has not accepted the legislature's expressed secular purpose as with *Epperson*, *Aguilar* v. *Felton*, 473 U.S. 402 (1985), and *Grand Rapids*. Yet at other times, it has accepted such alleged secular purpose even when it was highly unlikely that any significant benefits would accrue to nonreligious people (*Mueller*). Of course, no legislature would formulate its purpose as that of religious indoctrination to a particular religion. But the intent to benefit primarily even religion in general or all religions, if there be such, would still be illegal vis-à-vis the nonreligious posture.

[61]The "monitoring" presented an unacceptable picture of entanglement and "political divisiveness" of such aid. The *Lemon* Court which first elaborated the "political divisiveness" emphasized that although ordinary political debate and division is a "normal and healthy manifestation of our democratic system of government . . . political divisions along religious lines was one of the principle evils against which the First Amendment was intended to protect. . . . The potential divisiveness of such conflict is a threat to the normal political process" (*Lemon* at 602).

merely if the teachers were theologians or had professional ministerial degrees and/or allegiances.[62]

Opponents of religious studies in public universities might charge that the Free Exercise clause is violated if the religious studies courses count as distribution or general education requirements rather than as electives. This would be more likely if the class were accused of advocating ideals so different from the Western, democratic ones as to conflict with the basic grounding of our culture, of causing students to lose their religious faith, or threatening the existence of a religious communion.[63] And certainly the Court's assumption in *Tilton*, that college-age students are not very susceptible to religious indoctrination, is challengeable.[64]

In some respects, however, the Court recognizes public higher education to be considerably different from elementary and secondary education. Religious classes have been allowed in the latter only through "release" time, whereby the students actually leave the public school grounds for another location for instruction.[65] Yet the Court ruled that religious groups of university students should have "equal access" to the actual university campus facilities for religious study that were available to nonreligious student groups.[66]

In approving government loans for buildings to religiously affiliated colleges, the Court felt it could distinguish not only that the buildings would not be used for religious instruction; it also went to great lengths in defending the overriding nonreligious purpose of the schools themselves and their academic integrity in teaching disciplines according to the methods and standards demanded.[67] While the differences in charters, purposes, etc. of state and religious

---

[62]Despite the positive aspect of the holding of *Tilton* v. *Richardson*, 403 U.S. 672 (1971), a case involving government-funded buildings for religiously affiliated colleges, the aversion toward theologians or the professionally religious is apparent. The Court was assured that such religious professionals would not teach in the publicly funded buildings. This stands in tension with Justice Brennan's footnote in *Edwards* about never having opposed religious studies of theology in higher education unless the Court can distinguish the methods, motives, exact training and expertise of those "theologians" in the private schools from those in the public universities.

[63]This was the rationale behind *Yoder*. As unlikely as it may seem that it would be applied to religious studies classes in a state university, it is possible in light of the adverse effect Chief Justice Rehnquist expressed about secular higher education in *Thomas* (see his statement quoted above on page three).

[64]*Tilton* at 685-86: "College students are less impressionable and less susceptible to religious indoctrination" than elementary and secondary school students.

[65]*Zorach* v. *Clauson*, 343 U.S. 306 (1952).

[66]See *Widmar*. Whereas one was conducted by school personnel, however, the other was quite obviously a student organization.

[67]*Tilton* at 680, 686-87.

schools make this disanalogous, it does suggest that the Court views higher education in general as nonreligious in character.

Indirectly, the Court's approval of legislative chaplains and certain nativity scenes has some application to the issue of religious studies classes. The Court's decisions were based on at least four justifying features. It insisted that a mere ritual that appears to be religious is not a violation of the Establishment clause if through its long history it has not in fact caused an establishment.[68] Further, it insisted that we are a "religious" nation, so to root out all religious references would represent an unrealistic hostility to religion.[69] A third argument was that a public forum cannot be closed to speech or symbols merely because they connote something religious to some people.[70] Finally, the Court also insisted that so long as religious symbols make only historical assertions but not metaphysical assertions, they are not an illegal establishment.[71] So allusions to Jesus or even "Christ" may occur so long as the emphasis is upon the historical beginning of Christianity as a historical religion. As already discussed, however, the third and fourth arguments above have not previously prevented the Court from holding unconstitutional *all* religious instruction and symbols in public elementary and secondary schools, even against the argument that all the symbols and instruction professed to do was to make historical references or inculcate a general morality.

This brief review of cases in which the "tests" have been applied indicates well the complexities encountered with attempts to employ them. This ambiguity is only heightened by the Court's attempt at definition: definition of the proper relation of religion to the "inculcation" of moral virtues—a process the Court has deemed fundamentally important to processes of education in this country; and, even more problematic, the definition of religion itself.

---

[68]This was primary rationale behind the holding of *Marsh v. Chambers*, 463 U.S. 783 (1983).

[69]Thus Chief Justice Berger's overriding argument in *Lynch*.

[70]*Board of Trustees of Village of Scarsdale v. McCreary*, 471 U.S. 83, (1985), per curiam, affirmed by an equally divided Court.

[71]In *Lynch*, the Christian religious overtones of the crèche were neutralized not only by the presence of many nonreligious symbols and activities; it was also argued that since the birth of Jesus was a historical fact, and Christianity was a historical religion, therefore there need not be more than a heightening of historical awareness in such a display. But see also *Allegheny*, note 30.

IV. The Question of Values

Aside from the dicta of *Schempp*, the general holding itself and the Court's subsequent use of it have raised two further issues: 1) the question of the relation of values to religion; and 2) the question of whether the "religious" or "secular" content is not in fact derived more from the way the content *functions*, than from some inherently uniform characteristics.

Despite the state's argument that the reading of scripture was not a religious exercise but rather simply a long-standing tradition connected to the schools' legitimate role of inculcating values to its students, the *Schempp* Court rejected the idea. Even a claim of neutrality, it argued, cannot be used by a majority to restrict anyone religiously, a claim which includes forcing one to appear irreligious. Such is the essence of the Free Exercise clause.[72]

This rejection of the appeal to the inculcation of necessary moral values was repeated later in *Committee for Public Education* v. *Nyquist*.[73] To be sure, this case involved parochial rather than public schools; and the issue at hand was not teaching, but rather various forms of subsidies. All the same, an intriguing comment was made. In a footnote, the Court once again cited to *Schempp*, observing that although the state in that instance had argued that the purpose of the Bible reading was, "the promotion of moral values, the contradiction to the materialistic trends of our times, the perpetuation of our institutions and the teaching of literature," nevertheless, "without discrediting these ends and without determining whether they took precedence over the direct religious benefit, the Court held such exercises incompatible with the Establishment Clause."[74] The *Nyquist* Court reinforced its point by noting that the Virginia bill—promoted by Patrick Henry, and forcefully defeated in part by the wide dissemination of James Madison's "Memorial and Remonstrance"—was a bill that proposed tax-supported teaching of religion for the same reason: the indispensability of such teaching for the "morals of men" and the "peace of society."

This position, however, stands in tremendous tension with the Court's many other references to the necessity of teaching morality or ethics in the public schools. While the *Nyquist* reference to *Schempp* implied that the cultivation of good morals in students is not of sufficient secular purpose or effect to overcome a direct religious effect

---

[72]*Schempp* at 221-24.

[73]413 U.S. 756 (1973). The Court ruled the direct money grants, the tuition reimbursements, and the tax deductions all three as unconstitutional because of their religious effects, insisting that a proper secular purpose does not immunize the law in question form further scrutiny pertaining to its effects.

[74]Ibid., note 39 at 783-84, citing to *Schemmp* at 223 and 278-81, Justice Brennan concurring.

(which rendered it illegal), the Court has several times used Justice Brennan's concurring opinion in *Schempp* to emphasize how necessary it is that our public schools inculcate the values and morals that are so essential to our democratic form of government.

For example, in *Amback* v. *Norwick*, the Court cited to *Schempp*, along with many other cases, to emphasize that public school teaching "go[es] to the heart of representative government." Here, it spoke glowingly of "good citizenship," "democratic society," and "awakening the child to cultural values."[75]

> Today, education is perhaps the most important function of state and local governments. Compulsory school attendance laws and the great expenditures for education both demonstrate our recognition of the importance of education to our democratic society. It is required in the performance of our most basic public responsibilities, even service in the armed forces. It is the very foundation of good citizenship. Today it is a principal instrument in awakening the child to cultural values, in preparing him for later professional training, and in helping him to adjust normally to his environment.[76]

The same sentiment was expressed in *Plyler* v. *Doe*,[77] as the Court again quoted Judge Brennan (concurring) in *Schempp* within a long list of decisions emphasizing the crucial role played by public education in our country. The "acquisition of knowledge" is a matter of "supreme importance"[78]; and the public schools are "a most vital civic institution for the preservation of a democratic system of government."[79] These schools are "the primary vehicle for transmitting 'the values on which our society rests,'"[80] values very important to democracy, "freedom and independence."[81] The *Plyler* Court went further on its own, speaking of education as providing the "basic tools by which individuals might lead economically productive lives to the benefit of us all." It further emphasized the absolute necessity of all groups being educated so as "to absorb the values and skills upon which our social order rests."[82] It insisted that "these historic perceptions of the public schools as inculcating fundamental values necessary to the maintenance of a democratic political system have been confirmed by the observations of social scientists."[83]

---

[75]441 U.S. 68 (1979), citing to *Brown* v. *Board of Education*, 347 U.S. 483, 493 (1954), and *Sugarman* v. *Dougall*, 413 U.S. 634, 647 (1973).

[76]Ibid. at 76–77.

[77]457 U.S. 202 (1962).

[78]Ibid. at 221, citing to *Meyer* v. *Nebraska*, 262 U.S. 390, 400 (1923).

[79]Ibid., citing to *Schempp* at 230.

[80]Ibid., citing to *Ambach* v. *Norwick*, 441 U.S. 68, 76 (1979).

[81]Ibid., citing to *Yoder* at 221.

[82]Ibid.

[83]Ibid., citing to *Ambach* at 77.

Likewise the Court in *Epperson* cited to *Keyishian* to accentuate basic constitutional freedoms of the public classroom, even though not religious in nature.[84] The *Keyishian* Court emphasized that the public school classroom is peculiarly the marketplace of ideas, a forum essential for the maturity of citizens, a necessary exposure to diverse ideas en route to truth yet unknown, a vital process of free inquiry and evaluation upon which our constitutional government is founded and upon which our civilization's very life hangs.

The greatest irony to those who think *Schempp* itself justified only objective neutrality in teaching was the Court's citing of Justice Jackson's opinion in *Everson* which suggested that the separation of religious teaching from public schools would not negate the schools' inclusion of,

> all temporal knowledge and also maintain a strict and lofty neutrality as to religion. The assumption is that after the individual has been instructed in worldly wisdom he will be better fitted to choose his religion.[85]

Many have deduced from this statement that the inculcation of values therefore has an integral and unchallengeable place in the public schools.[86] More concretely, some scholars have interpreted this to mean that the nation has its own "civil religion."[87] The Court, however, has been unimpressed with the idea of "core" values of our society which would constitute such a "civil religion." This may be due to the fact that this designation retained the term "religion." After

---

[84]*Epperson*, citing *Keyishian* v. *Board of Regents of New York*, 385 U.S. 589, 602-3 (1967).

[85]*Schempp* at 218, citing *Everson* at 23-24. This could be viewed as only incidental, but sounds more like a religious purpose behind a secular purpose.

[86]For the importance of values-education in the public schools, see *Bethel School Disttrict No. 403* v. *Fraser*, 478 U.S. 675 (1986); *Rendell-Baker* v. *Kohn*, 457 U.S. 830, 848, note 2 at 848-49 (1982); *Plyler* at 221; *Ambach* at 76-77; *Nyquist* at 756; *Sugarman* at 647; *Yoder* at 221; *Brown* at 493. *Schempp* was cited in all of these except *Fraser* and *Brown*.

[87]Sidney Mead, Robert Michaelson, and Robert Bellah among others have developed this idea. Mead suggests that the historical development of this democratic ideal as the national or common "religion" of the American people had to be entrusted to the public schools for its promotion. For this analysis, see his *The Nation with the Soul of a Church* (New York: Harper & Row, 1975). Robert Michaelson has developed similar ideas with his, "The Public Schools and America's Two Religions," *Journal of Church and State* 8:3 (1966) pp. 380-400. See also Justice Frankfurter's concurring opinion in *McCollum* at 212-32. If there be such national ideals, even if in a state of change, and they function in a way equivalent to recognized religions, that would afford Free Exercise right according to *U.S.* v. *Seeger*, 380 U.S. 163 (1965), but could simultaneously violate the Establishment clause by being deemed to constitute a sect in itself. See Justice Brennan's observation in the following note.

Schempp, to embrace the religious over and against the nonreligious was considered illegal.[88]

If the Court will be satisfied only after the sources, instruments and means proposed for use in inculcating moral values in the classroom have been sanitized of all traces of religion, that betrays either a "hostility to religion" (which *Schempp* had allegedly deplored) or at least provides an artificial and truncated view of human life, as well as education, far beyond the decision of *Schempp.* Moreover, the states' intention to propagate any significant moral values will necessarily be frustrated, as morality is so intertwined with religion that either a religious purpose or a primary religious effect can disqualify the effort. That is, nearly all, if not all, specific religions in the U.S. have as one of their *primary* purposes that of effecting a more moral humanity. Further, they would be substantially, directly, and primarily (not merely incidentally) benefitted ("primary effect") by the schools' propagation of morals or values basic to society as a whole; yet the Court insists that such broad goals of society would not be considered a "religious" purpose or primary effect. But that is to say that purposes or effects become illegally "religious" only when any *content* (especially content consisting of what the Court thinks of as unverifiable metaphysical ideas) of the activity or curriculum becomes challengeable by its identification with some specific "religious" group, tradition, or idea.[89] If it is only its identification with specifically distinguishable religious groups that is objectionable, does this mean that *Everson, McCollum* and *Schempp* went too far in forbidding aid to all religions over and against the nonreligious, or that the Court should be more receptive to the idea of values com-

---

[88]Justice Brennan (concurring in *Schempp* at 286-87) argued against such a reduction of any particular religion which might simply create a new sect, a "public school sect." The Court's reluctance to admit such does appear in considerable tension with its high-sounding phrases of the "values on which our society rests." In *Schempp,* Justice Brennan felt he could distinguish the "uniquely democratic values" of public education from "religious" values (ibid. at 242); yet, the former *do* sound very similar to what has often been referred to as America's "civil religion." In Justice Brennan's own words, "It is implicit in the history and character of American public education that the public schools serve a uniquely *public* function: the training of American citizens in an atmosphere free of parochial, divisive, or separatist influence of any sort—an atmosphere in which children may assimilate a heritage common to all American groups and religions. . . . This is a heritage neither theistic nor atheistic, but simply civic and patriotic" (ibid. at 242, emphasis in original).

[89]This is what Justice Powell assured in *Edwards.* In *Stone,* the first several of the Ten Commandments made the enterprise objectionable, no matter how noble the idea of inculcating values, even as the predominantly religious instrument (the Bible) used in *Schempp* made the action illegal despite the alleged purpose of cultivating higher spiritual values in a materialistic age.

monly and critically held by both religious and nonreligious entities, even if the entity were called something other than "civil religion"?[90]

The Court's decisions on instructional materials other than books and state-prepared tests, field trips, and imported teachers for counseling or remedial services at the parochial school reveal its position that abuse of inculcation of values by the addition of the religious element is more likely to take place in public primary and secondary schools than in even church-related colleges. These decisions also suggest that proselytizing is much more apt to occur in a class on religion than one on science.[91] Ironically, however, in higher education—even in church-related colleges—the Court has allowed for the federal funding of buildings by insisting that these schools can be trusted to be primarily academic and secular rather than religious in nature and function. Curiously, this decision suggests that the Court has more confidence that a sectarian university could be used in a nonsectarian manner than it has that a sectarian document such as the Bible could be used in a nonsectarian manner. But Justice Jackson has insightfully noted that the elusive point of difference between instruction and religious proselytizing "is, except in the crudest case, a subtle inquiry."[92] In short, it is still not clear how the Court's goal of the inculcation of values can be realized without an Establishment violation.

Perhaps partial resolution of the dilemma can be found in cases in which the Court has protected a traditionally nonreligious content as if it were religious, or a traditionally religious content as if it were secular. In a Free Exercise case, for example, the required flag salute was equated with religious symbols, rituals or beliefs.[93] The Court ruled such salutes to be an unconstitutional coercion. *United States* v. *Seeger* and *Welsh* v. *United States* are two cases which brought the

---

[90]This would square more with the Court's utilization of Tillich's definition of "religion" in *Welsh* as "ultimate concern" as discussed below.

[91]See *Wolman* v. *Walter*, 433 U.S. 229 (1977); *Levitt* v. *Committee for Public Education*, 413 U.S. 472 (1973); *Meek*, *Lemon* and more recently *Grand Rapids* and *Aguilar* v. *Felton*. The Court in *Roemer* v. *Maryland Public Words Board*, 426 U.S. 736, 762 (1976), naively assumed that there is very little danger that "religion" could be inserted or taught in a class that is "ostensibly secular" such as "biology" or a "foreign language."

[92]*McCollum* at 236.

[93]With *Barnette*, the Court emphasized that symbols, rituals and beliefs, whether traditionally religious, political or nationalistic, cannot be sustained or made uniform by coercion. Rather, dissent and individuality must be preserved, since a "person gets from the symbol the meaning he puts into it, and what is one man's comfort and inspiration is another's jest and scorn" (at 632-33). "Those who begin coercive elimination of dissent soon find themselves exterminating dissenters. Compulsory unification of opinion achieves only the unanimity of the graveyard" (at 641).

Court to reconsider traditional definitions of "religion."[94] These cases, both involving conscientious objector status, brought the Court to a definition of "theism" which embraced more than Jewish and Christian notions of a Supreme Being. Drawing on the language of Paul Tillich, it equated religious moral conviction with an "ultimate concern" equal in function to a belief in God or a Supreme Being. Once again, the Court focused on *Schempp's* insistence that the state cannot prefer any religion over non-religion, just as it cannot support a single religion. It further held that the plaintiffs' convictions against war, though not derived from specific religious institutions, nevertheless qualified them for CO status since they held their convictions with the strength of traditional religious convictions. In this, the Court reduced the content issue not simply to its objective source, but to the way the content *functioned for the litigant.*[95] The *function* was more dispositive for the case than the question of internal or external sources of the belief or action, or the question of how logical or credible the belief or action was.

Whereas many Establishment cases would seem to indicate that religious content could never lose its illegal religious taint, *Lynch* and *Marsh* are cases which reveal the Court's position that even obvious traditional religious content can be understood, given their *function* as symbols or institutions, as either not "religious" or at least only innocuously and not unconstitutionally so. In *Lynch*, sufficient secular symbols—Santa and his reindeer—forming the context cured the otherwise religious symbols of the nativity scene of any illegal taint. In *Marsh*, the Court simply assured us that the history of a chaplain serving the Nebraska legislature had itself proven that no illegal establishment of religion had taken place; the practice, therefore, could not be construed as an illegal establishment.[96]

If the Court would further develop this criteria of *function*, it may be relieved of the more controversial tasks of weighing "excessive entanglement," or primary against incidental effects, as well as the especially undesirable task of challenging legislative purpose.

---

[94]*Seeger* at 185-88; *Welsh* at 341-44.

[95]Justice Harlan, concurring in the result in *Welsh*, also cited to *Schempp*, arguing that although Congress did not have to grant CO status to anyone, if it did so on the basis of the person's conscience or theistic religious belief, once it draws this line, "it cannot draw the line between theistic or nontheistic religious beliefs on the one hand and secular beliefs on the other" (at 357-58). The Court has not accepted this, insisting on its "religious" nature, but "religious" is not further defined by this. Interestingly, in *Smith*, the trial court utilized *Seeger* and *Welsh* to rule out certain textbooks as *functioning* for "secular humanism" in a "religious" way, though the appellate court overruled such characterization.

[96]Justice Brennan, dissenting, insightfully noted that a great many people participating in the chaplain's prayer would probably have been rather shocked to be told by the Court that its prayer was not really a prayer!

V. Conclusion

Those reflecting on the role of religious studies in liberal education have wrestled with the basic issues the Court addressed with its decision in *Seeger*: the locus of normative value can no longer be defined by "religion" as traditionally defined. They have also come to recognize that the values we hope to "inculcate" through public education cannot be generically derived from religion and other discourses as a "given." Confidence in the neutral ground of "objectivity" that once allowed for these assumptions has eroded. Some in the legal community have deemed this loss of "objectivity," coupled with the diffused definition of religion articulated by the Court in the *Seeger* decision, to afford legal grounds for treating "secular humanism" as a "religion." As noted by James McBride,

> Conservative Christian lawyers have argued that if traditionally nonreligious, nontheistic beliefs, e.g., "secular humanist" values held with "ultimate concern," were to be considered religious under the Free Exercise Clause, then such views should likewise be regarded as religious under the Establishment Clause. And if what is protected under the Free Exercise Clause is prohibited under the Establishment Clause, the religious status of "secular humanism" under the former should ensure that it not be "established" in the public school system under the latter.[97]

This approach insists that the hidden values in the value-free approach be unveiled, such as the value of separation of religion and state or the values inherent in the "value-free" discourse of public schools. The value of tolerance of religious pluralism, as vital as it is to all, is inherently threatening to the absolutistic manner in which many religions are experienced and espoused. With this concern finding greater prevalence in our courts, we find the tables beginning to turn with regard to the constitutionality of religious studies in the public school system. Rather than the ideal of "objectivity" serving as a solution, it is now beginning to be deemed the problem to the extent that it is propagated with "ultimate concern" to the detriment of religion.

---

[97]"Paul Tillich and the Supreme Court," *Journal of Church and State* 30:2 (1988) p. 247. McBride argues that this equation is a misinterpretation of Tillich's theology which leads him to conclude, "Whereas it was assumed that Tillich's idea of 'ultimate concern' encompassed only an affective attitude (in which case anyone might be considered religious), the incorporation of Tillich into the American legal tradition provides an objective standard of 'trancendence' as the criterion by which beliefs may be judged religious" (p. 247). Yet the Court has refused to get caught up in determining the adequacy of metaphysical claims; it therefore has necessarily to limit itself to the function of religion as discussed here.

Seeger and other recent decisions involving the Establishment Clauses signal that the issue will be settled by focusing more on issues of function than content. Justice Powell is probably correct in *Edwards* in insisting that the Establishment clause is violated only when the "particular" is promoted, but the "particular" must be defined under the Free Exercise Clause as having the "function" formerly associated with religious belief, that is, involving an uncritical or unquestioning obedience. At issue, therefore, will be not so much the subject taught—be it religion, literature, political science or economics—but the extent to which it is determined to be religious in function.

Were religious studies to face legal challenge, it may well be that the key word would not be "objective," but something more along the lines of "critical" which neither attempts to reduce notions of ultimacy within an "objective" interpretation, nor side-lines such notions altogether. As discussed above, the Establishment clause precludes agencies of the state from advocating an uncritical approach or propagating any particular symbol, narrative, or demand that would function as an ultimate concern. This would mean that *any* subject that was taught in a way that precluded critique—that is, requiring absolute consent or allegiance to an unquestioned ultimacy—would be subject to challenge on Establishment grounds. The only test would be whether the teaching assumes or advocates an ultimacy which cannot be brought into the realm of critical discourse. As long as critique and even self-criticism are present, it would not be considered "religious," no matter what the subject or content and no matter what the students' age level. This mode of discourse could then be governed by other civil and criminal law, so as, for example, to be subject to reasonable time, place and manner restrictions. But it would not be disposed of by the Religion clauses! The Court's previous decisions would be compatible with the Seeger definition of "religion" to the degree that the "purpose" and "effects" prongs of the Court's test can be subsumed under this idea of *exclusivity in function*, and that exclusivity is found in most of the cases.

Inasmuch as one of the goals of a liberal arts education is not simply to learn to analyze and argue a position, but to responsibly evaluate and commit for the well-being of humanity, it is a process that brings students into conversation with diverse modalities of ultimacy. This function fulfills the Court's goal of public education: the inculcation of values. But once again, this goal cannot be accomplished in an authoritarian or absolutistic way; its processes must be defined by critical dialogue. So long as dissent is encouraged as a part of the pedagogical process that leads to valuation, with no particular position absolutized, this engagement with issues of "ultimate concern" would not be scrutinized under the religion clauses of the First

Amendment, no matter what the field of study. Moreover, the comparison and diversity of subject and interpretive approach implicit in the critical process would prevent any party from taking unfair advantage of others—which is, after all, what the two religious clauses of the First Amendment are all about.

The contractual nature of our Constitution and the rights it ensures for its diverse citizenry presuppose that the vitally important things on which we citizens in a pluralistic society differ must be discussed openly and intelligently rather than being stifled by authority or be based on circumstances that no longer exist. It further assumes those values important enough to be mutually and fairly contracted for will be values rightfully enforceable. These assumptions require the serious and responsible interchange of ideas in the public forum, including the classroom. Only then will the dynamics making for true democracy be realized; otherwise, as stated by the *Barnette* Court, we will be living with but "a mere shadow of freedom."

FOUR MODES OF DISCOURSE:
BLURRED GENRES IN THE STUDY OF RELIGION[1]

Sheryl L. Burkhalter

In the spring of 1988, the debate over how a curriculum in liberal education might best be structured found its "fifteen minutes of fame." That issues in education should find this moment in the limelight was perhaps of some surprise; but it was also long in coming. While the debate itself was decades old, it had gained momentum in the more recent past with various controversial pronouncements made by William Bennett, first as head of the National Endowment for the Humanities and then as Secretary of Education. His critiques of American education were augmented by the startling success of Allan Bloom's *The Closing of the American Mind* which remained on

---

[1]This essay originated, as discussed below, from the sessions of the 1986 NEH Institute. At the end of each week, I summarized the presentations and discussions which followed. These summary statements, while hardly representative of the diversity of contributions made, provided a cohesive element to which participants contributed with their responses and critiques. It was this process that transformed Duane Friesen's suggestion that we adopt a heuristic model of differentiated discourse for our discussions into what proved to be a centerpiece for the discussions themselves. Perhaps more directly than the other papers in the volume, therefore, this paper gives an ear to what went on during the six weeks of intense discussion and debate celebrated with the Chicago Institute. Of course, there are other echoes to be heard: the readings that have brought me to engage in quite different ways with the memory of those discussions; and the various responses which the statement has evoked since it first took form at the Institute's end. In this regard, special mention must be given the 1989 meetings of the Project in Berkeley whose discussions led to a basic revision of the paper. I would also like to express gratitude to Frank Reynolds, who provided encouragement and critique throughout the process leading from the summary statements to this paper. Despite the transformations that have made for a statement quite different from that marking the end of the Institute, I trust that those who were participants will find represented in the following pages something of what we were about in those six weeks at Chicago—echoes of their voices, their contributions and critiques which at this juncture in time are impossible to trace.

the best-seller list for several months running. The eye of public attention was further drawn to such concerns by a presidential campaign whose candidates rode the wave, seeking to corner the market on educational issues. The import this agenda had assumed at this time came later to be mirrored in the title of "The Education President" that George Bush would claim for himself upon assuming office.

Perhaps it was the momentum built up by these events which made for the "fifteen minutes" that the nation spent with Stanford University when it decided to revise the reading list for its year-long "Western Culture" requirement.[2] The issues debated were familiar to curriculum committees across the land: defining a canon appropriate for liberal education. But for a time, the four walls of the committee room gave way to the four corners of a nation. And, not surprisingly, it was a spotlight which drew a public appearance from Bennett who referred to this decision as marking, "The Closing of the Stanford Mind." He later elaborated this statement on national television, where he described Stanford's decision as having emerged "not through intellectual discussion," but from "pressure politics" which "trivialize the academic enterprise"; he then emphasized this point by saying that what informed this decision was "a political agenda, not an intellectual agenda."[3]

That the most prominent representative of education in our land could dismiss as "trivialization" a debate which had been waged at Stanford during the previous two years is in itself remarkable. This, especially after his report as head of NEH, "To Reclaim a Legacy," had crystallized an argument which for years had been debated along similar lines throughout the academy.[4] Not only does the debate over

---

[2]See, for example, the exchange of editorials and letters to the editor published by the *Wall Street Journal* and now reprinted in *Essays on the Closing of the American Mind,* ed. Robert L. Stone (Chicago: Chicago Review Press, 1989) pp. 362-66.

[3]William Bennett in conversation with the President of Stanford on the McNeil-Lehrer News Hour, April 19, 1988.

[4]William J. Bennett, "To Reclaim a Legacy," *Chronicle of Higher Education* 28 (1984) pp. 16-21.

In the winter of 1985, Jonathan Z. Smith provided a most powerful critique of Bennett's, "To Reclaim a Legacy," for the annual Woodward Court Lecture at the University of Chicago (unpublished). It is with considerable restraint that I limit his discussion to the following quote:

The issue that troubles me most is not what has bothered others. It is not the haughty, jingoistic chauvinism, nor the pathetic limitations of Bennett's little list of thirty-two books and seven documents which he claims, "virtually define the development of the western mind . . ." Rather, it is that there are no apparent wrinkles on his brow when he speaks in so singular a manner of *the* "western mind" which has had, it would appear, a unilateral development from classic Greece to 20th cena canon appropriate for liberal education have a considered, and rather lengthy, intellectual history[5]; more significantly, it is also a debate which, drawing on the likes of Foucault and Said, has taken issue with the insular categorization Bennett is wont to make between political and intellectual agendas. Indeed, it is precisely the interplay of these categories in processes of cultural formation which has drawn many to rethink the cannon appropriate for liberal education in our time.[6]

To be sure, the limelight of the public eye has since moved on; but the heat it generated has made for much steam in the backwaters. Even today, the issues raised are deemed sensational enough to merit continued discussion in the morning papers.[7] The debate concerning

---

tury America. . . . Western civilization is assumed to be a self-evident, fully incarnate entity in a manner that makes self-respecting theologians blush with shame.

Smith further takes issue with Bennett's claim that "intellectual authority came to be replaced by intellectual relativism as the guiding principle of the curriculum," and that this "relativism" is a "self-inflicted wound" on the body of contemporary education; that it legitimates the subordination of everything to "contemporary prejudice"; and that in consequence "all meaning is [deemed] subjective and relative to one's own perspective." Smith's response: "Nonsense! This is to *trivialize* one of the major issues of western thought; one that has been central for centuries."

[5]A bibliography adequate to this history warrants an essay of its own. John Trimbur, however, sums up the direction it has taken in noting, "At this juncture in history, it is simply no longer possible to assume that there is a single self-evident canon of humanistic thought and texts that can be restored at the heart of the curriculum" (*Liberal Education* 72:2 [1986] p.111). The entire volume of this journal is devoted to the debate over canon. A similar collection of essays discussing the issue from the perspective of Religious Studies was published in *Soundings: An Interdisciplinary Journal* 61:3 (1978), and includes a wonderful contribution by Ralph Norman, "Necessary Texts: Pluralism and the Uses of Canon," pp. 236-46. The broader ramifications of the debate have been followed by numerous position papers published by the Woodrow Wilson Institutes.

[6]Jacques Derrida states the case well: "[A]s we all know, it is impossible now more than ever to dissociate the work we do within one discipline or several, from a reflection of the political and institutional conditions of that work. Such a reflection is unavoidable. It is no longer an *external* component to teaching and research; it must make its way through the very objects we work with, shaping them as it goes, along with our norms, procedures and aims" ("The Principle of Reason: The University in the Eyes of its Pupils," *Diacritics* 13:3 [1983] p. 3).

[7]The *Chicago Tribune* devoted an entire article (September 15, 1989; section 5, p. 3) to a discussion of the response which Bloom's best-seller received with Rick Simonson and Scott Walker's *Multi-Cultural Literacy: Opening the American Mind* (St. Paul: Graywolf Press, 1988). More recently, the debate again made headlines with the publication of Lynne Cheney's report as chairwoman of the National Endowment for the Humanities, "50 Hours: A Core Curriculum for College Students." In reviewing this most recent proposal for reform, the *New York Times* indicates the extent to which the debate is on-going and quotes one dean as re-

liberal education is now a public one. Taking this fact seriously requires that we pause for a time in our ready critiques of Bennett's
campaign, to remember that it was a campaign waged with more the
public than the academy in mind. With this purview, the ease of critique tends to give way as it requires that we abandon a familiar lexicon for a language more accessible to the general public. And, as Said
notes, for academicians this proves an increasingly difficult task:

> In having given up the world entirely for the aporias and unthinkable
> paradoxes of a text, contemporary criticism has retreated from its con-
> stituency, the citizens of modern society, who have been left to the
> hands of 'free' market forces, multinational corporations, the manipula-
> tions of consumer appetites. A precious jargon has grown up, and its
> formidable complexities obscure the social realities that, strange though
> it may seem, encourage a scholarship of 'modes of excellence' very far
> from daily life in the age of declining American power.[8]

The stance Said here assumes finds ironic consonance with that of
Bennett: this, in the extent to which they have both demanded that
academicians move beyond the comforts of the discourse which their
respective disciplines have made familiar, so as to take seriously the
students—and through them, the public—we teach. The lacuna these
two public figures have attempted to breach, albeit in their opposing
and most controversial ways, is certainly not new to the academy as
evidenced by such familiar phrases as "town and gown" and "ivory
towers." But in confronting this lacuna, those who hear the voice of
Bennett on the one hand and Said on the other have come to experience apprehension, if not considerable anxiety, over the outcome of
the debate.

Given the strength and stridency of these voices which have
awakened the concern and apprehensions of a nation, academicians
have no choice but to move beyond the domain of their familiar pos-
turing in the ongoing debate over liberal education. That is, the likes
of Said and Bennett require us to confront the ease with which we
tend to dismiss public scrutiny by brandishing insular categories of
our own, categories which we would be able to critique with a facility
equal to that assumed in our responses to Bennett and Bloom. The

---

sponding, "A reform that relies so heavily on the traditional Western civilization
courses runs the risk of a dangerous superficiality" (October 7, 1989; section Y, p.
11).

[8]Edward Said, "Secular Criticism," in *The World, the Text, and the Critic*
(Cambridge: Harvard University Press, 1983) p. 4. I have quoted Edward Said in
this instance, as his *Orientalism* represents a powerful argument undermining
Bennett's critique of "trivialization." Yet, Said is but one of a chorus of scholars
who have voiced the kind of lament quoted above. See, for example, Tzvetan
Toderov, "All Against Humanity," *New York Times Literary Supplement*, October 4,
1985, pp. 1093-94.

"fifteen minutes," in short, invite far more than a critique of dismissal: they occasion instead a moment to reflect on our own speech in discussions with those not of our academic specialization. With this reflection, we are asked to articulate with greater creativity and responsibility our claims concerning the contributions Religious Studies makes towards a liberal education.

Religious Studies in the Arena of Liberal Education

For Religious Studies, this self-critique of our own public posture represents a rather formidable task, as it requires that we leave open for debate the language which paved the way for Religious Studies' return to the academy. I refer, of course, to the differentiation between the teaching "of" and the teaching "about" religion. The language of this differentiation belongs in the first instance to the Supreme Court's ruling on the *Schempp* case, the decision which paved the way for establishing religious studies departments in large numbers of public universities across the country.[9] Though this sanction from the Court may have settled the case in the public's mind, scholars in the field recognized early on the ambiguities confronted in taking the "of/about" differentiation into the classroom: What pedagogical design rightfully merits the designation of "teaching *about* religion" as distinct from the "teaching *of* religion"?[10] The discussion this question generated among scholars is now beginning to make its way back into the courts. Royce Clark's contribution to this volume follows this discussion, indicating the extent to which the presumed definiteness of the "of/about" differentiation marks anything but an open and shut case.[11]

Whatever the future of religious studies in the legal arena, it will certainly be informed by how scholars in the field have come to understand and define their work within the broader academy. The "of/about" language continues to be heard in this regard, perhaps because the definitive slash represents the issue in a 30-second byte for those who have little interest in pursuing it further. Alongside

---

[9]Commenting on the *Schempp* decision, Justice Goldberg indicated that given the "opinions in the present and past cases," it could be assumed that "the Court would recognize the propriety of . . . the teaching *about* religion, as distinguished from the teaching *of* religion in the public schools" (*Abington School District* v. *Schempp* 374 U.S. 203, 306).

[10]See, for example, the debate sparked by Robert Minor and Robert Baird's article, "Teaching About Religion at the State University: Taking the Issue Seriously and Strictly," *Bulletin of the Council on the Study of Religion* 14:3 (1983) pp. 69-72. Their position evoked several responses in subsequent issues of the *Bulletin*.

[11]See his article in this volume, "The Legal Status of Religious Studies Programs in Public Higher Education," pp. 109-39.

Bennett, that is, many in religious studies continue to face the public with a simple dichotomy of their own; and, again with Bennett, it is a dichotomy which "trivializes" our enterprise, given the lack of consonance it bears with the kind of research and scholarship pursued by scholars in the field. The consequence of this "trivialization" is borne out in the demure—if not dormant—posture scholars in religious studies have traditionally assumed in discussions about the future of liberal education.[12] Defending the discipline with language that finds little theoretical support from its own discourse has assured that the scholarship of religious studies remain ensconced in the back waters of specialized discourse lamented by Said.

The "of/about" language thus continues to guard a lacuna between public and professional discourse in religious studies. It is, significantly, a lacuna which has gone far in muting the voice of the one discipline that came into the modern academy with discussions of normativity, of formation, and of canon very much to the fore; the discipline that had "hermeneutics" as an integrated concern long before this word found such prominence among the more traditional discourses of the academy; the discipline that addressed the epistemological issues of cultural contact long before these became a basis for rethinking curricular design; the discipline that self-consciously went "global" long before this term became a code word for new directions in American education. That such concerns now find high profile in the current debates over the future of liberal education, I will suggest, provides Religious Studies with an opportunity and a responsibility to become more vocal in the ongoing debate over how best to address the current crisis in liberal education.

Participation in this debate—beyond the critiques we are wont to make in the privacy of religion journals—requires that religious

---

[12]Jonathan Z. Smith made mention of this tendency in the paper he delivered at the initial session of this Project ("How I Would Teach an Introductory Course in Religion," *Sourcebook for the Berkeley/Chicago/Harvard Institutes* (1988: p. 18). Referring to the proposed arena of discussion, "The Study of Religion in the Liberal Arts," he remarked:

> I am delighted that such a topic has been proposed. If taken seriously, it marks the beginning of our potential for maturity as a part of the profession of education. Because of this, I note with sadness that this conference is the result of independent entrepreneurship . . . rather than being a major focus of our putative professional society, the American Academy of Religion, which still confines discussion of educational matters to a ghetto or limbo reserved for those feckless few whose work is too trivial even to be featured as part of the normal agendum.

Fortunately, whether by virtue of this Project or otherwise, the AAR has since instituted a section on "Academic Teaching and Study of Religion."

studies "go public."[13] It demands that we acknowledge the trans-formations in our discipline and in the larger academy which have taken religious studies beyond the place of being but a "stepchild" in the university.[14] To take this demand seriously is to move beyond the defence which the "of/about" language has long been assumed to provide. This price is but a trifling in comparison with the resources religious studies might contribute if its scholarship, rather than the rhetoric of its traditional defence, were to fuel its participation in on-going discussions about the future of liberal education.

Rethinking the Place of Religious Studies in the Academy

Moving beyond the "of/about" language requires an initial step back, with consideration given the broader context of the categoriza-tion itself and the priority it continues to assume as a starting point for such discussions about the place of religious studies in the academy. I refer in this instance not the decision of the Court which provided us these prepositions, but to the more general historical milieu which prevailed when religious studies returned to the univer-sity as a discipline in its own right.

Prior to its "exile," theology had reigned over the academic enterprise as the Queen of the Sciences: its interpretive discourse remained regnant among the disparate disciplines.[15] After a hiatus marked by the Enlightenment, religious studies would return to the university; but this, after the unitary structures of the monotheistic deity of medieval universities had long been replaced by the principle of Reason. In this context, the principle of "universal" Reason served as the unitary center through which knowledge was ordered and in-tegrated. This mode of rationality thus marked the door through which our discipline—albeit, somewhat uneasily—reentered the modern university.

Allow me to emphasize the adverb, "uneasily": In returning to the university under the sign of the Enlightenment, religious studies left the normative discourse of theology to institutions of religious

---

[13]Since writing this paper, I have discovered Martin Marty's expression of similar concern—albeit from quite different perspective—in his 1988 Presidential address for the American Academy of Religion, "Committing the Study of Reli-gion in Public," *Journal of the American Academy of Religion* 57:1 (1989) pp. 1-22.

[14]Charles Long, "Human Centers: An Essay on Method in the History of Re-ligions," *Soundings* 61:3 (1978) p. 402.

[15]This discussion, reflecting on the history of Religious Studies as a locus for rethinking the voice the discipline might assume in proposing future directions for liberal education, draws on an article written with Frank Reynolds, "Privileging the Periphery: Reflections on Religious Studies and the Liberal Arts," *Criterion* 26:2 (1987) pp. 2-6.

learning; normative for the discourse of religion in its return was the notion of universal rationality which mapped out a quite different topography for pedagogical design. The unease was generated by the fact that religious studies reappeared as a discipline of study by insisting that the relation between Reason and specifically religious discourse had been misconstrued by this topography as charted out by the more established disciplines. That is, religious studies came into its own as an arena of study within the academy by making waves, waves generated by an insistence that the discourse of religion required distinctive means of interpretation if its meaning was to be adequately explored within the context of the university.

Discussions concerning how this "distinctive means" might best be construed and defined remains, of course, the primary problematic of religious studies—and one to which this essay does not propose a resolution. Of import to the present discussion, rather, is the need to recognize that there has been a dramatic change in the *context* of the debate: no longer is the differentiation between subjectivity and objectivity discerned in the terms which initially structured the argument. The hierarchical relation that once characterized Reason as a locus of adjudication hovering over, and lending clarity to, subjective understandings of the world has long since given way.

Much ink has been given to critiques of the Enlightenment project throughout the decade past from all corners of the academy. Epistemologically, the knower and the known are now recognized to be integrally related, a relation conceding to the impossibility of "value-free" inquiry. Reason, as configured in terms of a given—an abstract and static norm defining the "givenness" of things—no longer serves as a singular locus of adjudication for discourse within the university. Its moorings have been traced; and its diverse—and sometimes contradictory—expressions, both through history and across disciplines, demand that the normative status traditionally accorded Reason as the "given" upon which the academy is based be questioned and investigated with a quite different eye, an eye which recognizes "just how unvirginal reason is."[16]

Given this critique, the radical oppositions of "knower/known," "subjective/objective," "intellectual/political" and—might I emphasize—"of/about" do not serve us well. Presented as alternatives, they conceal more than they reveal: the differentiation they afford misrepresents the case. The "simple logic" assumed to represent the preliminary dichotomy has time and again been shown to be anything but "simple." Once stripped of this simplicity, such absolute differentiations occasion an unfortunate, if not misleading, place of beginning. Representation is more adequately to be discerned—as Clifford

---

[16]Clifford Geertz, *Local Knowledge* (New York: Basic Books, 1983) p. 149.

Geertz, among others, has taught us—through the slash itself; and this, through its blurring.[17] Significantly, attention given this blurring has made for much of the most creative scholarship in the humanities throughout the decade past.

Implicit in a "blur," however, is a line: in this case, a line representing the role that the Enlightenment notion of reason has traditionally assumed in adjudicating balance within the interpretive enterprise of modern scholarship, a role that has generated and sustained the modern university. The door has been passed through and closed; it cannot be reopened. Religious Studies cannot forego the critical mode of discourse that is its inheritance and revert back to teaching in the humanities through the medium of theology or theologies. We cannot go back; but we can, and must, move forward.

This will require that we admit to the inadequacy of the "of/about" language which has represented (or misrepresented) our discipline for decades; but it will also, and perhaps more importantly, require that we make this admission while recognizing that the inadequacy stems not so much from what we do—or do not do—in religious studies, as from the transformations in what it is now possible to assume in the academy about the production and reproduction of knowledge. This process, the cornerstone of liberal education, has lost its innocence. As discussed above, the well-defined image of the educated person once imagined with the promise of Reason as a center to lend proportion to all other imaginations has given way. The smooth lines of the "classic," long assumed to give form to a liberal education, are now threatened by the "enormous multiplicity" which Geertz terms "the hallmark of modern consciousness."[18] Disparate— and often contradictory—modalities of reasoning are to be discerned among the academic disciplines themselves[19]; and this disparity is only compounded when placed within the context of the highly complex and differentiated global situation in which we now live.

Undermined both philosophically *and* culturally—alongside all the interfaces this "and" represents—the discourse of Reason and rationalities can no longer be imagined with the singular line of a seawall which the waves of "would-be" disciplines seek to reconfigure.[20]

---

[17]See Clifford Geertz, "Blurred Genres: The Reconfiguration of Social Thought," in *Local Knowledge* (New York: Basic Books, 1983) pp. 19-35.

[18]Geertz, *Local Knowledge*, p.161.

[19]Jonathan Z. Smith confronts us with the challenge which the disparate modes of reasoning represented by the academy present to anyone who takes issues of education seriously in his essay, "'Narratives into Problems': The College Introductory Course and the Study of Religion," *Journal of the American Academy of Religion* 56:4 (1988) pp. 727-40.

[20]The term "would-be" disciplines was coined by Stephen Toulmin to refer to knowledge communities within the academy that could not be easily accommodated within the scientific model of the university as configured by Enlighten-

The seawall has given way as much by force of transformations *within* the classic disciplines as by challenges that have come from the "would-be" disciplines on the periphery. The map of the academy has changed with the end of the twentieth century; and it has little place for "of/about" discourse. A new language of representation needs to be discerned.

In Search of New Discursive Patterns

It might be argued that religious studies has, from its inception as a discipline, been involved with critiques of Enlightenment notions of rationality. Of present concern, however, is not so much the nature of this theoretical involvement, as the extent to which this theoretical discourse has—or, more accurately, has not—been taken public. And it is precisely here, at the interface between theoretical discourse on the one hand, and public representation of that discourse on the other, where religious studies has contributions to make in redressing the current "crisis" in liberal education.

The promise of this contribution came through time and again during the six-week Institute which this volume in some sense represents. In this context, it soon became explicitly recognized by all involved in these discussions that every aspect of Religious Studies directly involves one with diverse communities of discourse. Yet, throughout these discussions we found ourselves spending an inordinate amount of time attempting to sort out these involvements through differentiations of various modes of discourse and their relation to one another. This led us early on to map out the following "four modes of discourse" as a heuristic model for addressing—and redressing—the differentiations in discourse often assumed in the praxis of religious studies.

> **Mode One**: the discourse of the believer, as encompassed by patterns of worship and practice. It is the discourse generally associated with expression which has often been deemed spontaneous, emotive, and uncritical; hence, "pre-logical" and/or "irrational." This discourse belongs to the realms of performance and ritual, and to the myth and symbol presumed operative within them.

> **Mode Two**: the language of second-order reflection within the tradition itself, language attempting to integrate the discourses of mode one within the broader scheme of what is deemed to be true; and in terms of that understanding, to structure the commitment and action of those

---

ment-oriented notions of Reason. See his discussion in *Human Understanding: The Collective Use and Evolution of Concepts* (Princeton: Princeton University Press, 1977) pp. 378-95.

who adhere to that understanding. Within this mode, we find theologi-cal and philosophical reflection on the one hand, and legal codes and prescriptions for community behavior and order on the other. In both instances, this praxis has been recognized as an attempt to present a distinct identification with the tradition which serves to differentiate it from those who do not adhere to the said tradition.

Mode Three: the language of the academic, language which imposes the critique of Enlightenment sciences—historical, psychological, anthropo-logical, philosophical, sociological—on modes one and two, and which tempers interpretations of the practitioners' speech with the interpretive analyses of the human sciences.

Mode Four: the discursive practices of the student, discourse which cuts across the other modes in reflecting the travails of one who must inte-grate them all in ways that are personally meaningful and communally relevant. This mode defines a language and situation of judgment and evaluation.

While this model afforded clarity to Institute discussions, it came to play a more important role in facilitating critiques of assumptions so often implicit in the pedagogical design we tend to bring to our courses. This critique, in turn, brought us to review the case fre-quently made for having such courses incorporated within a liberal arts curriculum. For example, in first working through how this model plays out in a classroom situation, we time and again caught ourselves referring to its differentiation in terms of "levels" of dis-course. Though not intending—much less, prepared—to defend a hierarchical model that places mode two "above" mode one, and mode three "above" modes one and two, the word choice brought us to contend with the extent to which this hierarchy continues to be as-sumed despite our theoretical formulations to the contrary. This cri-tique could not be silenced with the mere substitution of another word, such as "mode": the model brought us to place the hierarchies of knowledge operative in our pedagogy alongside the hierarchies we tend so readily to critique with our scholarship. In this, we found that the "of/about" debate needed to be situated within the much larger context of the cultural aspects of the production and reproduction of knowledge within the academy.

The heuristic value explored with this "four modes of discourse" model might be intimated in taking up the history of religious studies at a more concrete level. The discipline—perhaps more accurately represented by the term "disciplinary matrix"—came into its own with a readjudication of hierarchies of knowledge within religious studies itself. Whatever the tradition studied, this required a rethink-ing of the "universals" assumed by the third mode of discourse. Among others, an early target taken on was the evolutionary schema of religious thought which mapped out religious history between the polar oppositions of "primitive/ civilized," with the latter assumed to mark the ending of religion through the process of "civilization" (liberal education writ large).[21] Already at this juncture, the "of/about" dichotomy was being questioned; the attempt to keep religion at bay by displacing its meanings and translating them within a discourse structured by Reason was being challenged.

Religious studies would later push the point further by insisting on different rules of translation: as discussed above, neither the discourse of "theology" nor the discourse of "Reason" afforded an appropriate hermeneutic. Interpretation had to be sought, and forged, in the in-between. Thus, religious studies early on disrupted given hierarchies of knowledge with an insistence that the religious arena of human meaning cannot be appropriately adjudicated either through reference to theological discourse alone, nor through the exclusive use of the version of third mode discourse that it had inherited from the Enlightenment.

The instance of studies in Hinduism provides a more defined arena within which to discuss the case. Early scholarship, as initiated by F. Max Müller, focused on the theological traditions as articulated in the Sanskritic texts of the Hindus, with particular prominence given the Vedas and Upanishads. That is, Hinduism first found voice in Western scholarship through the classical texts of the religious elite, the theological locus of "mode two." Later scholars came to recognize that interpretations stylized by the textual tradition had silenced other theological voices of Hinduism as expressed in the ritual and oral performance traditions of "illiterate" believers, the discourses of mode one. Studies of such rituals and performances throughout the Indian subcontinent have demonstrated that the religious meanings explored and expressed by these participants represent interpretive styles and categories of their own. Discursive practices once dismissed as emotive, irrational and uncritical have revealed highly systematized meanings. Thus, the discourse of colonial British officers who first brought the South Indian buffalo sacrifices into the discourse of mode three comes to tell a quite different story when the interpretive strategies of an Enlightenment orientation lose their normative valence in being juxtaposed with those of the tradi-

---

[21]Charles Long brought to the Institute his exploration of the meanings concealed by the slash dividing "primitive/civilized." His presentations urged the group to consider the import this slash might have for discerning a new discourse regarding the meaning of religion in a post-colonial era. As evidenced by this essay, the problematic of "continuity/discontinuity" he recognizes in the slash was frequently returned to as a locus for rethinking some of the issues contributing to the current crisis in liberal education.

tion itself. (See, for example, the brilliant analysis Richard Brubaker affords with his study, "The Ambivalent Mistress."[22])

At this juncture of the discipline's history, the discursive practice of "mode one" could no longer be subsumed within the interpretive discourse of "mode two"; no longer could they be mapped out as the "little traditions of the unreflective many" and the "great tradition of the reflective few."[23] The classic hierarchy of knowledge as the normative mode of inquiry gave way; yet—and this is crucial—the modes of discourse did not meld one into the other. Instead, scholarship has come to revise the dynamics assumed in the categorization itself in recognition of the fundamental interplay of various discursive styles and practices of interpretation. In this, current scholarship has come to afford a portrait of Hinduism quite different than that to which we were introduced by Max Müller.

Needless to say, the portraits now provided by academic scholars are also quite different from those presumed by the elites of the traditions being studied. When Berreman tells of the religious life of the Hindus of the Himalayas[24], he presents an analysis quite different from that we would be afforded by the gurus of Hardwar or Rishikesh. So too, when Lawrence Babb studies the Divine Hierarchy operative in a rural town of Madhya Pradesh[25], he reveals a hierarchy quite different from that assumed by the Pandits of Raipur's main temples. In part, this difference might be attributed to an indifference within the religious traditions themselves. As Ashis Nandi puts it:

> In spite of recent attempts to show the rationality of the savage mind *à la* Lévi-Strauss, the savage mind itself has remained on the whole unconcerned about its own rationality. Both the science of myth and the scientific status of myth continue to be a predominantly modern concern.[26]

This "savage mind" has variously found integration within the diverse hierarchies of knowledge operative in Hinduism. Yet, the indif-

---

[22]Richard Brubaker "The Ambivalent Mistress: A Study of South Indian Village Goddesses and their Religious Meaning" (University of Chicago Dissertation, unpublished, 1978). This study illustrates well the possibilities Renato Rosaldo envisions with his suggestion that "Rather than discarding distanced normalizing accounts, the discipline should recover them, but with a difference. They must be cut down to size and relocated, not replaced" (*Culture and Truth: the Remaking of Social Analysis* [Boston: Beacon Press, 1989] p. 62).

[23]Robert Redfield, *Peasant Society and Culture* (Chicago: University of Chicago Press, 1960) p. 41.

[24]Gerald D. Berreman, *Hindus of the Himalayas* (Berkeley: University of California Press, 1963).

[25]Lawrence Babb, *The Divine Hierarchy: Popular Hinduism in Central India* (New York: Columbia University Press, 1975).

[26]*The Intimate Enemy: Loss and Recovery of Self Under Colonialism* (Delhi: Oxford University Press, 1983) p. 59.

ference to which Nandi refers makes for considerable difference when the elites of two quite separate arenas (the knowledge communities of mode two and three) interpret the meanings of the phenomena in question.

Religious studies, as mentioned above, has from the start privileged this difference: it is not one that can be adjudicated within the "objective" discourse of mode three as traditionally conceived. Richard Schweder has provided a wonderful analysis of the problem with an essay which draws the world of Oriya temple priests in India into conversation with current discussions of the nature of human reason and rationality. This brings him to conclude:

> I think what we have come to realize is that if rational thought is restricted to inductive and deductive logic, we will have very little of a rational sort to say to each other. No presuppositions. No analogies. No semantic or pragmatic implications. . . . Yet if rational thought requires a "third sort" of logic or a nonlogical necessity, it is not the kind of constraint that anchors us to a unitary external world of objects. It is more like the kind of thing that makes it possible for two Marxists, two psychoanalysts, two radical behaviorists, two Muslim fundamentalists to have rational discussions within their respective versions of reality but not across them. Rationality seems to have that peculiar bounded quality; it requires deductive and inductive logic, but deductive and inductive reasoning goes on within the framework of a third sort of logic that is bound to something neither uniform nor unitary. What we seem to need is a concept of divergent rationality.[27]

Whereas the basis for that "third sort of logic" was once a notion of Reason that was assumed and allowed to define the "objective" and "value-neutral" discourse of mode three, it is an understanding of Reason that has now given way; and in the process, the hierarchical relationship which traditionally defined the Enlightenment understanding of mode three as intrinsically separate from the discourse of mode two has been displaced.

Schweder's use of the term "divergent" in this context, however, draws to the fore another aspect of the contestation of elites mentioned earlier, and reveals the extent to which the hierarchy of knowledge between modes two and three remains in tact. Although we have come to recognize diversity in patterns of human reasoning, we continue to assume a norm not argued for, a norm from which other patterns of rationality are understood to "diverge." Where we admit to relativism in theory, we have yet to realize it in fact; and for this we should perhaps remain grateful, as this reality would (as

---

[27]"Divergent Rationalities," in *Metatheory in Social Science: Pluralisms and Subjectivities*, eds. Donald Fiske and Richard Schweder (Chicago: University of Chicago Press, 1986) p. 170.

Schweder points out) leave us very little to do in our scholarship or teach in our classrooms.

But gratitude does not erase the problem of the normative; rather, it confronts us with the extent to which the "contestation of elites" is a product of the invasion of Enlightenment reason upon the otherness of the world of India. From this perspective, the background of the contestation is colonialism; but the implications of the debate are not erased with the demise of colonialism. It continues to constitute the problem of knowledge and hermeneutics: correlations between the value claims of intellectual cultures and the structure of social power can no longer be hidden.[28]

This continuation reveals that there was another aspect to the "invasion" of Enlightenment reason into a place such as India: the invasion, as is the case with most, did not mark out a one way street; the colonial relationship that it enforced proved to be reciprocal. While it was a relationship which brought us to think again about hierarchies of knowledge in the traditions studied, it is also a relationship which has brought us to rethink with care our enterprise itself, drawing us to recognize what Todorov refers to as "the humanist camouflage of European colonialism."[29] Our increasing self-consciousness concerning the chapter of colonialism thus draws us to "invade" the boundaries demarcating various modes of discourse by forcing us to recognize the extent to which they have been determined by an era of history which is now past.

This period of colonialism cannot be erased from our memory, nor can it be hidden; our only alternative is to work through the meanings we have inherited so as to assume for ourselves the critical morality it has left as its legacy. This involves coming to new understandings of not only what "the Hindus"—with emphasis now given the plural—know to be true, but also of what *we* have come to understand to be true through this juncture in human history. Making this point with reference to a quite different chapter of this history leads Octavio Paz to write of,

> . . . the ambiguity of history, which always oscillates between the relative and the absolute, the particular and the universal. If it is no longer metaphysics but history that defines man, then we must put at the center of our meditations, in place of the key word *to be*, the key word

---

[28]The writings of Ashis Nandy (including *The Intimate Enemy* cited above) explore and lend considerable insight to this problematic.

[29]Tzvetan Toderov, "All Against Humanity," *The New York Times Literary Supplement*, October 4, 1985, pp. 1093-94.

between. Man . . . at the center of time, between the past and the future;
between his myths and his acts.[30]

Our present situation has usurped the metaphysics of both theology
and reason, bringing us to lend a quite different valuation to the *relational* dynamics implicit in that key word, "between."

The case of colonialism does not frame *the* problem for religious
studies, any more than the study of Hinduism frames *the* problem.
Yet their specificity intimates the extent to which *relational* dynamics
between disparate modes of discourse inform and structure interpretation. Moreover, they serve to remind us of the extent to which we
must remain responsible for the configuration given these relational
dynamics in the production and reproduction of knowledge as represented by the university. It is this larger problem that might be cred-
ited with making for the current crisis in liberal education: reason itself has come to be recognized as the subject, rather than norm, of interpretation. Ironically perhaps, the unified posture of critique that
Reason defined has given rise to a quite different posture which ac-
knowledges that the "norms" of what had previously been presumed
to be true must be questioned and reformulated.

Fourth Mode Discourse and the Process of Initiation

Plato told us that all education is initiation; and since his time,
"initiation" has remained a favored metaphor for the role of liberal
education in the academy. The metaphor mirrors the normative dimension of education, the process of cultural formation that makes
for citizens responsible and creative within the public arena. As noted
by Allan Bloom, "Every educational system has a moral goal that it
tries to attain and that informs its curriculum. It wants to produce a
certain kind of human being."[31] The present crisis in liberal education
is born of this desire in confrontation with the "enormous multiplicity" referred to above. In our time, the "moral goal" of liberal education cannot be defined in terms of a set of generic nouns preserved by a given authority, religious or otherwise. The "crisis" thus
challenges the way this term has been appropriated in asking, "To
what is the student now to be initiated?" In answer to this question,
no noun—given the "multiplicity" of modern consciousness referred
to above—will suffice.

---

[30]"Foreword" to Jacques Lafaye, *Quetzalcoatl and Guadalupe: The Formation of
Mexican National Consciousness 1531-1813*, trans. Benjamin Keen (Chicago: The
University of Chicago Press, 1987) p. xxii.

[31]Allan Bloom, *The Closing of the American Mind: How Higher Education has Failed
Democracy and Impoverished the Souls of Today's Students* (New York: Simon and
Schuster, 1987) p. 26.

From the perspective of religious studies, however, the metaphor continues to serve well as it visits us with Victor Turner's notion of the liminality invariably marking this rite of passage, the period of crisis as well as transformation, where boundaries give way in the discovery of quite different horizons of meaning. Religious studies weathered this "crisis" with its [re]initiation into the academy; the discipline is thus afforded a strong position to work with students as they—in the course of their initiation into the discourses of liberally educated persons—face a similar "crisis."

The encounter with worlds of meaning not one's own—whether this be an encounter with the worlds of other cultures or the worlds of other disciplines—engenders new vision not so much through the data or entities introduced, as through the processes of interpretation that lead to new understanding. That is, if interpretation is to prove adequate to the data, it necessarily entails that new perceptions of the world be structured, new meanings be generated, and new modes for being human in the world be recognized. For taking on this agenda, religious studies is particularly well-placed in the academy precisely *because* of what is taught and studied in Religious Studies.

It is difficult to find anything that might be termed "religion" without encountering hierarchies of knowledge and authority which define the *givenness* of what is known to be the case. It is the immediacy of this disjunction—the notion of "givenness" that defines the locus of our discipline, with the "hermeneutics of suspicion" which is a basic element in the interpretive posture of our scholarship—that provides religious studies a rather fortuitous place to find voice in processes of liberal education. This disjunction has often been cited as a basis for what we have come to term "easy relativism" when referring to students and "cognitive relativism" when referring to our colleagues: without access to objective discourse and interpretation, all discourse and interpretation is deemed equally valid.

The heuristic model we are employing here, however, suggests that quite different horizons might be explored through the disjunction. It *does* draw attention to the impossibility of defining the normative in education in terms of a given tradition as defined by either second mode discourse or by the third mode of discourse as traditionally conceived in the academy. But at the same time, it also draws attention to an alternative—namely, to the notion that the "moral goal" of liberal education can and must come to be understood as a process that involves the ongoing formation and cultivation of interpretive skills. As Jonathan Z. Smith is wont to insist, "Value has meaning only in connection with issues of interpretation, of translation, of recognizing the consequentiality, of accepting responsibility for outcomes."[32] The model likewise highlights, however, that such value is always dynamic—that, as Schweder puts it, *all* interpretive discourse presumes a "third sort of logic that is bound to something neither uniform nor unitary."

Because religious studies is self-conscious in its exploration of diverse configurations of reason, the immediacy of this disjunction between "givenness" and "suspicion" affords particular purchase on introducing and addressing the problem of interpretation and critique: this, by introducing and cultivating ways of thinking about how the world is put together and how it operates; of understanding the processes by which we come upon these interpretive strategies; and of how this knowledge is variously adjudicated with alternative interpretive strategies.

When the dynamics involved in interpretation are thus made explicit, one establishes a position from which not only to determine the adequacy of a given interpretation, but also—and more importantly—to engender interpretive skills themselves. That is, it allows for the *students'* re-creation for themselves of the dynamic which has made for the discourse of the academy. It allows them to engage in what many have come to recognize as the primary task of liberal education: cultivation and enhancement of the courage and conviction now required for finding one's own creative voice of vision, of affirmation and critique within the public arena. That is, it allows for the creation of the fourth mode of discourse in our model.

The cultivation of values is implicit in the formulation of this discourse. But if such formulation be the factor defining the particular import of liberal education, it is also the primary problematic. For, as emphasized throughout this essay, this process is necessarily normative. The normative dimension that is inherent in our third mode of discourse is closely related to the presence of critical analyses of various sorts. In engaging in such "critical strategies," students are necessarily drawn to rethink—to lay bare to criticism and to reconfigure—other modes of discourse. This process will bring them to rethink their own motives and assumptions and those of the communities and cultures from which they come. In many cases, the application of these approaches to the students' own beliefs and traditions will not be addressed directly in classroom pedagogy. This said, if the learning experience fails to move a student towards these new horizons of meanings, if it fails to provide a language that allows students to find a new voice with which to articulate their own religious and symbolic affirmations and negations, it will be difficult to define the experience as "educational."

---

[32]Lecture presented for the 1986 Chicago Institute, "Religious Studies and the Liberal Arts," (July 20, 1986).

Admitting this normative aspect of all educational enterprises necessitates that a very different articulation be given the use of "initiation" as a metaphor for liberal education. No longer can it be drawn on as a metaphor for the process whereby subjective worlds were drawn into a rational world as formed through a singular strategy for Reason. This loss of Reason as an objective center to adjudicate all interpretation, however, brings the normative element implicit in the critical attitudes and strategies of mode three to the fore. This is true not only in religious studies, but throughout the human sciences. From this perspective the initiation metaphor continues to serve us well by reflecting the *processes* whereby all discourses in the academy impinge on the formation of the fourth mode of discourse, the mode involving the personal and communal appreciation of value as cultivated by a liberal education.

What is imperative for those who wish to address the current crisis in liberal education is that they take seriously the extent to which "the normative" has been transformed from a set entity into a process within the academy. Classical notions of the liberal arts presume the kind of normativity which our model locates within the arena of mode-two discourse: they presume an ideal for what an educated person should be, an ideal which assumes not only a singular cultural tradition but, more problematically, a singular standard of truth and rationality.

We live now in another world, another time. The normative agendas of the liberal arts can no longer be framed in terms of a mode-two discourse that is either theological *or* positivistic; they must shift to the normativity of a new kind of mode-three discourse, a mode of normativity which bespeaks ways of exploring and adjudicating the conflict and disparity that have come to characterize knowledge in our time. As we now recognize Reason's failed promise of a value-neutral turf on which to stand while examining a given subject of study, so too we must admit to the lost turf from which to assume the values once understood to be defined by Reason as "a given." In the processes of formation that a liberal education is understood to represent, the noun of initiation has given way to the verb and all the complex relational dynamics it is known to encompass.

Religious Studies and Liberal Education

Once we take seriously the context of the academy which has made for a crisis in liberal education, we find ourselves in a very different position from which to consider what Religious Studies might contribute to a liberal arts curriculum. And we find, through an embrace of the peripherality born of having been a "stepchild" within the academy, a creative voice with which to address the malaise that presently engulfs the proponents and practitioners of liberal education.

Octavio Paz writes of our time:

> We Mexicans always lived on the periphery of history. Now the center or nucleus of world society has disintegrated and everyone—including the European and North American—is a peripheral being. . . . Now history has recovered its unity and become what it was at the beginning: a meditation on mankind. [33]

For religious studies to participate in this meditation, the field will do well in reflecting on its own history of peripherality within the university: the modes by which it has adjudicated the normative dimensions of education as defined by the theological structures of its subject; and the modes by which it has critiqued the normative valences of its own past on the one hand, and the legacy of Enlightenment Reason on the other. By bringing this struggle—rather than an easy differentiation between "of" and "about"—to the public, religious studies will assume a posture from which to address, with far greater creativity and engagement, a new vision for liberal education in the coming years.

Scholars in religious studies have long been engaged in encouraging students to recognize, appreciate, and adjudicate the symbolic and imaginative aspects of diverse worlds of meaning. In this, they have provided curricular support to what Kenneth Bruffee has defined as the two most important things to learn in acquiring an education: "how judgment is made within an assenting community," and "how knowledge grows within an assenting community."[34] The discipline has addressed these issues both through study of these processes among "other" peoples, and through critical reflection on the processes whereby we come by such understandings of the "other." Students are thus drawn to cultivate interpretive postures which bring them not only to rethink the ways they have come to configure the rest of the world, but also—through this process—the way they have configured their own world. In fostering this critical reflection, religious studies contributes to a style of liberal education that supports creative and effective participation in the kind of interaction born of the global situation in which we now live.

To be sure, it is a style of liberal education at odds with more traditional conceptions which remain confident of the possibility of

---

[33]*The Labyrinth of Solitude* (New York: Grove Press, 1962) pp. 171-72.
[34]Kenneth Bruffee, "The Structure of Knowledge and the Future of Liberal Education," *Liberal Education* 67:3 (1981) p. 184.

initiating students to universal notions of "the true" and "the good" as a "rational" basis from which to safeguard social values. With the academy now undermining the epistemological support that the Enlightenment project long afforded this "rational" agenda, however, it provides religious studies ample opportunity to assume a more public profile with the contributions it might make to the liberal arts. And with liberal education now understood to define more a process than an ideal, religious studies would do well to cultivate a greater self-consciousness about its involvement in this process. Instead of the "of/about" language, the discipline would best draw to the fore the relational language highlighted by the model discussed with this essay—a language which must be explored, critiqued, and more carefully articulated if our society is effectively to engage in the processes that make for a democracy. Global involvements and cultural plurality can no longer be left to the periphery; our situation now demands that they be addressed not only in theory, but in practice as well.

BEYOND OURS AND THEIRS:
THE GLOBAL CHARACTER OF RELIGIOUS STUDIES
James H. Foard

The global character of religious studies seems virtually a given. In large state and major research universities, religious studies departments offer courses throughout a staggering cultural range, generally wider than any other department in the school. Two sorts of justifications have conventionally been given for this state of affairs, professional ones and educational ones. The professional are the older, for the discipline and perhaps even the notion of "religion" were born from global encounter; and certainly in the shaping of our theories and categories, we have had to consider pertinent data from many cultures throughout human history. Also, a minimal breadth has long been politically desirable in the academy in order to deflect suspicions that we were promoting a particular religion.

None of these justifications, however, has any necessary relationship with teaching undergraduate, general studies students. Unless we assume that our purpose in teaching such students is to introduce them to our professional scholarship—and I see no reason to make such an assumption—we cannot claim that the global necessities of the field dictate similar necessities for students. Of course, there have long been educational purposes claimed for studying the religions of the world: understanding "others," gaining perspective on one's "own" tradition, and so forth. Within the more general discussion of liberal education, however, such purposes might be deemed trivial, impossible, or, as I hope to show, largely wrongheaded.

For now, at least, the global range of our curriculum remains as it is, seeming not to require more careful reflection. Yet recent events have challenged the presence of "non-Western" studies in the curriculum in ways that have attracted the attention of the general public, and which demand responses. I am referring to the popularity of Allan Bloom's *The Closing of the American Mind*, and to the controversy surrounding the core curriculum (what I call in this paper "general studies") for undergraduates at Stanford University. While neither event emphasized religious studies specifically, the justification for anything "non-Western" can no longer be taken for granted by any discipline. Moreover, religious studies is not just any discipline when it comes to this argument: it has a special stake in its outcome, as well as a particular contribution of its own to bring to the discussion.

This is not to say that we should accept the terms of the current public debate. In both the Bloom volume and the Stanford controversy, the issue of "non-Western" studies was discussed by all sides in terms of "canon"; that is, under the assumption that the university must select a limited collection of books whose contents define an authoritative tradition to be passed on to the young. Hence the argument made in both cases focused on the inclusion or exclusion of certain books or kinds of books. In one sense, such argumentation is of little consequence, as the entire discussion of canon is patently derivative. All sides justify their nominations for the canon with something more basic, something they wish to happen to students during their four years at the university: their inheritance of a "legacy," the raising of their "consciousnesses," whatever. If different views of what education is for lead to different canons, it is certainly possible that some views will lead to no particular canon at all. It would follow that the first task is to clarify what we wish education to do to students, then figure out how to do it, and pursue the idea of a canon only if it suits those purposes. If it does not, we should not bother with it.

This essay will seek a justification for the global character of religious studies by claiming that a global character helps us do with students what we do best. I begin with a proposition about a feature of religious studies that I call "multiple discourses." I then suggest that this feature permits us to develop with unique efficiency certain intellectual faculties in students. The next section supports this claim by indicating how this educational goal is hindered by the "Western tradition" canon that has been so publicly advocated by Allan Bloom and William Bennett. I suggest that any such distinction between Western and non-Western—even within a curriculum of global scope—obstructs rather than facilitates the development of these faculties. Finally, I conclude by showing how the global character of our teaching enhances our ability to do what we should be doing.

In taking this route, I am sympathetic to Jonathan Smith's notion that we teach students not a body of information, but what some people might call an approach or even an attitude toward "religious" things.[1] Even so, we must have far greater specificity about what sort

---

[1] Jonathan Smith has presented this argument in many forums and publications, though perhaps most recently with his essay, "'Narratives into Problems':

of attitude this is before it can become a really useful pedagogical idea. In getting specific, I will be outlining what Lee Yearley might call "intellectual virtues" rather than what are often referred to as "methods."[2] Methods are for majors. What we wish to give general studies students are more, well, general. They may be less than what the word "virtues" implies; but, on the other hand, they probably represent a more realistic goal, given the short four years of an undergraduate education. I thus make use of a more banal phrase, "intellectual faculties," in referring to the intellectual habits and abilities that we seek to develop in our students. In a companion essay, I will suggest that these faculties can only be developed through some specific and fairly traditional sorts writing exercises.

Throughout this discussion, I draw principally from my own experiences at a large state university where I teach classes in World Religions and East Asian Religions. In doing so, I will at times make claims about what goes on in a classroom that are admittedly based only on the experiences of my department. Others may have different experiences, though I fear this prospect less than empty theorizing.

Religious Studies in Liberal Education

Religious studies is, in fact, a discipline. By this, I do not imply that it has any single, or even singular, method; rather, I use term "discipline" to refer to an ongoing discussion—"discourse" is the fashionable word—concerning religion, in which there is sufficient consensus for mutual intelligibility, disagreement, and agreement on a shifting but coherent variety of issues. One segment of educational thought, represented by Perry and Hirst, would have us believe that liberal education consists principally of initiating students into several distinct areas of discourse—lets them into the discussion, so to speak.[3] In so doing, we provide them with essential means for what Hirst calls the "structuring of experience." This model of initiating students into a discourse may be very appealing, as it seems to fit so well with current hermeneutical philosophy and literary criticism: the university is an arena for "interpretive communities" within which there are distinctive "discourses," which precede knowledge and

---

The College Introductory Course and the Study of Religion," *Journal of the American Academy of Religion* 16:4 (Winter, 1988) pp. 727-39.

[2]See his article in this volume, "Education and the Intellectual Virtues," pp. 89-105.

[3]Paul Hirst, "Liberal Education and the Nature of Knowledge," in *Philosophical Analysis and Education*, ed. by Reginald D. Archambault (N.Y.: The Humanities Press, 1965) pp. 113-138. W.G. Perry, *Forms of Intellectual and Ethical Development* (N.Y.: Holt, Rinehart, and Winston, 1970).

contain it.[4] These "interpretive communities" are represented by departments; and their discourses are, of course, the disciplines.

Surely we initiate students into a disciplinary discourse in religious studies as well. While there is no single model for areas or methods (are there for any of the humanities and social sciences?), our majors, at the very least, will become familiar with the various "studies" of religion—historical, sociological, textual, and the rest—as well as some specific traditions. Does this mean, though, that religious studies is just a disciplined discourse concerning the disciplines that study religion? If so, there is little to recommend it in general education, for it would be a rather derivative discipline into which we initiated students.

The justification for religious studies in undergraduate general education lies elsewhere: that is, in the object of its discourse, namely religion. The suggestion that we are merely initiating students into interpretive, discursive communities cannot accommodate this object. For such a model would suggest that there is no particular object of discourse apart from the disciplinary discourse itself. To be sure, there are objects of study—the material world, historical documents, or whatever—in other disciplines; but these objects are contained by the discourse itself. By "contained," I mean that the objects of study do not challenge the very premises upon which that discourse takes place, however independently they exist from it.

Not so with religion. When we teach students in religious studies, we always initiate them into at least two discourses, and often more: we initiate them into the discourse of religious studies, but we also initiate them into the discourse of religion and, more specifically, the discourse of one or more traditions. If I offer a course on Buddhism, for example, students will be initiated into the discourse of the discipline *and* the discourse of Buddhism. If it is Islam, we will have the discipline paired with another discourse. I am not saying that this *should* happen; I am saying it *does* happen, even if the professor tries to avoid it. If there is one skill students have developed by the time they reach college (and I sometimes think it is the *only* skill they have developed), it is the ability to adapt themselves to a new discourse. They have, in fact, been trained by reward and punishment to do so.

This rather simple fact—let us call it the presence of multiple discourses—sets religious studies apart from other disciplines in the university. The extent that other departments, especially literature and history, share this is usually a measure of how much they are talking about religion. This does not mean that we traffic in the irrational. Quite the contrary, the rationalist tradition of the university

---

[4]Here I am thinking principally of Stanley Fish, but virtually all of the currently influential philosophers of hermeneutics, including Derrida, could be included here.

rightly provides the ground rules for the discourse of our classes, and religious traditions themselves can hardly be slandered as irrational. Nevertheless, the two sorts of discourses are different, and, I think, mutually challenging. Indeed, the ability to say *something* comprehensible to the academy and general public about religious expressions without smothering them with social science generalities is very much what we are about.

Multiple Discourse and Intellectual Faculties

This fairly simple, though exceptional, feature of religious studies courses also dictates those intellectual faculties which religious studies can develop in students, if not uniquely, then uniquely well. I term these faculties: 1) simple location; 2) complex location; 3) humanistic encounter; and 4) an appreciation of the value of judgment.

1. Simple location. First of all, the information which students should receive, even in an introductory course, helps them locate themselves in time and space. It does so by impressing them with how vast the world is and how varied human experience has been. Included in this awareness is the realization that religions are, in fact, imbedded in culture and history. For some students, this could happen in a world religions course; but it could happen just as easily in a course devoted to the history of Christianity or to Chou Dynasty thought. I am fond of telling people that I became a student of Japanese religions because I took a course as a sophomore on Islamic Civilization, the point being that that course gave me the awareness of the breadth and depth of human experience that made my later studies possible. I see precisely this sort of thing happening to students all the time, and very little evidence that they get it elsewhere in or out of the university. Religious studies can develop this awareness particularly well because its multiplicity of discourses involves students with the most fundamental means humans have used for ordering individual and social experiences.

2. Complex location. The second intellectual faculty begins with the students' realization of their own historical contingency, and proceeds through the process of comparison. If the first faculty required only a rather rudimentary "mapping" according to geography and chronology, this second involves mapping according to various kinds of categories. Just as the first could develop in a course on virtually any tradition, this second could develop through the discussion of virtually any sort of reasonable categories. The important thing is to develop in students the notion of what comparison involves. Many departments, and certainly my own, have witnessed rather lengthy debates regarding whether the introductory course should be structured by a survey of religious traditions or by the categories employed in the study of religion; in other words, whether it should be "if it's Tuesday it must be Tibet," or "if it's Monday it must be myth." Once we think in terms of educational consequences, however, we no longer have to survey anything, although we may if we want. The important thing is the results we hope to achieve with our students.

The further development of this complex location should include the placement of religious studies within the map of its own making, the map it created for understanding its object of discourse. That is, no religious studies course should avoid placing itself within its own schemes and categories. Even in an introductory survey of religions, the sharper students will do this anyway: they will realize we are performing a task that is itself locatable in time and space, a task that has its own historical contingency. This is not as elaborate an endeavor as it may appear, for usually it involves little more than making explicit a relationship already implicit in the relationship between academic categories and the religious phenomena we are presenting. Once again, therefore, we see the special potential of multiple discourses in religious studies.

This potential can also mean that religious studies is where the whole Enlightenment rationalist critique which the general studies student encounters, not only in religious studies but everywhere else in the university, is itself critiqued. Following Derrida, we might say that this is the only place in the university where the reason of the university is challenged, where its basis in "unreason" is exposed.[5] At times, this may be true, though I think religious studies is far less threatening than that. More common is simply the ability to see academic discourse, rather than just presume it.

3. *Humanistic encounter.* But there is more going on in religious studies than locating students, important as this may be, since the multiple religious discourses, encapsulated by terms such as "Buddhism," "Confucianism," and "Christianity" that are brought into the classroom, are never just the "others" by which we define ourselves. Nor, to go back to our metaphor, are they but parts of our conceptual map. Rather, we are mapping maps that map us in turn. Furthermore—and here I must depart from the metaphor—these other discourses have proven themselves cogent for individuals, including geniuses and whole societies; surely it is asking too much to expect that our students will somehow be immune from such discourse. In fact, my own experience assures me that, to the degree that I teach well and sympathetically, students will respond with remarkable powers for imagining what it would be like for a given tradition to be true. This is not to say that they will convert to anything, much

---

[5]Jacques Derrida, "The Principle of Reason: The University in the Eyes of Its Pupils," *Diacritics* 13 (Fall, 1983) pp. 3-20.

less that they will even begin to approach the experience of a believer. But it does imply that I find them doing more than limiting these traditions to mere objects of analysis: they try them out—crudely, often playfully—in the safety of the classroom. And they often keep things when they leave: the Buddhist notion of mental constructions, the Confucian sense of self-cultivation, the Japanese intimacy with divinity, the Muslim insistence on universality. For now, though, I want to emphasize that the religious traditions of humanity do more than locate us and our students. They provide unique and compelling expressions of what it means to be human, in an inexhaustible and dizzying supply. There seems to be no end to teaching and learning about them; no survey, let alone canon, is ever really sufficient. This is perhaps the most powerful consequence of the multiplicity of discourses in religious studies.

4. *Appreciation of the value of judgment.* This is something like leaving home, getting a job, and learning to appreciate the value of a dollar. One learns how hard it is to earn a dollar—its cost, in other words—as one learns also how truly necessary it is. In a religious studies course, students first learn of the tremendous cost of their most fundamental judgments, judgments they had largely taken for granted. These costs include the sheer intellectual work of becoming informed and working through a humanistic issue carefully, as well as the potential costs to others in a world of conflicting visions. At the same time, students also learn the necessity of making such judgments for anything approaching an authentic human life. Once again, both senses of this appreciation are fostered by the multiplicity of discourses in religious studies. It is, after all, not the academic language of religious studies, but rather the discourses of religious traditions themselves, that challenge the unreflective assumptions of students. Encountering these discourses provides the most thorough encounter with cultural relativism available on the campus, a relativism which makes judgment sometimes so awful. At the same time, though, religious traditions illustrate to students, better than anything else available to them, that these judgments have to be made and that they have consequences.

Each of these four faculties grows from what is unique to religious studies courses: namely, the presence of multiple discourses. Each is desirable in a liberal education, and each can to some degree be developed in a single course. What, then, does the cultivation of these faculties suggest about the issues of canon, of Western and non-Western studies, and the rest? First of all, it suggests that the teaching of religious studies is hindered by whatever interferes with the multiplicity of discourses and the cultivation of the intellectual faculties that depend on it. More specifically, it is hindered by the very notion of a canon which restricts the multiplicity, and by the division of even a generous multiplicity into Western and non-Western, which inter-feres with the use of that multiplicity in the cultivation of the facul-ties. I explore these two hindrances in the next two sections, and then suggest how one might select objects of study that serve—rather than hinder—the cultivation of these intellectual faculties.

The Canon Dismantled

A canon will always restrict the multiplicity of discourses that we may introduce into the classroom. For it demands that, among the discourses available for use, some may be considered and others may not. While the notion of "canon" might not make our job absolutely impossible, it certainly makes it harder and less successful. Once we recognize the canon to be the unnecessary intrusion that it is, we can see that no canon—no matter how reformed—can help us pursue our legitimate purposes. This means that efforts such as those expended at Stanford to expand the canon so as to include minorities, women, and the non-Western world are of little help to us.

If the issue of canon is allowed to structure the debate, propo-nents of the "Western tradition" will inevitably win. Of all the disci-plines in the university, we in religious studies should know what a canon is. There can be no canon without limits on both text and, yes, community. However, once we begin to argue for the inclusion of the *Chuang-tzu* and the *Bhagavad-gita* in the canon of "great books," while ridiculing our opponents for narrow-mindedness or worse, we be-come trapped by a rather pious rhetoric about a virtually unlimited quantity of texts and a community of all humanity. In other words, we justify adding things *ad infinitum* to the canon, and inevitably ad-vocate the absurdity of unlimited limits. Our opponents know this; and we should concede the point. Instead of reforming the canon, we should attack the very idea of it.

Ours and Theirs

The danger to cultivating intellectual faculties, however, comes not just from limiting the traditions to be considered by a canon; it can also come from distinctions made among traditions, even if all are open for consideration. Such distinctions are signalled by certain polar terms, especially "Western/non-Western," but also "our tradi-tion/their tradition," or simply "ours/theirs." These pairs divide the religious discourses of our classrooms into two groups in order to prescribe two quite separate agendas within the disciplinary dis-course of religious studies. The agenda for teaching about "our tradi-tion" is to learn about where "we" have been, where "we" are now, and where "we" are going. In exploring other traditions, our study helps us rather to understand the "exotic" religions of "others," by which we mean figuring out how their most troublesome features fit within their society and culture.

While such a study may permit the multiplicity of discourses in the classroom, its assumed division will subvert each of the four intellectual faculties discussed above. Although students may find a simple location within a prescribed tradition, it is of a one-dimensional sort: namely, over and against the history of that tradition. Other traditions are different simply because they are "other"; beyond that, they do not inform a student's sense of location. Similarly, since one is no longer comparing like things, complex location suffers. (Indeed, one could say that the comparative language of religious studies depends on imagining every religious tradition as "other," and in this, all religious traditions are alike.) Humanistic encounter, of course, becomes possible only with one's "own" tradition, which can be taken seriously as raising issues in the student's own existence. In the case of other traditions, the issues are the generalized (and largely anthropological and sociological) ones of religion in human society and culture. Finally, judgment is cheapened because students cannot appreciate the cost of their most basic judgments, only of their secondary ones.[6]

In the end, the distinction between "ours" and "theirs" is just the canon creeping back in the guise of yet another, self-evident "given." But if it is a given, surely we are entitled to ask just where we might find the locus of a tradition thus deemed "ours." More specifically, we must demand to know how it finds representation within the classroom; only then will we be able to discern the contours of the "our" with which we are dealing. Is it the cultural inheritance students collectively carry into the classroom? If so, we are simply stating that "our tradition" is the student body's immediate world of discourse; and that, surely, is the one thing the university need not teach. Are we then saying that the tradition is not the culture of the students but of the university, specifically the rationalist critique bequeathed by the Enlightenment? If so, it is already privileged in the discourse of religious studies, as I have described, and we have already taken care of it. Are we then saying that it is the religious

---

[6]If the problem of this division is twofold—limiting ourselves to a preordained tradition and accounting for others according to social science generalities—then we can say that there are two variations on this division, each of which preserves only one of these problems. The first, inter-religious dialogue, limits "us" to some preordained tradition, but does not treat "others" as objects of social science. The second, world theology, does treat "others" as objects of social science, but treats "us" that way as well. It does so by elevating social science generalizations to transcendent truths.

community to which a student belongs? If so, then where is the locus of this "our"? I teach, at once, Mormons and Navahoes, Japanese and Jews, Protestants and Sikhs, and a large number of indefinables (the largest group). If I taught in an institution committed to a religious community, I would have my answer; but I do not.

If we cannot, outside of religiously committed colleges, find "our tradition" as a given present in the classroom, we might claim that, regardless of student knowledge or religious allegiance, there is a Western tradition that has shaped the dominant culture of the country in which students live—a tradition delineating its laws, delimiting the parameters of its literature, and discerning the structures of proper cultural formation. In other words, if "our tradition" is not in the classroom, then perhaps it is around it, in its social and cultural milieu. Just what that milieu is, however, is nearly as hard to define as the collective "tradition" of my students. Were we to define it as the Western tradition, there would be deep and justified objections from many quarters of our society. Nor do we have the option, as Charles Long has pointed out, of solving this dilemma by just adding those "other" traditions onto the Western tradition we presume.[7] In fact, this whole encounter of traditions and the consequent setting of boundaries is what much of religion is all about. This being the case, we would do well to leave such issues open for our classes.

If "our tradition" is not an indisputable given, then why has it seemed so? The answer is fundamentally political, with ramifications far beyond what I pursue with this essay. Yet, we might do well to ponder Victor Turner's observation that, "the culture of any society at any moment is more like the debris or 'fall out' of past ideological systems, rather than itself a system."[8] The claim that "ours" is "the Western tradition" is unreasonable—and is defended with dogmatic fury precisely because it is unreasonable—and seeks incessantly to create this tradition while asserting its givenness. The canon of that tradition, as many realize now, helped define what was finally human and what was not, as it also helped define an elite who were initiated into it through liberal education. More than any other discipline, religious studies can expose the mythic power of this idea of a Western tradition, as well as its social consequences. We would do well to do so.

With its disguise, however, this version of the canon is even more insidious than its more conspicuous version—particularly when ac-

---

[7]In this volume, see his essay, "The University, the Liberal Arts, and the Teaching and Study of Religion," pp. 19-40.

[8]Victor Turner, *Dramas, Fields and Metaphors: Symbolic Action in Human Society* (Ithaca, N.Y.: Cornell University Press, 1974) p. 14. Turner is paraphrasing Harold Rosenberg.

companied by pious pronouncements about how we must understand others in a pluralistic world. Students tend to narrow their
sense of themselves as they expand their knowledge of the world.
They become more certain and unreflective than ever of the community in which they belong, its boundaries and its rules. While this
could be interpreted by some as self-discovery, in fact it is a cunning
defense against real indeterminacy and the reflection which can follow from that. As someone who has been deeply involved personally
with more than one culture, I can testify to the confinement one feels
when hearing how "we" are now in a pluralistic world which
changes how "we" think about "our own" tradition. Somehow, I
never find myself in the presumed categories; and I suspect that those
who can share common allegiances with the speaker, allegiances
which are being irrationally reasserted. My discomfort is probably
akin to that felt by minority students in a class that continually refers
to "our" tradition.

Little changes, however, when students react by identifying
themselves with the "non-Western." It just means that there is more
than one "we," and more than one "they." The problems that I described will still be present. I caution my students on the first day to
watch their pronouns. When a student begins a statement with
something like "We think . . . ," I will ask what they mean by "we."
More often than not, the answer will be "Christians" or "the West" or
"black people." Whatever the accuracy of their statement, the shift to
the third person marks the commencement of self-reflection; while
the preordained distinction between "ours" and "theirs" prevents it.

Selecting What to Study

If notions of both "canon" and of "Western/non-Western" be
dispensed with, what then are religious studies courses to study? The
goals I have set do not require that any particular tradition be studied, that any particular comparative category be used, or that any
particular humanistic issue be raised. All that is required is that the
multiplicity of religious discourses introduced into the classroom be
sufficient for the cultivation of the intellectual faculties. In other
words, the diversity of religious discourses examined in the classroom should be sufficient for students to locate themselves in time
and space, to practice the comparative language of religious studies,
to encounter a breadth of humanistic meanings, and to understand
the necessities and consequences of their judgment.

This, in the end, is the justification for what I have referred to as
the "global scope" of religious studies. The phrase is deliberately
vague. Obviously, it cannot mean the study of all religious phenom-

ena everywhere; nor does it necessarily refer to the agenda of "world religions" textbooks. What it does mean is: 1) nothing in the world is made off limits by a canon; 2) nothing is treated differently than anything else according the labels of "ours" and "theirs"; and 3) we should freely employ anything that provides sufficient diversity in cultivating the intellectual faculties that religious studies cultivates best. Other factors, particularly those involving students' educational background, may guide the selection. At my university, for example, where few students have ever studied a culture outside the United States, the traditional "world religions" survey finds some justification because it develops the first intellectual faculty. At some of the more elite schools, comparatively fewer traditions, or even one, may be sufficient. In general, though, the greater the global scope, the more efficiently the intellectual faculties will be cultivated. Obviously, a law of diminishing returns will always be in effect, as the global scope approaches practical and pedagogical limitations; but these are the only legitimate limitations, by which I mean that they are the only ones that help us pursue our educational objectives.

Conclusion

I began this discussion by examining what religious studies does uniquely, not as a professional guild of scholars, but as one discipline in the general education of undergraduates. Its basic feature, the multiplicity of discourses introduced into the classroom, indicates that it can with unique efficiency cultivate in students intellectual faculties for: 1) simple location; 2) complex location; 3) humanistic encounter; and 4) an appreciation of the value of judgment. I then argued that both a canon and a distinction between "our" and "their" traditions interfered with this cultivation, whereas an undifferentiated, generally global scope enhanced it.

In conclusion, I would like to point out how this position answers two common accusations which advocates of a Western canon tend to make about their opponents. The first is that, in the absence of a canon, virtually anything can be taught. Indeed, some who oppose a canon do make this claim, as if such sheer randomness were, indeed, a possibility. I trust I have shown that not just anything goes, and that principles other than canonical ones can guide the selection of what is studied in any particular course, namely educational principles concerning what should happen to students. Moreover, I would maintain that different principles of the same type underlie even the advocacy of a canon. Rather than claiming that my position opens the floodgates to just anything, then, advocates of a canon must argue that their educational principles—what they hope happens to students in the course of their undergraduate education—are superior to mine.

In effect, this is what they do by claiming that only a canon saves students from cheap relativism. Nothing that I have proposed, however, leaves students in that condition. On the contrary, by maintaining the multiplicity of discourses—including our own scholarly discourse—in our classrooms, we cultivate students' incessant questioning, the ongoing relationship between their critical thinking and the values of all people, including themselves, that will be essential if students are to lead responsible lives in the twenty-first century. The multiplicity of religions and values is something they cannot escape, either collectively or individually; they must contend with it. We should therefore not think of introducing students into normative positions, but into the work involved in achieving them: normative positions must be taken, but only through the intellectual tasks of which most students have little awareness. Simply to pass on a "legacy," even while tacking on texts by women, minorities, and "non-Western" cultures, leaves students unable to make the ethical choices that will be required of them by an ever-changing world whose cultural and religious complexity will not go away by academic fiat.

PART IV: STRATEGIES AND TACTICS

Religious Studies and Exposure to Multiple Worlds in the Liberal Arts Curriculum

Judith A. Berling

Profound demographic and social changes since World War II have changed the face of liberal education in the United States fundamentally and probably permanently. Faculty are quite naturally aware of these problems, since they affect their lives within the university. These changes have also created difficulties for students. The collapse of the old consensus about the liberal arts has not been replaced with a new consensus which can help students understand the broader aims of their liberal education courses. It is no wonder, then, that students question and complain about general requirements, since many institutions have been unable to make a coherent and persuasive case for liberal education which would give students a sense of purpose and direction.

This essay flows from five assumptions about the nature of liberal education which should be made clear at the outset. First, while a liberal education is defined curricularly as a set of general requirements and a specialization in a major, it is the courses which fulfill the general requirements that embody the school's philosophy of liberal education. This is not to argue against the importance of the major, for learning in depth and acquiring some sophistication in one mode of critical thinking is central to a sound education.[1] However, the very diversity of the disciplines and departments results in rather striking differences among the majors. Whereas biochemists and mathematicians generally offer a rather strict sequence of courses, humanities majors often have a bewildering and loosely structured set of options.

---

[1] For a provocative and thoughtful proposal for a religious studies major, see "Study in Depth in Religion: A Preliminary Report," prepared by Steven Crites and the Task Force on the Religious Studies Major, sponsored by the Association of American Colleges. The preliminary report was presented at the 1989 Annual Meeting of the American Academy of Religion in Anaheim, and is available through the offices of the Academy.

Second, while majors always have as an important component of their design the preparation of students for further training in the discipline, general requirements, which embody the liberal arts philosophy, are designed for any student, even the average student.[2] Promising and highly motivated students caught up in the pleasure of intellectual inquiry are always a special joy and responsibility. No teacher would be satisfied with a course which did not aspire to engage and stretch such students. However, in those courses which fulfill general education requirements, it is the general student who is the special object of pedagogical concern. The highly motivated student will, after all, take many more advanced and challenging courses and is more likely to pursue independent learning, but the general student has usually not yet discovered the joys learning. Especially in these days when many students pursue vocationally-oriented majors, teachers in the humanities and human sciences (and even in the basic sciences) often have only a few chances to educate future citizens in the basic issues of their disciplines before they move on to specialized vocational courses. Their liberal education depends almost entirely on the general education requirements, and that is a weighty responsibility.

Third, because of the expansion of college education beyond the demographic limits of a narrow upper middle class elite, liberal education needs to be cognizant of the origins and the future roles of its students. The demographic changes in university population have led to a broader understanding of "tradition" and of the human heritage. The authors of this volume wrestled deeply with the canonical issues facing liberal education today. On the one hand, we believe in the virtues and merits of the traditional classics. Great literature, arts, and music—the monuments and historical achievements of European civilization—are indeed worthy of study, but they are not the boundaries of human civilization. If students come from and are to live in a global and pluralistic world, they need also to be exposed to traditions and heritages which were for a time ignored, excluded, or marginalized. To find the balance between the "classics" and the riches beyond them is a matter which will require careful reflection and extensive conversation. One of the aims of this volume is to offer some specific proposals which might be the gateway through which

---

[2]Some faculty at a number of leading institutions have argued that general education courses not only should not count toward majors, but should in fact transcend the bounds of any single discipline; however, the implementation of general requirements often undercuts this principle. See William A. Graham, "Rethinking General Education at Harvard: A Humanistic Perpsective," in *The Humanities: A Role for a New Era, A Colloquium* (Santa Barbara: Educational Futures, International, 1978).

these conversations might move forward in departments and institutions.

Fourth, liberal education is designed for the sake of students, not for the sake of the faculty. Statements about liberal education need to be embodied curricularly and pedagogically in a manner effective for the student population. The nature of the institution, of the students, their backgrounds, their social and intellectual development, their concrete difficulties in understanding and even relating to the subjects taught are germane to our theoretical reflections. To say this is not to propose that the curriculum pander to student fads, or that "market issues" set the agenda for liberal education. Rather, it presses the issue of what a liberal education should do not just for those who are prime candidates for doctoral studies, but for students who will not go on to graduate education, who will be the educated citizens of our society.

Fifth, liberal education is not simply an ideal hotly debated by faculty committees and canonized in college bulletins; it is the defining task of any liberal arts college. The definition of a liberal education is mere verbiage unless it is embodied in the curriculum and pedagogical practices of the college. In turn, the curriculum is a sterile structure and teaching an empty exercise if they are not effective in bringing students toward the stated intellectual goals. The theory, practice, and audience of liberal education are intimately interconnected. In wrestling with the issues of liberal education, I am ineluctably drawn back to courses and students, to the continuing struggle to find more effective ways to engage them in those intellectual virtues and pursuits which are central both to learning in general and to my work as a scholar. It is through the dialectic of reflection on theory and praxis that I have struggled towards a new position. It is in this way that I can present that position most honestly and effectively.

This essay will consist of four parts: 1) the implications of the model of liberal education which sees it as the intellectual confrontation with the issue multiple worlds; 2) the challenges, both cognitive and psycho-developmental, in the exposure to multiple worlds; 3) the case that religious studies courses are well-situated to expose students effectively to the issue of multiple worlds; and 4) a case study for a practical approach to teaching multiple worlds.

Liberal Education and Exposure to Multiple Worlds

The authors of this volume began our deliberations by setting aside a week to reexamine collectively our thinking about liberal education. Toward the end of that week, we produced a "manifesto" which, although by no means unanimously endorsed in all its particulars, in many ways captured the direction of our discussions. The statement began: "A liberal education should inculcate a love of learning and teach students, as individuals and as members of communities, how to apprehend the personal and social worlds in which they and others live; discern how these worlds have come into being and how they are maintained; evaluate those worlds in a variety of ways in their relationship to one another; and participate creatively in the discovery and construction of worlds in which they live." While this statement does not encompass all that a liberal education might and should do, it points in two directions: first, toward a theoretical understanding of the social construction of meaning in a pluralistic and changing world; second, toward a number of central issues in the educative process.

This section will develop some of the implications of the statement. The discussion of this statement in no way intends to rule out other readings or to prescribe its intention; indeed, part of the merit of the manifesto lies in its plurivocity. Rather, it will attempt to play out one reading which may help to envision a distinctive potential of religious studies courses for fulfilling the aims of liberal education.

First, students need to apprehend, to become aware of, the multiple worlds in which they live. Liberal education exposes students to the striking plurality of modern culture, with its variety of ethnic and regional traditions. It also exposes the diversity of cultures in the world and their impact on our lives in the global village. Modern communications and the networks of international trade and industry have created intimate interconnections among cultures around the globe. Yet few Americans have recognized how fully their lives as citizens of the modern world have placed them in a network of relationships which extends far beyond the boundaries of the familiar, much less faced up to the challenge of cross-cultural understanding.

On a very different plane, the apprehension of multiple worlds in the late twentieth century must include some grasp of the mind-stretching views and implications of contemporary science and technology, which open up radically new ways of envisioning the many dimensions of our functioning as organisms in relation to the physical environment, the planet, and the universe. In the context of liberal education, science does not simply offer up physical reality "as it is," but represents one distinctive human enterprise seeking to define and make sense of the world.

The apprehension of multiple worlds does not stop with recognizing the fact of plurality; it also seeks understanding, learning about the distinctive points of view which these many worlds possess and offer. How, for instance, is the world seen and defined through the eyes and experience of an Appalachian woman, an eskimo fisherman, or a theoretical physicist? What are their ways of life, their beliefs and values, and their picture of the functioning of the world? In order to understand, the student must become familiar with information about these worlds and with the symbolic forms and practices through which the inhabitants of those worlds express and sustain their understanding of reality.

This task of understanding leads naturally into the second phase of exposure to multiple worlds: discerning how they come into being and how they are maintained. Students should study the influences of material culture, physical environment, types of labor, historical institutions, religious beliefs and practices, psychological or physiological forces in shaping how persons and communities view and live their lives.

Historical and religious forces introduce a whole new dimension of multiple worlds, namely the persistence of the past in the present. Students begin to appreciate that they and their culture have been profoundly shaped and informed by a long past and heritage. To complicate matters, that past was impelled not only by its own internal momentum, but was also shaped by encounters with other cultures and traditions. A glimpse into the complex dynamics of history can expand a student's sense of the world almost as radically as when an elementary school student first grasps with amazement the immensity of the universe.

As students study the impact of these various forces on individuals and communities, they explore various disciplinary versions of the process of world construction. Each version or discipline analyzes a particular world construction on the assumption that the forces in its domain of study are active in the constructive process and that those forces shape both individual and collective behavior. Each discipline also posits competing theories about the human agencies, institutions, means of communication, or forms of control which continually sustain and readapt the world of meaning to fit evolving views of reality.

At the next level, liberal education assists students in evaluating these worlds in a variety of ways in relationship to one another. Students begin to assess critically both various disciplinary versions of the world-constructing process, and to compare and contrast the claims of the various worlds of meaning themselves.

The former strikes to the heart of the current intellectual debates, both within disciplines and among them. Many students, familiar with the functioning of computers, have learned in a practical way that what the data yield depends on the program used to analyze them; as the saying goes, "garbage in, garbage out." They thus have some grounds to understand that different disciplines and different theories within a single discipline see very different processes of world construction and maintenance, and also posit different worlds. Part of liberal education is exploring such disagreements and assessing the relative merits of various positions.

A more immediate aspect of diversity is the variety of worlds (cultures and dimensions of culture) in which human beings live. Liberal education stimulates students to juxtapose these various worlds for the purpose of mutual criticism and analysis; no world, they learn, is complete or has solved all human problems. The plurality of cultures and worlds of meaning is one way in which humans confront the limitations of any single world.

Liberal education also teaches students how to participate creatively in the process of discovery and construction of worlds. Once they understand the process of world construction in its various forms, they can be active and effective participants in professional, social, artistic, religious, political, or other worlds which they inhabit. They can, to recall more traditional language about liberal education, exercise critical and independent judgment and become active participants and leaders in their communities.

The Difficulty with Multiple Worlds

While it is arguably central to the task of modern liberal education, the intellectual confrontation with the implications of multiple worlds of meaning is intellectually, culturally, and even psychologically difficult for most entering college students. Today's students bring a diversity of life experiences with them to college. There are increasing numbers of older students in the classroom. Despite recent alarming statistics about declines in the numbers of African-American and Hispanic students enrolling in, and graduating from, college, and despite the serious decline in financial help available to economically disadvantaged students, the ethnic and socio-economic diversity of the college population is still dramatically greater than in the pre-World War II era.

The diverse life experiences of the students, however, need to be sharply distinguished from their ability to understand and appreciate the multiple worlds in which they move, to negotiate readily among them, and to assess critically how they might contribute to the process of shaping those worlds. Lived experience is not the same as a life reflected upon. Moreover, the plurality of cultures, disciplines, and issues embraced in the university will ask students to reflect on their worlds from a variety of intellectual perspectives, and about worlds and experiences beyond the bounds of their own lives. A sound liberal education is and should be, in the words of Jonathan Z. Smith, "a living day-to-day challenge to [student's] limited worlds of experience."[3] Liberal education calls into question their unexamined assumptions, opinions, and values; it asks them to understand and "try out" a number of conflicting ways of viewing and being in the world; and it exposes the limitations of virtually every position and perspective. To many students, especially in their first year of college, the critical analysis and questioning required of college courses seem to take away all of the certainties without providing any substitute. Students resist the questioning or anxiously look to the professor for the right answer, seeking to fill the void with a new solid certainty. This anxiety may be expressed in terms of course requirements ("Tell us what we have to know for the test"). The deeper issue, however, may have to do with their sense that their unexamined views of themselves—their locations in their narrow worlds and various broader worlds—have become decidedly messy and uncertain.

Some students respond to the plurality of perspectives which they confront in college by clinging to their personal opinions and values with a black-and-white dualism and parochialism; they posit their limited and relatively unexamined world as the one and only world. Such students talk about "we" as though it included all decent people ("we Christians," "we Americans," "we students"); but in fact, the "we" is rather narrow, reflecting the limits of the world with which they are familiar, and to which they cling as their authority for the normal, the good, and the right.

Other students, overwhelmed by the sheer diversity of perspectives and values not only in their academic work, but also among their peers in the university environment adopt an equally rigid relativism that says "anything goes," "people do their own thing," or the like. Such students deny there is any basis on which to judge right or wrong, or to evaluate various positions. They are unwilling to judge critically their own lives or those of others. They adopt an easy, uncritical relativism masquerading as a tolerant "live and let live" attitude.

While these categorizations of students are posed here as extreme "types" seldom met in pure form, their cognitive dispositions are met frequently in the classroom. Both uncritical dualism and easy relativism are fundamentally at odds with the critical thinking which liberal education aspires to nurture. First, both positions are unreflective; neither type is willing to examine the assumptions underlying his or her position. Dualists hold to their position by asserting that it is right without feeling they have to identify or defend the assumptions by which they could make the assertion. Relativists, on the one hand, are unwilling to examine the values informing any position.

[3]Jonathan Z. Smith, "How I would Teach an Introductory Course" for the Conference on Religious Studies in the Liberal Arts, Pacific Lutheran Theological Seminary, Berkeley, California, June 17-23, 1985.

Thus both types can follow their inclinations without taking critical responsibility for their choices. Second, they are at odds with the goals of a liberal education in that both types are fundamentally unwilling to engage, understand, or have meaningful contact with other points of view, other worlds of value and meaning. Both are ultimately isolating positions: they avoid real contact with the diversity of worlds in which humanity in fact exists. They cannot begin to apprehend, understand, or reevaluate the multiplicity of human worlds nor participate creatively in the construction and discovery of these worlds. They are hiding from the very process of world discovery and world making.

Theories of cognitive development can help to document the resistance many students exhibit in confronting other viewpoints. It is overwhelming to be thrust suddenly into such a chaos of meaning. What professors sometimes assume to be intellectual laziness is often students' fears that if they were to examine their positions critically, or significantly appreciate the positions of others, the tenuous self constructed out of their life experience might collapse. Such fears make students wary of disturbing questions, whether about the limits of present scientific paradigms, the social construction of gender, or the impossibility of an authoritative interpretation of a text.

William Perry's research on cognitive development, based on a fifteen-year study of Harvard undergraduates, provides ample evidence that student discomfort with the pluralism of world-views and values they confront in college can be found even at our most elite institutions.[4] This is not simply a "curse" of public universities or less eminent colleges. Considerable education and reflection is required to develop the capacity to understand and learn to live with the ambiguity and diversity of the multiple worlds in which we live.

Perry's analysis of student interviews led him to posit a nine-stage schema of moral and cognitive development. His sample of students was a rather narrow base on which to construct a general development schema, if indeed such a universal schema is possible.[5] However, even if Perry's nine stages of development may not hold up to broader scrutiny, his long-term study of students' attitudes and values is extremely valuable. It is all too easy for faculty unconsciously to expect students to live up to some norm of intellectual

---

[4] William G. Perry, Jr., *Forms of Intellectual and Ethical Development in the College Years: A Scheme* (New York: Holt, Rinehart, and Winston, 1970; first published Cambridge, Mass.: Bureau of Study Counsel, Harvard University, 1968).

[5] Richard A. Shweder's article, "Divergent Rationalities," in *Metatheory in Social Science: Pluralism and Subjectivities,* ed. Donald W. Fiske and Richard A. Shweder (Chicago: University of Chicago Press, 1986) pp. 163-197, seems to argue against any universal schema of cognitive development, for there is no universal rationality on which it could be grounded.

readiness or maturity which bears no relation to the reality of their situations. Perry's study has challenged many thoughtful faculty to think again about their students, and not to dismiss student discomfort with certain modes of thinking and analysis as laziness or lack of promise. Liberal education has the task of inculcating cognitive skills and habits which require careful nurture and training.

Insofar as a liberal education teaches students how to apprehend, understand, reevaluate, and participate in the construction of a multiplicity of human worlds, its courses will raise basic human issues and concerns. It is generally recognized that it is a pedagogical error to presuppose that the general student can simply "pick up" at the professor's level of sophistication and maturity and immediately begin to think critically with him or her. It is also misleading, however, to approach teaching about human issues as if they were disembodied, purely intellectual skills with nothing humanly at stake for the students. If a liberal arts curriculum is engaging the issues it should, it will be profoundly challenging humanly as well as cognitively for the students.

The challenge may be stronger, and the human implications more profound, for those students who come from backgrounds in which their immediate relatives were not liberally educated. Since those in a student's immediate world have not been exposed to these intellectual virtues and habits of thought, these skills will seem doubly alien and threatening. All too often, the seemingly gifted students in a freshman class turn out to be simply those who come from highly educated families, where the habits required of college students have been ingrained from birth. Likewise some students who seem lazy because they nag for more quizzes and about what will be on the examination sometimes turn in the long run to be very bright.

During my second year of teaching, I heard a program on National Public Radio's "Options in Education" which put this in some perspective for me. The program discussed the effects of working-class versus middle-class socialization on student performance in college. Middle-class parents, the program noted, typically raise children to internalize general principles of behavior for which the rewards are neither immediate nor tangible, but long-term and indirect. Working-class parents, on the other hand, by and large assert arbitrary authority ("Why? Because I say so!") and give immediate feedback of punishment or praise. The basic structure of college courses fits the middle-class model. Generalized intellectual expectations are stated at the beginning of the course, but the feedback comes only occasionally—often through a midterm, paper, and final. There is no way for students to be sure in the first few weeks whether they are fulfilling the professor's expectations. Naturally, students from working-class backgrounds are even more prone than middle-class students to think that success in the course comes from "psyching out the professor," as though his or her expectations were arbitrary and idiosyncratic. Moreover, when such students adopt more sophisticated critical styles of thinking, these are not likely to be affirmed by those at home.

Even bright and highly motivated students, then, often face very real cultural, social, and psycho-developmental challenges in adapting to the modes of thinking and intellectual virtues of liberal education. Freshmen courses designed to meet general requirements are the locus in the college experience where students need to be given guidance and opportunities to make the transitions they need to make toward new intellectual approaches. On the one hand, the course standards and the professor's teaching need to model the aims of liberal education; on the other, the course's structure and process need to offer some clear steps through which the students can move toward and approach those goals and aims.

Religious Studies in Liberal Education

Religious Studies as a field is well-situated to confront the problem of multiple worlds. It represents a reconfiguration of concerns and reflections about human meaning and value, anciently taught under the rubric of theology and more recently as history, sociology, philosophy, and English until the professionalization of these various disciplines largely peripheralized such general value issues. The modern field of Religious Studies continues to address these concerns while recognizing the radical multiplicity of worlds of meaning. The field attempts to understand how, in a variety of cultural and historical circumstances, humans have struggled with vexing concerns about meaning, value, and the ineffable dimensions of life; how they have apprehended, understood, and reevaluated various worlds of meaning; how they have encountered others and assimilated those encounters into their worlds. Like traditional philosophy, Religious Studies raises questions about value and meaning, ignorance and wisdom; like anthropology, it raises questions about the diversities of human cultures (constructed worlds of symbols and practices). Like the humanities, it studies the highest expressions of human ideals; like the social sciences, it analyzes actual behaviors which are not always consistent with those ideals. It cuts across the humanities and the social sciences with its focus on human issues of meaning and value: the nature of selfhood, its relationship to nature and to the ultimate; the ways in which human communities find their foundations in transcendent symbols; strategies to cope with human frailty, deviance, ignorance, and mortality.

When students take a course in Religious Studies they become engaged in a significant intellectual confrontation with pluralism. Such courses introduce them to traditions of other cultures which are based on values, beliefs, and premises strikingly different from the narrow "world" of their own upbringing. They also introduce the diversity of "our" world or heritage, expanding students' notions of Western civilization, of American culture, of their ethnic and religious heritage. Courses almost always expose the otherness of what students thought was their own heritage, when the "world" which was so familiar, yet relatively unexamined, becomes the object of critical analysis, looked at from both the emic (insider's) and etic (outsider's) perspectives. This process defamiliarizes the unexamined and exposes it to public scrutiny.

For students from secular backgrounds, the otherness of Religious Studies may rest in taking seriously the fact of the religious dimension of culture, as the very idea of *homo religiosus* may be entirely new to them. Religious Studies courses may reveal significant religious dimensions even of secular culture, and make visible ways in which cultural symbols and structures create, support, and reflect the values and orientations which are usually seen as "choices" of individuals.

Religious Studies does not simply provide information or neutral data about these various worlds; like scholars in any discipline, we assume that those forces in our domain of inquiry contribute to the shape of culture and history. Study of the religious dimensions of human life recognizes the fact that persons claim that their religious practices, beliefs, symbols, and tradition provide a meaningful center for their lives. By implication, any human being, including the students, should be able to appreciate the human meaning of a religion; this does not require them to adopt or accept it, but rather to imagine what it would mean to do so, and what implications this would have for how the world would look. Insofar as they take seriously the religious commitments of others, students hypothetically explore a broad range of human situations, and thus intellectually expand their range of experience and understanding.

Someone in another field might object that true understanding always entails this intellectual stretching of the self into a new context. To understand biology thoroughly, for instance, students must begin to think like a scientist, raising the questions and adopting the procedures of verification that a scientist would. To do this successfully, they must transcend the layperson's acceptance of nature as a given in the world of everyday experience, and begin to view all phenomena with a vivid curiosity and sharp analytical eye. This is quite true. The content of Religious Studies, however, is distinctive in that it deals with beliefs, values, and life orientation. The content of

Religious Studies courses addresses and challenges students' attitudes toward central concerns of human life, including their own struggles with human issues. Students have to work hard to keep an open mind about alien ways of life precisely because they assume that their own beliefs, practices, and values are at the very core of the identity which they are struggling to establish and maintain as they negotiate the critical questioning of liberal education. Some students begin with conscious resistance to strange religious ideas: not boredom or disinterest, but active dislike. This dislike, however, gives rise to a question: "Why would anyone believe or do such a thing?" Other students are mesmerized by the very otherness, the exotic flavor of the new ideas. Out of these two positions—unreflective critics and uncritical admirers—a healthy pedagogical conversation can begin. Students usually have opinions about religion—not sophisticated opinions, but strong ones. The teacher can use these reactions as part of the teaching process.

Students need reassurance that once they have made an honest effort to understand and evaluate the other worlds on their own terms, they will be able to make their own personal judgments. This is acceptable in the classroom as long as those judgments are supported with intelligent and critical arguments. "I don't agree with Buddhism" is not an adequate statement in a paper or on an exam; but, "There is a problem with the Buddhist world-view for the following reasons . . ." can be an excellent piece of academic work, as long as it also demonstrates an understanding of the religion which it is criticizing. One of the benefits of comparative study is that it gives students a more thoughtful perspective on their own values and heritage; some affirm their heritage with considerable confidence and intellectual sophistication; others become quite critical of their past. For most, it is a complex mixture of affirmation and criticism which is the beginning of a nuanced and mature approach to their own world.

In order for Religious Studies courses to encourage students' abilities not only to apprehend and appreciate multiple worlds, but also to make critical judgments about them, these courses must go beyond a mere idealization of the religious worlds which are studied. The ideals, achievement, and contributions of religious communities need to be seen in relationship to the human contradictions in the institutional forms, political and social realities of religious life in the culture. Religious Studies looks not only at the human meaning of religions, but how religious communities have actually responded, or would respond, to vexing and tragic issues, and the use that has at times been made of religious institutions and ideas to support destructive enterprises. The juxtaposition of the ideals of religion with the historical realities of religious life can help to undermine the overly tidy sense of human moral integrity which many students want to demand of the world.

If Religious Studies courses take seriously the fact that religious communities make serious truth claims, students are urged to evaluate those claims against the evidence of how lives within those communities are actually lived. In turn, this process of evaluation can be applied to their lives and those of their peers. One of my most memorable class sessions was sparked when a student asked how a Taoist practitioner of "non-action" would deal with a drunken friend who wanted to drive. The campus newspaper had been running a series on the tragic effects of drunk driving. I tabled the remainder of the day's agenda to engage the students in a lengthy discussion which exposed how the Taoist view could be used either to avoid the issue by not getting involved, or to model for one's friend a radically different approach to life and responsibility. Religious Studies courses do not teach students to embrace uncritically the plurality of the world, but rather to recognize it, analyze the implications of the various worlds of value, and critically reevaluate them in light of their own evolving ideals.

Some Practical Approaches to Teaching About Multiple Worlds

a) Comparison and the Teaching of Multiple Worlds

While the content of Religious Studies is admirably situated to confront the problem of multiple worlds on a cognitive level, the use of comparison in courses can help to engage students productively in this discovery of multiplicity. Minimally, this means including emic and etic (insider's and outsider's) perspectives on the community's beliefs and practices. This distinction can be made in part by the contrast between primary evidence (primary narratives, symbolic objects, thick descriptions of rituals and practices) which expresses the story of the community in its distinctive language, and the critical analysis of such evidence by the teacher and students which uses language generated outside of the religious community. Similarly, emic and etic perspectives may be developed by means of the tension between the ideals of the tradition expressed in classic myths, rituals, or sacred texts, and the actual behavior of the religious community and its institutions in the larger socio-historical context. Courses on a single religious tradition and community may also introduce a comparative dimension by highlighting the diversities within the community so that there is no single, normative standpoint against which all is measured. The beliefs, assumptions, values and practices of any religious community become visible only in comparison with alternative viewpoints.

At the next level, comparison may examine the interaction of communities (Jewish-Christian, Muslim-Christian, Buddhist-Hindu, Buddhist-Taoist). Most religious communities have experienced encounters with other traditions at crucial points in their histories. Including these encounters in courses helps students to understand the evolution and reinterpretation of ideas and practices within a single tradition. Students occasionally have difficulty understanding the reinterpretation of traditions: they tend to take the "original" teaching to be the true and unchanging core of the tradition, not aware that even the presentation of the "original teaching" is generally a reconstruction by the community at a key point in its early history. The study of confrontation of religious communities helps them to perceive what kinds of situations stimulate radical reinterpretations of beliefs and practices.

Comparison provides a stance of multiple worlds beyond the parochial experience of students, a stance from which they can raise questions about the emphases of any given community. It can highlight certain issues and/or reveal what is missing in a given example. Comparison is the foundation of discursive thought; the human mind understands any concept only in comparison with what it is not. At a relatively simple level, such as distinguishing classes of physical objects such as clocks, we take this ability for granted; yet rigorous philosophical analysis can demonstrate how fraught with complexities this "simple" ability actually is. On the conceptual level, we must learn to be careful about our distinctions and assumptions, since the disconfirming evidence may not be apparent until we open our eyes to it.

The most notorious and familiar case in Religious Studies is surely the concept of "religion" itself. Many freshmen level courses include some consideration of the narrow and inadequate assumptions about "religion" which any student brings to a class; the diversity of religions in the world forces us to expand our sense of that concept. Other central concepts, such as "scripture," "revelation," or "church," are equally problematic. Comparison provides the examples which stretch and challenge our preconceptions, and thus expose our assumptions to scrutiny.

An example may help to illustrate the potential of comparative examples as a pedagogical strategy in a general education course. A colleague who teaches a freshman-level course on Religion and Social Issues has a unit on sexual ethics which begins with a discussion of the creation of sexuality in Genesis. This is the first moment in the course in which the students read the Bible, and the first class on sexuality. In order to defamiliarize the Genesis story and to demonstrate its significance as a cultural myth constructing gender, he introduces Plato's myth of the origin of human sexuality from *The Symposium*. The Platonic myth tells us that humans began as Siamese twins, joined at the side to a partner who might be of the same or the opposite sex. The hubris of these creatures caused Zeus to divide the halves, and so humans spend their lives yearning for their lost other half. The implications of the Platonic myth are fundamentally at odds with the Genesis story, even though Plato is also squarely within the "Western" heritage. Read alongside Plato's myth, the Genesis account no longer seems a given; it contains assertions about the nature and purpose of gender and sexuality which are by no means inevitable, and hence are significant.

This example illustrates how a comparative example can be used as a tool to sharpen the students' appreciation of a text germane to the aims of the course. However, it is not comparative in a second sense; that is, my colleague deliberately removed the Platonic myth from its context, not even addressing whether in fact this passage stands as a statement of Plato's views on sexuality. The professor's purpose was not to give the students a comparative understanding of two views of the origins of sexuality, but rather to use the comparative example as a foil to highlight some aspects of the Genesis text. This is a legitimate, though limited use of comparison. If the goal of the course, however, were to teach the students to do comparative analysis, then the illustrations would be equally contextualized and weighted, so that each may be analyzed in terms of the other.

Good comparison is always demanding, but teaching comparative thinking is far more difficult than doing comparative research. The researcher presumably has some basic grounding in the contexts she or he is comparing. However, such a grounding has to be built into a course. If several examples are to be given equal weight of analysis, and if the student is to be anything more than a passive observer of the teacher doing comparison, then some selective introduction to each of the contexts has to be built into the course. As difficult as these courses are to structure well, they offer enormous rewards: the comparison or contrast of two or three different examples directly nurtures those cognitive skills and intellectual virtues needed to understand and reevaluate the multiple worlds of meaning in everyday life.

b) *Student Diversity as a Tool in the Classroom*

When we consider the resistance of some students to confronting the plurality of perspectives in the world or the cognitive challenges of being introduced to two or more foreign cultures (or distantly removed historical contexts) in an introductory level general education course, we sometimes feel overwhelmed. But the same is true if we try to explain and understand how we can teach someone to walk or drive a car: it is far more difficult to explain theoretically how we do it, than it is to do it. The simple fact is that all human beings in all cultures have in fact lived in relation to other groups and communities and in that sense have been engaged in comparisons and confrontations with "others" from the dawn of humanity. Moreover, as noted above, all human understanding is rooted in comparison. Thus, teaching comparison simply refines and extends a skill which is crucial to human life. It builds on that skill and nurtures it to a more intentional and critical level.

Moreover, current student demography can be an extremely valuable asset in the teaching of comparison and the introduction to multiple worlds: the teacher can make use of the diversity of the student population itself. The mix of students in any given classroom can be one of the keys to opening students to the reality of multiple worlds and to comparative modes of critical thought. The first step in taking advantage of this diversity is, obviously, to uncover the actual diversity of the students in the class. This process will vary from institution to institution and from class to class. One of the great challenges of teaching—and a delight if one is able to embrace it—is that in a very real sense one cannot teach the same course twice because the students will be so different.

All institutions offer a diversity of students, but the mix varies considerably. I have taught at a variety of institutions, but primarily at Indiana University in Bloomington with 35,000 students and freshman classes of from two hundred to three hundred.[6] At IU, there was almost a bell curve of both social backgrounds and intellectual promise; it was there that I taught both my very brightest undergraduates and also the least promising. The challenge for teachers at IU was to cope with the astounding diversity one met in every class. I learned to acquaint myself as quickly as possible with the specific mix of students. There are many ways to do this, but my personal choice was to request a written self-introduction from them, partly structured by my questions and partly designed by them.

In order to use the mix of students to pedagogical advantage, the teacher must devise an approach to teaching which had room for the backgrounds and experiences of the students. These students are not blank slates waiting to be imprinted; there are increasing numbers of undergraduates who may be older than many of their teachers. It has been argued that the new demography of higher education makes the notion of "pedagogy" anachronistic, since the root of the term refers to the instruction of children. According to the O.E.D. the primary meaning of "pedagogue" was, "a man having oversight of a child or

---

[6] I have also taught briefly at Columbia-Barnard, Stanford, University of Chicago, and the Graduate Theological Union in Berkeley.

youth: an attendant who led a boy to school." An alternative term, "andragogy," suggests the teaching of adults, a less hierarchical, more collaborative model in which students as well as teachers bring life experience and wisdom into the classroom.

This does not mean that the focus of the class shifts to the students' life experiences and away from the material, but it can provide a way to turn the dynamic away from the teacher-and-material versus the students, to get the students more involved in the act of interpretation and comparison. One simple way to do this is to build into the very earliest parts of the course some discussions in which the students can bring their experiences or opinions to bear on a topic germane to the course: What does a given symbol or tale, for example, suggest to the students, as opposed to what it suggested to the community for which it was originally created? By getting students to experience early in the course that they have opinions, interpretations, and ideas different from those of their peers, they begin to see that the "others" they are learning from and about are not simply the teacher and the materials in the textbook—but also their peers and colleagues.

In order to nurture more sophisticated skills of analysis and interpretation, the teacher needs to provide models for the step-by-step analysis of a different world of meaning. Initially, the comparison and analysis should be relatively straightforward, first modeled by the teacher and then done collaboratively by students so that they can learn from each other. This move to collaborative learning is especially important in dislodging the false notion that the teacher has all the right answers. Most teachers want students to learn to think for themselves; this can happen more readily when teachers remove themselves from the center and work to facilitate a group process of learning. Moreover, the variety of interpretations and analyses produced by the group not only provides a rich lesson in the range of possible valid interpretations; the interaction of the group should also demonstrate that some interpretations simply do not hold up to critical scrutiny. Finally, group collaboration focuses on the process of interpretation, rather than on the "answers." As Kenneth Bruffee has observed, education is largely a communal act of inculcating the next generation into the current patterns of discourse.[7] Bruffee's view may exaggerate the consensus in any intellectual milieu; but if we do not consciously teach students how to talk about and approach intellectual problems, they will remain simply passive auditors.

A second way to encourage student participation is to assign a comparative paper early in the course, challenging each student to work out his or her own approach to the material. This moves them

---

[7]Kenneth A. Bruffee, "Liberal Education and the Social Justification of Belief," *Liberal Education* 68:2 (1982) pp. 95-114.

from a passive to an active mode, demonstrates what they are trying to accomplish, and offers a sense of at least partial achievement. If the paper is assigned early, the students have to use the skill actively early in the course. An excellent follow-up is to structure small or large group discussions on the issues of the paper assignment so that students can learn from each other that they took distinctive approaches to the topic. The course can then build on what is learned from this experience to go on to more complex comparisons or analyses. However, students' insecurities require the teacher to clarify the purpose of the assignment and to show how what is learned will be used in the remainder of the course; otherwise, students will want to plead for more time before committing themselves to writing.

c) A concrete example

With some trepidation, I would like to offer the example of my attempts to solve the problems of a general education course at Indiana University not as a model, but as a narrative for grappling with these problems in concrete terms. "Religions of the East" (R153) at IU was a large, freshman-level course which fulfilled humanities distribution and culture-studies requirements. It was also one of a handful of courses outside of the English department which could be taken to fulfill the freshman composition requirement, so that the composition sections engaged in the cultivation of writings skills in ways similar to those outlined in Jim Foard's paper. It drew an exceptionally wide range of students, two to three hundred per semester. It was highly recommended by the business school for their undergraduate majors. There were two lecture sessions per week and one small-group discussion session (a second small-group composition section for composition students). This course was taught in rotation by three colleagues who agreed to cover five major "traditions": Hinduism, Buddhism, Confucianism, Taoism, and Shinto. Beyond that, each of us was free to structure the course as we wished.

Over the years, I tried to improve the course in three respects: 1) to make it effective and accessible for the average freshman, while still stimulating to the very brightest students; 2) to build in a comparative dimension so that it was not simply a "tour" of Asian religions; 3) to build in increasing levels of sophistication in analysis to avoid the trap of survey superficiality (the lists of three "this"es or four "that"s). I never solved all of the problems to my satisfaction, but in the process I became clearer about what I was trying to achieve and how I was attempting to do so.

The first radical revision attempted to create a sounder gradual introduction to comparative thinking by abandoning my strong historical predilections and arranging the course in a sequence governed by pedagogical intentions. Rather than presenting an historical evolution or a story of the diffusion of religions, I selected a few critical and comparative issues to present and highlight in each of the traditions, and then constructed a course around them in a pedagogically coherent sequence. The course began with the varieties of ways of being religious[8] represented in Asian religions, underscoring the notion that all Asian religions are not one. The comparative dimension was built around a series of very broad critical questions: What did these communities, at several key moments in time and space, see as the fundamental challenges to a meaningful human life? What were their solutions to key problems or obstacles in human existence? What practices led to those solutions? How did they understand the interconnections of the previous three questions?

The sequence I chose was: Shinto, Confucianism, Taoism, Hinduism, Buddhism, Asian religions in the contemporary world. The first three were a useful means through which to lay the groundwork for issues which would then be elaborated as a comparative framework in the later sections of the course. However, the order reflects not the inherent qualities of the traditions, but rather my pedagogical instincts and interests. What was vital in the successful evolution of the course was liberation from notions of coverage and historical development, to the selection of a number of key issues and concerns upon which to construct a pedagogical strategy.

Scholars of non-Western religions are increasingly skeptical of the appropriateness of "traditions" as the lens through which to view religions. I am sympathetic with this view, but felt constrained by two factors: a) the availability of textbooks and readings suitable for freshmen which still overwhelmingly assume the "traditions" approach; and b) the students' reasonable desire for some convenient categories through which to get a hold on the dizzying wealth of symbols, practices, terms, and ideas encountered in such a course. While continuing to use units based on "traditions," the pedagogical strategy of the course was formed around key issues and questions, and not around the "traditions" or geographical divisions. These concerns, which cut across the "traditional" boundaries, served to question or stretch those boundaries as the course progressed. Even if there were available texts and readings which would allow a non-"traditional" way of structuring courses, whatever broad categories were used to provide students a means through which to approach materials would have to be balanced by some counterstructures with which to question the categories initially provided.

---

[8]This phrase is from Frederick Streng. I have found his typology of the four ways of being religious a useful heuristic device for introducing students to ways of analyzing religious differences. *Understanding Religious Life* (Encino, CA: Dickenson; Second Ed., 1976) pp. 66-125.

The very general questions around which pedagogical strategies were structured in Religions of the East threatened to make the story too simple; to ensure that the emic as well as the etic perspective was introduced, virtually every class session included some attention to a primary text in translation or a symbol, painting, ritual act or other primary representation of the religion. These were treated in lectures, discussion groups, and assignments. Average students were asked to grasp some basic issue presented in the primary evidence, and were exposed to a sufficiently complex discussion or assignment so as to be at least aware that there were many dimensions they were not engaging. Better students were challenged to go as far as they could in unpacking layers of meaning, both within the "tradition" under study and in comparison to others. As the students gained some background, the texts and examples assigned became more challenging. The first short quiz was designed primarily to assure students that they could understand these foreign ways; the quiz was so basic that even average students could do well unless there were major problems in their study habits. Each successive short quiz required more sophisticated judgment and analytical ability, thus demonstrating to students their progress and challenging them to apply the cognitive skills they were learning.

About halfway through the course, students were challenged to a major exercise in comparison: it could be, for instance, a debate between students assigned to represent various religions on large issues—such as peace or the environment. This exercise also helped the students to prepare for the final examination which required essays in comparative analysis which did not simply regurgitate a single lecture or class session; instead, students were asked to do their own comparison, building on material they had studied.

The course ended with a unit on Asian religions in the modern world. This unit began initially as a response to student interest, but I gradually came to see it as an appropriate capstone to the course, providing a comparative synthesis of the religions in light of the challenges of the modern and post-modern world. It was in this unit that students began to see some basis on which to make critical judgments about the adequacy or potential of these religions as possible worlds.

Religions of the East, then, evolved as a series of responses to student interests and needs. I have presented this course not as an exemplary model of what a Religious Studies course should be, but rather as an illustration of how one teacher in a particular context sought to respond to contextual challenges by refining course structures and aims. As the course evolved, it came to be self-consciously designed around the issue of multiple words.

The issue of multiple words was addressed in part through the use of Frederick Streng's varieties of ways of being religious. Streng's four types were not in themselves the point of the course; they were used as vehicles to help students perceive the scope of the diversity of religious approaches, on the one hand, and some general similarities among examples from different cultures, on the other. Streng's models were useful because they supported both aspects of the comparative enterprise: marking similarities and differences.

The comparative issues or threads of the course posed very general questions which arise naturally in virtually any religious community, though the ways in which they arise may vary markedly: a) challenges to a meaningful or wholesome life; b) answers to central problems or challenges of human existence; c) practices for realizing or attaining solutions to problems and for a wholesome life. The intention was to assist students in making the human connections not only between themselves and the communities they studied, but also between the various communities and examples in the course. That is, they attempted to help students evaluate various worlds in relation to one another.

In the first third of the course, lectures and discussion sections raised general issues about the basic definitions of religious experience and feelings. These very general issues invited students to test their own observations of religious experience in the world around them against the examples in the readings and lectures. Such exercises quickly revealed the diversity of experience and observations among the students themselves; they introduced the reality of pluralism through their own interactions as a class, an interpretive community. These early exercises helped students open themselves to the diversity and range of human beliefs and practices; the diversity is not just in "them," it is in "us."

In the middle section of the course students were asked to analyze debates within and among Asian religious communities about social problems and ways of life. They began to understand the deep and often irreconcilable differences of opinion and practice which constitute human discourse, and to see on what basis communities and individuals made normative judgments and choices. Lectures in this section of the course described the context, issues, and implications of such debates, and discussion sections invited students to assume various Asian perspectives to debate closely related problems posed for a more contemporary context.

In the final section of the course, students studied Asian communities' responses to the modern issues, and thus began to engage in a contemporary critical analysis of the viability of these positions in today's world. This section introduced live human faces to represent contemporary Asian positions by using films or other materials which communicated to an audience broader than the narrow religious community of the spokesperson. Thus the case was, as far as possible, addressed to an audience like the students themselves; this helped them to respond more thoughtfully and critically. Such skills would help the students to be able to engage in the discovery and construction of worlds of meaning.

The final examination tested all of these modes of critical encounters with multiple worlds. It consisted primarily of several essay questions handed out a week in advance of the examination, but to be written in class and without the help of notes. The advantages of handing questions out in advance were several: 1) the questions could require thoughtful analysis and more precise supporting material, since students could choose their questions in advance and research their answers in preparation for the exam; 2) answers could be expected to be coherent and informed, since students were urged to outline and think through their answers; and 3) the exam did not unduly favor students who were simply good at "thinking on their feet." This examination format asked for both comparison and critical analysis, and students were able to demonstrate their facility in the skills they had acquired in the course. Many students reported their sense of real achievement in being able to do something at the end of the course which would have terrified them at the beginning of the semester.

In the last several weeks of the course, discussion leaders would pose a key issue of the week in the form of a comparative essay question, and the group would collectively construct an answer, or answers, to the question. This exercise helped students see two things: a) there was no one "right" answer to a comparative question, and b) there were better or worse answers, depending on the coherence of the argument and the evidence adduced. In this comparative exercise, student diversity was used to demonstrate that students were free to appropriate critically the material in a variety of ways, but that there were intellectual skills involved in justifying their positions. Because these skills had been introduced gradually throughout the course, students came slowly to have confidence in their ability to compare and make judgments.

Conclusion

"Religions of the East" is merely one example of how Religious Studies courses are powerfully situated to contribute to liberal education, especially that aspect of liberal education which seeks to help students learn to apprehend, understand the evolution of, reevaluate the function of, and participate in the discovery and construction of worlds of value and meaning. This is in part due to the distinctive content of Religious Studies which always includes central attention to belief, value, and life orientation—central human issues which undergo intensive reexamination in the process of education and maturation. Other Religious Studies courses in ethics, sacred texts, mythology, American Religious history, or special issues are also well-situated to confront these issues, though they would engage them in their distinctive ways. In each case, however, the course structure and assignment would need to be designed to enable students to confront the issues of diversity successfully and with critical acumen.

Religious Studies courses, when taught intentionally as liberal education courses, can serve an integrative function in the education of the student. They bring together the approaches of disparate modes of knowledge focused around the study of human values and meanings. Religious Studies is not a discipline in the strict sense; it is an interdisciplinary field of studies. Thus it has a central role to play in integrating the cognitive and skill aspects of liberal education with issues of human meaning and value, which arise all too infrequently in today's highly professionalized university. It provides an intellectual base from which students might learn to integrate, or at least bring together in creative tension, the disparate worlds of meaning and value which at first appear so overwhelming and threatening. Moreover, Religious Studies courses can provide powerful examples of the juxtaposition of human ideals and the realities of life as lived, and thus urge students to a more complex and nuanced sense of human morality. Religion is by definition about meaning and value. Although relatively new as a separate field, Religious Studies provides courses that preserve and maintain a concern with human issues which have been vital to education for many centuries.

WRITING ACROSS THE CURRICULUM:
A RELIGIOUS STUDIES CONTRIBUTION

James H. Foard

In my earlier article for this volume, I argued that religious studies should have the effect of developing in students the following intellectual faculties: 1) The capacity for "simple location" of religious traditions in histories and cultures, including the realization that religion is, in fact, imbedded in history and culture; 2) The capacity for "complex location" of academic discourse concerning religion, including a realization of its difference from religious discourse; 3) The capacity to understand sympathetically the humanistic meanings of particular religious expressions; 4) The awareness of the value of judgment, including both the cost of judgment and its necessity. Having claimed this, I said that any canon or any distinction between "our" and "their" traditions interfered with our ability to cultivate these intellectual faculties, while a global character enhanced that ability; but I did not specify what strategies would, in fact, cultivate these faculties.

With this essay, I suggest how such cultivation can be initiated with a single course at the introductory level. Of necessity, I describe the transformation of a particular course in my own department at Arizona State University.[1] While situations at other universities may require different strategies, this case may prove valuable, particularly to those teaching as I do in a large state university. The main feature of this transformation, however, should remain constant for any course in any department: that is, as one's goal shifts from passing on a canon to cultivating intellectual faculties, the course itself is no longer governed by lectures, tests, and a paper or two, alongside a fat

[1]Work on this transformation was conducted through a program of the College of Liberal Arts and Sciences, Arizona State University, with support from the Ford Foundation. I would also like to acknowledge the excellent assistance of John Lindamood.

textbook or a tall stack of "classics"; rather, the course is structured by a consistent program of writing assignments.

The Course and the University

The course in question is titled "Religions of the World," and has been taught uncountable times by many people for nearly fifteen years. Although there have been several changes, the general format has remained the same: a survey of religious traditions through lectures and a textbook, and a series of tests that asked for information in some fashion or another. Despite the fact that a survey by the dean's office one year identified it as one of the most difficult introductory courses in the College of Liberal Arts and Sciences—surpassed only by Physics, Chemistry, Biology, and Political Science—it has proven exceptionally popular with students. It is a "service course"; perhaps two percent of the students have gone on to become religious studies majors, although a larger percentage have taken another course in the department.

The course has certainly served a need. Until recently, there were five social studies requirements in Arizona high schools: United States government, Arizona government, United States history, Arizona history, and Free Enterprise. Setting aside the last one, notice that there is nothing that could have taken students outside the borders of the United States. Since general studies requirements for the university were virtually non-existent until three years ago, and since most students matriculated into vocational, especially business, colleges rather than liberal arts programs, we could feel confident that the course provided nearly all students who took it with their only opportunity to encounter the larger world.

Furthermore, the course served the department's need for large enrollments. As with any large university—and ASU is now the country's fifth largest—only what is quantifiable is real, and teaching "production" is measured in "student credit hours." Over the long run, this has proven an important number for the health of the department. Under existing circumstances, any tampering with the course, especially any effort to make it writing-intensive, would certainly have threatened that health.

I mention these factors to show that no course can be changed without reference to the curriculum and political climate of the larger university. Were we to have introduced writing into this course alone, enrollments would certainly have dropped severely; and, since writing must be reinforced throughout the curriculum to be effective, little would have been gained by those students who remained. The benefits for them would hardly have been worth the cost to the department.

Obviously, then, the first step was to change the university, specifically its general studies requirements. This had been tried before, only to meet defeat in the Faculty Senate due primarily to opposition from the colleges of engineering, business, and others who had limitations on their flexibility imposed by outside accrediting bodies. I was deeply involved in another effort, which consulted those colleges from the outset, and which saw its more modest program adopted in 1986. Included in these new requirements were those for "global awareness," "historical awareness," and for writing-intensive courses, beyond freshman English, to be offered throughout all departments on both the Freshman-Sophomore and Junior-Senior levels. At the time the program was adopted, in a university of over 33,000 undergraduates, there were only five courses in the catalogue that met the guidelines for the lower-division, writing-intensive requirements.

Within these new circumstances, our department's introductory course could be transformed with no fears about enrollments and with some assurance that writing would be reinforced throughout the university curriculum. In addition, the College of Liberal Arts and Sciences at this point received a grant to launch a writing-across-the-curriculum program of its own. Several of us in my department were active in this as well. Unfortunately, the college's program was initially directed at upper-level, low-enrollment courses. I pushed to have the large, lower-level courses included as well; in fact, my work eventually became a test case of whether writing could be carried on with extremely large enrollments. The course I will describe involves well over two hundred students, one professor and one teaching assistant. Barring unprecedented funding and restructuring of the university, this situation will not change, so it is irresponsible not to deal with it.

In addition to the sheer numbers, there are other features of ASU students which have influenced the transformation of the course. A large percentage were raised in a language other than English, a huge majority cannot write a coherent paragraph, and many come from backgrounds that have severely restricted their global and historical awareness. Their greatest contrast to the students of the "best" universities, however, is that many work full time and some are older than the professor. The "non-traditional" student has been around places like ASU a long time.

The Place of Writing

Let us begin by being very clear about why we must require student writing. The intellectual faculties I have outlined are to be cultivated, not taught; and this cultivation can be achieved only through practice. What is practiced, however, is not precisely the intellectual faculty itself, but a specific sort of task whose repetition serves to cultivate this faculty. That is, as one perfects the performance of these tasks through repetition, one cultivates their corresponding intellectual faculties. In the end, each of these tasks must be a writing assignment. I see no other possibility, since there is too close and exclusive a relationship between writing and the kind of thinking one does in a university.

One could therefore argue that there is but one sort of task—writing. But writing is always an act in a particular rhetorical setting, a setting which changes the character of writing. Therefore, advocates of what is known as "writing across the curriculum" have unanimously stressed that writing is different for each discipline. If they are correct, and I think they are, then those teaching religious studies must be absolutely clear as to what rhetorical situations are appropriate for their discipline. The notion that we teach a particular attitude toward religion could well be a way of saying we teach a literary voice; but just as that attitude must be broken down into its components (what I have called faculties), so too that voice must be developed in specific rhetorical situations.

In the end, "rhetorical situation" is just a fancy term for an assignment worthy of the name. What I will describe, then, are assignments that cultivate the intellectual faculties I advocated in my earlier essay. They will seem possible only if one remembers that the principal purpose of writing-intensive courses is to get the students to write—not the professors to correct—and that there is no evidence that the traditional practice of correcting grammar, spelling, and so on does any good whatsoever. In fact, insofar as it deters professors from giving assignments in large classes out of fear of the time it would take to correct them, it actually harms students. Also, the professor's "corrections" are really proofreading that the student should, and nearly always could, do. Rather than correct spelling, it is far better to indicate that the spelling on the paper makes it unacceptable and return it unmarked. Only through such tactics will the student ever learn to check his or her own spelling in the first place. As for punctuation and so forth, it is far better for students to consult a style manual out of fear than to glance over the professor's red ink after checking the grade.

An analogous situation exists in the contemporary teaching of foreign languages. Instead of detailed and intrusive corrections of their writing and speech, students are constantly placed in situations in which they must communicate as best they can. They learn words and grammatical patterns through using them, rather than just learning about them. Through their own efforts, then, they develop "communicative competence" in the language.[2] Similarly, through the assignment of rhetorical tasks in religious studies, students will be habituated in, and not just learn about, the academic study of religion.

The faculties I have outlined require fairly constant practice of the following specific tasks: summarizing, for simple location; comparing, for complex location; interpreting, for humanistic encounter; and criticizing, for an awareness of the cost of judgment. (From here on, it will be useful to refer frequently to the chart below on "Course Structure.") The details of the assignments will vary according to the situations of various universities, particularly with respect to the basic writing skills that can be expected of students. In my situation, summarizing is best practiced through journal writing, and each of the other three through paragraph writing. In fact, these are probably the two best techniques to use in extremely large classes. All this practice leads to identical writing tasks on examinations, which are designed solely to test these writing skills. I will describe each of these—the journal writing, the paragraph writing, and the examinations—in detail. Please note, though, how they fit together as a system for developing the intellectual faculties of religious studies.

Course Structure

Faculties	Skills	Practice	Exams
Simple Location	Summarizing	Journal	Information question
Complex Location	Comparison	Paragraphs	Paragraphs
Humanistic encounter	Interpretation	Paragraphs	Paragraphs
Appreciation of judgment	Criticism	Paragraphs	Paragraphs

---

[2]*Initiatives in Communicative Language Teaching: A Book of Readings,* eds. Sandra J. Savignon and Margie S. Berns (Reading, Mass.: Addison Wesley Publishing Co., 1984).

Journal Writing

In order for students to develop the faculty of simple location, they must practice organizing large amounts of information into memorable and retrievable structures. That this was a problem was taught to me by the countless students who would come to my office after a rudimentary objective quiz and tell me how much they had studied, all to no avail. In examining them further, I discovered that they had indeed underlined every sentence in the book, and had made lists of definitions of key terms which they then memorized as one would a vocabulary list in a language course. All was a swirling dust storm of data that stung their eyes and parched their throats, rendering them incapable of reading and responding to the simplest of questions. The most successful way of treating them, I discovered, was to have them imagine I was their grandmother and that they were to explain to me what we had just covered. Gradually, and in response to my naive questions, they would organize the details of what they knew into categories and generalizations. The dust would settle, and the general lay of the land would become clear.

The journal writing assignment makes routine this rhetorical situation. Students are asked to choose a person they know (the grandmother is optional) who is totally unfamiliar with the subject. They are then given lists of key terms and proper nouns and are told to write, after every class session, a summary for that person while using each of these terms. In writing their summary, they are directed not just to give definitions, but to relate the terms to each other.

These journals are turned in once early in the semester, to make sure everyone has the idea, and after that on the days of examinations, since students will need them the rest of the time. They are not to be "corrected," but checked simply to see that students are doing them conscientiously.

Paragraph Writing

I use paragraphs rather than "essays" for these assignments, because I truly want just one paragraph. Most students cannot, in fact, write a good paragraph; and for those that can, a paragraph is a sufficient vehicle for finding their "voice" in the academic study of religion. My use of paragraphs is based on Bean's notion of "microthemes" as used in large lecture classes.[3] His guiding ideas are widely shared by others pursuing "writing across the curriculum."[4]

For each skill (comparison, interpretation, criticism), students are provided with generic instructions that apply to each of their assignments in that writing skill, as well as a preprinted page for the respective skill on which they are to type their paragraphs. Each of the instructions provides five criteria for their grades in that skill, and these five are repeated in abbreviated form as a check sheet at the bottom of preprinted page they turn in. (Of course, these five are not, in fact, equally important; but that does not matter, as the use of points is just to get the students' attention.) For each particular assignment, students will be given a short text and a question about it, with intructions to use one of the three generic instruction sheets and its respective preprinted page for typing their answers. Grading is simply a matter of checking off the list at the bottom of the page and adding up the points. With a little practice, virtually anyone can grade fifty in an hour. This efficiency permits paragraph writing to be assigned almost constantly.

Each of the three skills practiced in these paragraphs—comparison, interpretation, and criticism—is, of course, the subject of voluminous methodological literature since each is an essential element of virtually all humanistic scholarship. Rather than commence with lengthy and unnecessary discussions of them, I have included below the actual instructions for these skills that I pass out to my students. As will be apparent to the informed reader, these instructions are hardly methodologically neutral. Within this context, however, the important thing is that they are appropriate for beginning writers. The instruction sheets read as follows.

I. Comparison

Comparison is making a statement about the significant similarities and differences between two (or more) things. To be useful, a comparison should teach us something about the things being compared that we would not know from either one alone. (Indeed, there are some things we know *only* from comparison—for example, that a particular automobile is a large one.) Comparison requires more than merely listing similarities and differences, a process that might prove endless; you must select those similarities and differences that are significant, which means that: 1) you assume a point of view that is independent and distinct from the two objects of your comparison,

---

[3]John C. Bean, Dean Drenk, and F. D. Lee, "Microtheme Strategies for Developing Cognitive Skills," in *Teaching Writing in All Disciplines*, ed. by C. Williams Griffin (San Francisco: Jossey Bass, 1982) pp. 27-38.

[4]See *Writing Across the Disciplines: Research Into Practice*, eds. Art Young and Toby Fulwiller (Upper Montclair, N.J.: Boynton/Cook Publishers, 1986).

and 2) you select those similarities and differences that appear note-worthy from that point of view. This point of view will generally be an abstract category or model that applies, as equitably as possible, to both things you are comparing, and will be the basis for bringing these two things together in the first place.

To illustrate this last point, suppose you were asked to compare basset hounds and motorcycles. You would probably respond, "Say what?"; and rightly so. There is no category they share (or at least nothing very promising), and hence no point of view, independent of each, from which you can begin comparing them. Suppose, though, you are asked to compare basset hounds and dachshunds, or motor-cycles and bicycles. Then you have a category (short-legged dogs or two-wheeled vehicles) that embraces both objects of the comparison equitably and gives you an independent standpoint to begin your comparison. From that standpoint you might note that, say, the basset hound is the larger dog, or that the motorcycle is the faster vehicle. (You could have said that the motorcycle is faster than the basset hound, but that would be silly—silly, precisely because there is no common category.) Notice that certain features of basset hounds and motorcycles become significant (while others do not) by virtue of the fact that they play a role in your comparison from the point of view of a particular category.

To return to the subject of this course, suppose you are asked to compare the Christian eucharist (communion) with the Jewish seder (Passover meal). You could say that the former is Christian and the latter is Jewish. That would be a true, though useless comparison, since you have said nothing that is not already obvious from examin-ing each alone. To say something significant, you would have to be-gin by discussing both according to an independent point of view, in this case a category of "ritual," that seems to apply equitably to both. (Ignore for the moment the possible historical relationship between the two.) Since you will have previously learned something about ritual, you would note that both reenact important stories in their re-spective traditions and therefore let their celebrants participate in those stories. Having pointed this out, you can then observe that both involve sacred meals during which the elements consumed have de-tailed symbolic references to those stories. You might then notice differences: the seder is performed at home by a family, the eucharist at church by a community; the seder is held only during a specific, annual celebration, while the eucharist is performed many times during the year; and so on. This is real comparison. True, each of the features mentioned could be seen from looking at each ritual alone (e.g., we could see that the seder is done at home whether we look at the eucharist or not), but these particular features, out of all that *could* be listed for each ritual, become significant precisely because they have roles to play in comparing these two phenomena as rituals.

Obviously, there is more to comparison than this. After making the above comparison of the eucharist and seder, you might ask why there are these differences. To answer that question would, however, require exploration of historical and theoretical areas beyond this introductory course, and so you will not be asked it in your comparative assignments. (It is entirely legitimate to think about it anyway.)

Since we will be asking you to compare two things in your assignment, we will obviously have selected the category according to which we expect you to think about them. (Otherwise, we would have no reason for bringing these things together in the first place.) We will tell you what this category is. In the above case, we would ask you to compare the eucharist and the seder as rituals. You will be taught something about such terms as "ritual" beforehand.

Finally, although it does not affect your assignments directly, you should be aware that terms such as "ritual," and even "religion" itself, are essentially comparative terms; that is, they grow out of the effort to compare traditions and cultures, an effort that emerged from contact among peoples, particularly the conquest and colonization of much of the world by European powers over the last few centuries. This fact implies two very important considerations. First, such words are academic terms, the products of the scholarly effort to categorize and understand, rather than products of the traditions being studied. (The Jew believes that he or she performs the seder, not "a ritual.") Hence, such terms refer not to concrete entities, but to products of the scholar's theoretical imagination, which is always subject to modification. In fact, much of the study of religion involves the application and refinement of the language we use to talk about religion. Second, there is always the risk that in using such terms we are imposing standards and categories that distort, rather than illuminate, what we are studying. Given the history of unequal relationships among cultures, we must be cautious that the language we use to compare religions does not simply impose one culture's expectations concerning religion upon another.

The following criteria will be used in evaluating your paragraphs in comparison:

1) You must work from the *point of view* of the category provided by the question. Stick to this independent point of view and avoid speculating about what one side would say about the other.

2) You must find similarities and differences between *comparable things*. Say that cows have four legs and chickens two, not that cows have four legs and chickens feathers. Avoid point-

ing out that "x" is present in one thing and absent in the other.

3) You should be *fair to both sides*, treating them in their own contexts rather than yours or each other's.

4) The writing should be *mechanically correct*: grammatical, with correct spelling and punctuation.

5) Your essay should be *organized*. You should begin with the similarities that both share by virtue of being in the category given. Then you can either give further similarities first and differences second, or group similarities and differences within a particular subcategory or topic together as you go from one subcategory or topic to another. Do *not* list all the features you want to point out about one side and then all those from the other (e.g., do not give all the features of the eucharist and then give all the features of the seder).

II. Interpretation

Interpretation is saying something about what a text means. (By "text," we refer not only to the written documents of a tradition, but also to such things as its rituals and visual arts.) An interpretation makes a statement, not made in the text itself, about the meaning of a text, a statement that is both accurate with respect to the text and intelligible to the interpreter's audience. At a minimum, then, when you interpret a text, you must: 1) say something about the meaning of a text other than merely quoting or paraphrasing it; 2) accurately, fully, and reasonably use evidence from the text; and 3) address a particular audience, such that they can understand and evaluate what you say.

For your paragraphs in interpretation, you will be given a text to read and a question to answer. By answering the question, you will be giving an interpretation. In other words, the questions will *force* you to say something about what the text means that is not already stated in the text itself. So the first thing you should be sure to do is answer the question.

Your paragraph should begin with a sentence that states clearly, concisely, and as definitively as possible what your answer is. This is your thesis. The other sentences should develop your thesis and offer evidence for it from both the text and what you have learned about the tradition that produced it. You should not have any sentences in your paragraph that do not support your thesis.

While writing, imagine your audience to be the class, a diverse group representing many religious and nonreligious backgrounds, engaged in the academic study of religion. A good test of whether you are really addressing this audience is to ask yourself whether or not, theoretically speaking, virtually anyone in the class could have written your paragraph. If not, then chances are that you have relied on some particular beliefs, claims of authority, or definitions that not everyone in the class could fairly be asked to share. Try to write a paragraph that everyone in the class could discuss according to common standards of academic reason.

There are many theories of interpretation, but all would agree that it involves both a text and an interpreter. Notice that any interpretation that would fit the above definition must be a product of both, rather than either one alone. In other words, while you should not merely summarize the text, you should also not "read into" the text just whatever you wish it to say. Furthermore, a successful interpretation requires an awareness of the different contexts, or cultures, surrounding both the text and the interpreter. It is necessary for you to have this awareness so that you can avoid the all-too-common mistakes of expecting a text to deal with issues and ideas that are important to you but not to the culture that produced the text, or discussing only how the text agrees or disagrees with your own ideas. Agreeing or disagreeing do matter, but this discussion must come later. Your task in this assignment is to discuss what the text means in the context of its own culture.

There are no absolutely right interpretations, but not all interpretations are equally good. The following criteria will be used in evaluating your paragraphs in interpretation:

1) In the first sentence, there must be a clear *thesis* that *answers the question* clearly, concisely, and definitively. The thesis should not declare your agreement or disagreement, fascination or disgust, with the text. It should also not announce that you will be listing several points or issues.

2) The paragraph must address an *audience* engaged in the academic study of religion. It should not rely on personal beliefs or private definitions.

3) You should be *fair to the text,* treating it in its own context rather than yours. Do not ask it to respond to issues and ideas that are totally foreign to its time and place.

4) The writing should be *mechanically correct*: grammatical, with correct spelling and punctuation.

5) The essay should be *organized and logical,* with ideas leading to other ideas in a rational manner. Every sentence should support your thesis.

III. Criticism

There are many forms of criticism in religious studies, not to mention all those in the study of literature. For this course, criticism will mean saying something about what someone else says about religion. Criticism does not mean finding fault, although it may require that. It means, rather, viewing someone else's statement about religion from the perspective of your own knowledge of it, in order to: 1) identify the purposes and presuppositions of its author, which are often unstated; 2) evaluate the consistency and adequacy of its thought or argument in light of those purposes; and 3) judge the accuracy and balance of its evidence concerning religion. Notice that these three are specific intellectual tasks, none of which can begin easily with the words "I agree . . ." or "I disagree . . ." Notice also that, in the sense we are giving the term, you can criticize something you agree with. (Often, though, in the act of criticizing a statement you think you agree with, you discover problems with it and reevaluate your own thinking.)

You will be asked to criticize nonacademic statements about religion, that is, statements made outside of the academic study of religion, including those from journalism, fiction, travel literature, political discourse, and religion itself, to name a few of the possibilities. We will not give you obviously foolish or bigoted statements, but ones that actually say something reasonable. They will also be fairly recent.

For each of these assignments, you will be asked a specific question that involves one or more of the three tasks listed above. As in the interpretation assignments, the key to a successful paragraph will be answering the question with a clear, concise, and definitive thesis statement in the first sentence. The rest of the paragraph should support and develop your answer.

Also, as in the interpretive assignments, your audience should be the class, that is, those engaged in the academic study of religion. Try to write a paragraph that everyone in the class could discuss according to common standards of academic reason.

The following criteria will be used in evaluating your assignments in criticism:

1) In the first sentence, there must be a clear *thesis* that *answers the question* clearly, concisely, and definitively. The thesis should not declare your agreement or disagreement, fascination or disgust, with the text. It should also not announce that you will be listing several points or issues.

2) The paragraph must address an *audience* engaged in the academic study of religion. It should not rely on personal beliefs or private definitions.

3) In your critique, you should *employ what you have learned from the class*, either specific points about traditions or general knowledge about the nature of religion.

4) The writing should be *mechanically correct*: grammatical, with correct spelling and punctuation.

5) The essay should be *organized and logical,* with ideas leading to other ideas in a rational manner. Every sentence should support your thesis.

I distribute each of these three instruction sheets along with a preprinted page on which that kind of paragraph must be typed. At the bottom of these pages will be the check list for grading that kind of paragraph. For example, at the bottom of the sheets for interpretation paragraphs will be the following:

1. Thesis answers question   ( )   Total: _____
2. Audience addressed   ( )
3. Fair to the text   ( )
4. Mechanically correct   ( )
5. Organized and logical   ( )

In addition to offering generic directions for each assignment and, as we will see, for examinations, these statements are referred to many times throughout the course. After lecturing for a while, I will stop and point out that I have performed one of these sorts of tasks. Not only does this reinforce their understanding of them, but students also become convinced of the importance of the tasks. This process contrasts sharply with how "methods" of religious studies are introduced in every world religions textbook: they are described at the beginning and never mentioned again.

Examinations, Grades, and Outside Help

The examinations test only these writing skills. For summarizing, which students have practiced in their journals, they are provided with terms and asked informational questions the answer for which must contain all of those terms. For comparing, interpreting and criticizing, they are given short texts in the previous class session and questions at the time of the examination. The paragraphs they write in response to these questions are graded exactly as the assignments have been.

Grading is used solely to discipline and motivate students in their performance of these tasks. I would think that in any course, this would be the case; but I rarely see grading systems designed and presented to students in ways that reflect this purpose. In my course, the system is designed to get students to practice and then reward them for mastering the writing skills. It seems patently unfair to punish them for not having mastered beforehand what we intend to teach them in the course, although this is precisely what most humanities courses do. In contrast, mathematics courses strive to give students daily exercises of increasing difficulty with a few points each time to keep the students honest, and then test mastery of skills by examinations that have greater weight in their eventual grades. That is a good model to follow in any course that develops skills. Therefore, the points assigned to the paragraphs in my course are far less than those for the examinations, but are just enough to motivate students to do them. There is even an allowance for missed or miserably done assignments. As a result, it is possible to do poorly in the beginning, improve, and get a decent grade.

Finally, there are always students whose writing ability is so limited that the course has nothing to develop. These students need help beyond the course itself. In my university, they can find it at a Writing Center and, for other problems, a Center for Learning Disabilities. In my experience, the Writing Center can do things that no professor can do—or should even attempt. On the other hand, such a center does no good unless the student is working in it for some course. In fact, without a requirement for writing across the curriculum, such centers would have little to do, since the students who need them would not be identified. The establishment of a Writing Center with adequate staff and computers should be on the agenda of any university serious about liberal education; and anyone planning to teach the kind of course I have outlined in a university similar to ASU should push for one.

Conclusion

As circumstances vary among universities, so will the details of such introductory, general studies courses. I would suggest, however, that my experience at Arizona State may have four universal messages. First and foremost is that the shift from a curriculum centered on canon to one centered on intellectual faculties (or virtues, or point of view, or whatever) will always require a program of writing assignments. Second, one does not decide just to have students write; one must be very clear as to what faculties can be developed best in this course, and what rhetorical situations will foster that development. Once these things are decided, everything in the course must serve them. Third, the goal is to force the students to write as much as possible, not to see how much red ink can be wasted by the professor. Worrying too much about whether they are making mistakes along the way can impede students' practice. Even in extremely large classes, then, constant writing is both desirable and possible. Finally, benefits for students will not be worth the costs to the department unless the climate of university itself changes. For many, that must be the first step.

Both my papers for this volume have begun with close attention to what the teaching of religious studies can and should do to students. One would think that this subject should always command our attention, but it rarely does. When it is discussed at all, it is largely in terms of initiating students into what we do as scholars, what we call "the field." As I suggested at the beginning of the first paper, however, these scholarly goals may be quite different from those of our teaching, even though the former informs the latter. The increasing professionalization of all the humanities, while it may be good in other ways, only heightens this difference. Indeed, the more "professional," i.e. removed from public discourse, our scholarly problems become, the more we must address our educational ones separately.

Moreoever, students often represent the general culture—its needs and questions—in the academy, and hence our inattention to them indicates a lack of public purpose for the humanities. This lack has left plenty of territory for the academic conservatives to claim. They are more squatters than invaders, having simply moved into an area that most humanists have abandoned, namely that of educating citizens for reponsible life in a democratic society. This is the very thing that the public, rightly I think, expects us to do; but when stripped of the "classics," the humanities, religious studies included, seem unable to articulate how they are going to do it. Simply lobbing post-structuralist shells in the conservatives' direction, in order to return quickly to our professional concerns, only confirms the public's suspicion that the humanities as they are currently taught are hostile to any development of students as citizens.

As one of the humanities, the task for religious studies, then, is to demonstrate how it educates citizens for a responsible life in a diverse democracy within an international setting, and that it can do so better than the Allan Blooms of the world. This task requires not only a view of the world different from that of Bloom, which is easy, but also a clear educational purpose for students entering into that world, which is hard. These two papers, one theory and the other practice, are one articulation of such a purpose. Others in this volume present different views. What matters is that everyone teaching must address the problems of educational purpose and method as seriously and as explicitly as they would scholarly problems. Unless we do so, we will become further estranged from our students and the public at large.

PART V: EPILOGUE

DEARTH IN VENICE

William R. Darrow

In Memoriam Hans W. Frei

Venice May 7, 1987 The government of this city so beloved by travelers acted today to limit the influx of tourists who come here to gaze at the canals and palaces. A directive issued to travel agencies announced that to avoid overcrowding only a controlled number of tour buses would be allowed to approach Venice. The authorities acted after a series of holidays drew huge crowds and the police repeatedly had to untangle human gridlock in the narrow streets.

"New York Times," May 8, 1987 A5

This paper began as a reflection on the current state of graduate education in religion, but became bound up with my fascination with the image of Venice today as a trope for all the monuments of Western civilization. If a college education is in part dedicated to the task of allowing students to understand the legacies of the cultures from which they come, we do well to find ways to think about those legacies. Endangered by the sea, overrun by tourists, and increasingly bereft of people who can afford to live there, Venice is in danger of ceasing to be a living city and is now edging on becoming but a monument. Only a massive engineering project can save it physically; saving its soul will be more difficult.

I originally entitled this paper "Dearth in Venice," with the intention of writing the emptiness of a city which tourism has gone far to deplete of all but its monuments. I then discovered that this title had been used for an article—not unexpectedly—in *Gentleman's Quarterly*. Since I did not have the courage to order the article through our Inter-Library loan librarian, I do not know what that article is about; but in searching through newspapers for accounts of contemporary Venice, I discovered the report that now stands at the head of this paper. I changed the title to "No Dearth in Venice" in recognition of Venice's complete lack of space, even for tourists. Now that I have finished the article, and explored in its conclusion the empty space filled by memory, I have returned the title to "Dearth in Venice." Yet, in attempting to write not of lack, nor rupture, nor decay, but rather of duration, memory, and transformation, it may still be better to call it "No Dearth in Venice." I will leave it to you to determine which, if either, title is more appropriate.

*   *   *

We are perhaps accustomed to thinking of our students as Mongol hordes, but less accustomed to thinking of them as Kublai Khan. Yet the portrait Italo Calvino gives in his *Invisible Cities* of Marco Polo's entertainment and instruction of the Great Khan parallels closely our task as teachers.[1] Marco Polo is the archetypal traveler. As teachers we are travelers; our students are tourists, a feature which they share with the Great Khan. Paul Fussell has written on the relation between tourism and travel. Tourism and travel share many things. They are both movements over space and time; both are mechanisms of escape from the routine. They are almost always a movement into the past, either of geological or human history. In this, they are movements into the timelessness of the "other," a timelessness that we construct for the "other."[2] They also mark a social movement, an upward movement of class identity, be it living in a posher style or viewing the poverty that marks much of the world. Both seek relief from the drabness, boredom and ordinariness of one's everyday life. They are founded on the pleasure of learning new things and celebrate that pleasure somewhat indiscriminately. Finally, both share a quest for identity. Home cannot in our modern world provide identity, only hollow memories. Quoting Jonathan Culler, Fussell concludes, "[Identity] exists only in the past . . . or else in other regions or countries."[3]

But here the resemblances end. Travel is an intensification of the senses, an experience of wisdom and ecstasy. It is not relaxing or consoling; rather, it is strenuous work. And it is lonely.

> If travel is mysterious, even miraculous, and often lonely and frightening, tourism is commonsensical, utilitarian, safe, and social. . . . Not self-directed but externally enticed, as a tourist you go not where your curiosity beckons but where the industry has decreed you shall go. Tourism soothes, shielding you from the shocks of novelty and menace, confirming your prior view of the world rather than shaking it up. It

---

[1] Italo Calvino, *Invisible Cities,* trs. by William Weaver (San Diego: Harcourt Brace Jovanovich, 1974).

[2] Johannes Fabian, *Time and the Other: How Anthropology Makes Its Object* (New York: Columbia University Press, 1983).

obliges you not just to behold conventional things but to behold them in the approved conventional way.[4]

Tourism is as much the pleasure one takes in one's fellow tourists as it is the objects perceived. A tourist is protected from the contingencies of travel as much as possible, always moving in a secure caravan. Invoking Walker Percy's phrase, the tourist is characterized by a "busy disregard." "Tourism invites, or rather requires, an obsession with things that are not travel—the mechanics, rather than the objects and sensations of displacement."[5] Finally, tourism is embarrassingly, flagrantly, politically reactionary: a contrived encounter with the "other" rendered part of a timelessness that is of our own making. It is not a coincidence that the development of mass tourism coincides with the development of mass education. Both hold out a debated but largely shared canon of a common core, of things that one must see/read if one is to be traveled/educated. Both share a confidence in the utilitarian knowledge one gains. It will be good for something.

Travel, on the other hand, distinguishes itself from this utilitarian view in the name of a "liberal principle of disinterested and non-utilitarian perception and contemplation."

> Motivated purely by curiosity, you pursue liberal understanding neither to be nice to people nor to put money in your pocket but to glorify your human nature and to augment your awareness of your location in time and space. You pursue liberal understanding to deepen your sensitivity to ideas and images and not least to sharpen your sense of humility as you come to realize that your country is not the "standard" for the rest of the world but is just as odd as all the others.[6]

I do not want to be heard as simply ragging on the image of the tourist here, especially since I recognize that part of being a tourist is to hold other tourists in contempt. Nor do I want to neglect Fussell's concluding insight that the distinction of traveler and tourist may now be dissolving in the post-tourism world which he considers a sign of post-modernity. Post-tourism is characterized by a "doubt that the world available for scrutiny is a place where any stable understanding, interpretation, or even enjoyment is likely."[7] He points to contemporary travel writing as "characterized by boredom, annoyance, disgust, disillusionment and finally anger."[8] I shall return to

---

[3] Paul Fussell, "Travel, Tourism and 'International Understanding'" in *Thank God for the Atom Bomb and Other Essays* (New York: Summit Books, 1988) pp. 154.

[4] Ibid., p. 157

[5] Ibid., p. 159.

[6] Ibid., p. 164.

[7] Ibid., p. 169.

[8] Ibid., p. 168.

the problems of post-modernity in the body of this paper; but for now, let us accept the trope of the divide between travel and tourism.

It is in graduate school that tourists become travelers. Learning to travel is the skill that graduate school must impart; that in itself is more than enough of a task. But after graduate school, we will spend the rest of our lives teaching often eager and delightful tourists, with the hope that one or two may also become travelers; but with the more realistic expectation that we may help our students critically to inspect and enjoy the experience of being a tourist. There is comparatively little graduate school can do to prepare future teachers for this, beyond the obvious effort to get graduate students to teach and to think about teaching. I am not convinced that most of what I have to say would have been intelligible to me in graduate school, so I do not in any way present these thoughts as a positive program of reform for graduate education in the study of religion. Rather, I would like to explore three aspects of our task as teachers of religion in conversation with Calvino's rendition of that overdetermined encounter between Marco Polo and the Great Khan.[9] These are: the character of our students' expectations; the character of our subject; and finally, the character of educational processes.

These considerations occur while recognizing some features of the present moment of graduate education in the liberal arts generally, and of religious studies in particular. There is the general crisis of the university characterized as the crisis of reason, of the canon and of what Derrida calls "orientation."[10] Western culture's long-standing ambiguous relation to reason remains in complicated play. The question of the literary canon in many fields of the humanities is hotly debated: Are there things that every educated person should have read? And if so, what are they? Finally, the inextricable involvement of the university's structure of knowledge in the power

---

[9]The genius of Calvino's account is that he stresses this encounter. A fuller treatment of the paradigmatic encounter of the Western merchant and the Mongol sage-king in *Il Milione* would also have to treat Marco Polo's relation to his European audience, which brought to fruition the romance of the East represented by Rusticello's editorial approach to Marco's tales, and the vexing question of the nature of Marco's mission as propagandist for the Khan. These two points remind us of the complexity of the site of our teaching: the preconceptions that our students bring and the power dynamics of our teaching, which were raised by Edward Said for most of us in his *Orientalism*, but can be placed to the side in this essay. For a careful recent introduction to the first issue, cf. Mary B. Campbell, *The Witness and the Other World: Exotic European Travel Writing* (Ithaca: Cornell University Press, 1988); for the second, Leonardo Olschki, *Marco Polo's Asia: An Introduction to His "Description of the World" Called "Il Milione,"* trs. John A. Scott (Berkeley: University of California Press, 1960).

[10]Jacques Derrida, "The Principle of Reason: The University in the Eyes of Its Pupils," *Diacritics* 13:3 (1983) p. 12.

relations of society are currently being inspected; we now see with increasing clarity the character of the academy that we have created since the second world war.

We construct our curriculum and our departments according to disciplines and offer multiple courses; in the natural sciences with a sequence of developing skills, otherwise without an obvious sequence.[11] This curriculum creates an approach to knowledge that emphasizes its plurality, divisibility and masterability. The plurality of knowledge means that there is no one text or field that everyone must master. What we need to know is arbitrary and up to individual choice. Here is the place where our mostly illusory individual freedom is celebrated. One interesting result of this structure—appearances to the contrary not withstanding—is that there is no hierarchy of knowledge generally acknowledged by the academy. Divisibility into courses reinforces the features of plurality and underlines that education is control of discrete topics, methods, and fields. Masterability of discrete, arbitrary units of knowledge and of disciplines in a pluralist context is the format of curriculum in the contemporary college or university.

Into this world, the study of religion has been born: neither comfortably a field nor a discipline, religious studies is often, but not always, a department. This area of study has valued, perhaps too much, its liminal character celebrating a cross-cultural, multi-disciplinary orientation on a global scale. Its self-definition, however, makes sense only in an academy composed of fields and disciplines. In addition, the notion of the academic study of religion has solved the highly culture-specific problem of the place of religion in the modern American academy by affirming the dubious distinction between studying religion and studying about religion.

I think we ought to acknowledge that in the present period, religious studies has come of age. It is established as a cross-disciplinary field at the moment in which the genres of our disciplines have begun to blur, and it remains a significant player in that blurring.[12] The old battles to establish religion in the academy appear to be over. The generation that is now active cut its teeth in those departments that were founded in the 1950s and 1960s. It is a generation that works with a canon of sociological, psychological, anthropological and theological approaches to the study of religion that have allowed it to create its object. Significantly, we have created our object of study, i.e. religion, without the formulation of a common paradigm of the study

---

[11]I have in mind here the clarity of the *trivium* and *quadrivium* in the classical liberal arts curriculum as the model of a sequence of developing skills.

[12]See Clifford Geertz, "Blurred Genres: The Reconfiguration of Social Thought" in *Local Knowledge: Further Essays in Interpretive Anthropology* (New York: Basic Books, 1983) pp. 19-35.

of religion which some, perhaps too informed by Thomas Kuhn, had hoped for; but maybe such things do not exist for second-order concepts such as religion.[13] Our identity is, however, firmly grounded on the existence of the object we have created for ourselves and on the disciplines between which we choose to stand. It has also been characterized by the increasingly higher level of technical training demanded by the area of comparative religions. Much more explicitly than in previous generations, language study has become the union card to the field. Technical expertise is perhaps the most important mark of contemporary training in graduate schools, though this training is never considered to be as thorough as that of area specialists.

I think we can be confident that these necessary preconditions of our identity secure us in the academy. Nonetheless, if we do nothing else for the next generation of graduate students, we must prepare them for the changes that will inevitably appear in the configuration of power/knowledge that made possible the formulation of religious studies since the war. There is no more sobering experience than to examine a college catalog in fifty year intervals—not with any confidence in the progress of knowledge, but just with the traveler's gaze into the reality of change. Earlier generations did things differently, and our grandchildren will do so as well. The rise of national history as a field of study was only really completed two hundred years ago in a development intimately tied to the rise of nationalism. It has been but a century since English completed its struggle for acceptance in the face of a surviving emphasis on classical languages. Fifty years ago, the natural sciences were fighting to be independent both of natural philosophy and of each other. The growth of religious studies has been part of independence movements in the social sciences and of the rise of area studies. Although I do not know what kind of a curriculum my grandchildren will study, I have some idea of what the next battles will be; and I have no reason to think there will be a religion component in their curriculum as that component now exists. Educational institutions change too dramatically for me to be so confident of such stasis.

*   *   *

"The other ambassadors warn me of famines, extortions, conspiracies, or else they inform me of newly discovered turquoise mines, advantageous prices in marten furs, suggestions for supplying damascened blades. And you?", the Great Khan asked Polo. "You return from lands equally distant and you can tell me only the thoughts that come to a

---

[13]Jonathan Z. Smith, "'Religion' and 'Religious Studies': No Difference at All," *Soundings* 71:2-3 (1988) pp. 231-244.

man who sits on his doorstep at evening to enjoy the cool air. What is the use, then of all your traveling?" . . .

Marco Polo imagined answering (or Kublai Khan imagined his answer) that the more one was lost in unfamiliar quarters of distant cities, the more one understood the other cities he had crossed to arrive there; and he retraced the stages of his journeys, and he came to know the port from which he had set sail, and the familiar places of his youth, and the surroundings of home, and a little square of Venice where he gamboled as a child. . . .

. . . "Elsewhere is a negative mirror. The traveler recognizes the little that is his, discovering the much he has not had and will never have."

Invisible Cities, pp. 27-29

Let me return to the focus of this meditation: Marco Polo as teacher and the Great Khan as student. We may resist thinking of ourselves as Marco Polo for two reasons which we should address first. Marco Polo was a mere merchant, a businessman; the book he wrote needed a ghostwriter and was the worst form of vulgar popularization. Nothing so much characterizes the academy as its resistance to the business world. If I had more time, I would investigate the character of this resistance which clearly has something to do with the fact that most of our students will make more money than we ever will, although much else is obviously involved. One might also wish to classify Marco as a mere geographer. This is a related, though more complicated, resistance. It may be of some relevance that Marco's hugely popular account of his adventures was scoffed at by professional academic geographers, in which case the academic resistance to seeing Marco as one of us has a long history. Of more relevance is the status of geography as a field. If ever there was a field that was self-consciously interdisciplinary in the days before it was fashionable, it was geography. Combining the natural sciences, social sciences, and humanities, geography provided the context for a truly integrated approach to the study of the human experience. It also developed almost universal scorn in the academy among both students and faculty. Although I have no statistics, I have the impression that geography departments are the ones that have been successfully dismantled at a number of colleges and universities. We do well not to think of ourselves as geographers.

The Great Khan, I hope, will be a less troubling metaphor for our students. As a student, he is first of all singular; and we do well in insisting to our graduate students that they always remember the individuality and singularity of each student they teach. As the passage I quoted shows, the Khan—like our students—is a practical man seeking to maximize his profit. He wants useful knowledge. He is not quite sure that his teacher-traveler has anything useful to offer him, or that all the fuss and effort Marco has expended has actually achieved anything. But he is willing to listen, to be entertained and amused.

The Khan is also rootless: heir to a tradition of the nomadic steppe, he is now separated from his ancestral home and in a new Chinese environment that is at once enticing and repellant. It may be that rootlessness and homelessness have always been a feature of some portion in each generation, but today nothing is so vociferously affirmed and attacked as the experience of displacement, of rootlessness—the dilemma of the immigrant come either as conqueror or as refugee into a land where s/he does not belong. One cannot understand the furor over Salman Rushdie without understanding both the reality of being homeless and the irrational fury that such homelessness invokes in those who think they have a home. Our students are away from home for the first time; and while it would be ludicrous to equate their experience with that of the voluntary or involuntary immigrant, I think it would be wrong not to recognize the analogy of these experiences.

You may object that the Khan's age and status make him an atypical student—what we would technically term a "non-traditional student"—whom many of us are teaching more and more. I would not disagree. But the cynicism of the young shares something with the cynicism of the emperor. Calvino deliciously captures what is shared with the shift in person of the following passage, with which he opens his book.

> In the lives of emperors there is a moment which follows pride in the boundless extension of the territories we have conquered, and the melancholy and relief of knowledge we shall soon give up any thought of knowing and understanding them.[14]

Our traditional students come at the beginning of their conquests; the Khan is at his end; but the shared arrogance and cynicism of the two is clear.

The Khan shows, even towards the end of his instruction by Marco Polo, a confidence that he might still master the rules, understand the system, and then finally possess his empire. He has not quite given up the hope of true mastery. Finding the rules that make mastery possible is a wonderful image of the quest for reason. In the end the Khan becomes a total structuralist. The goal of the Khan's education becomes the mastering of the rules of the chess game he plays with Marco. With this, the great Khan becomes the bodiless model of all human activity. In the moment of mastery over the game, its purpose eludes the Khan and he is still unable to possess his empire.

---

[14]Ibid., p. 5.

The Great Khan tried to concentrate on the game: but now it was the game's purpose that eluded him. Each game ends in a gain or a loss: but of what? What were the true stakes? At checkmate, beneath the foot of the king, knocked aside by the winner's hand, a black or white square remains. By disembodying his conquests, to reduce them to the essential, Kublai had arrived at the extreme operation: the definitive conquest, of which the empire's multiform treasures were only illusory envelopes. It was reduced to a square of planed wood: nothingness . . . [15]

The stance of the Khan might be positioned within William Perry's scheme of intellectual and ethical development in the college years. In that scheme, a college student moves from Dualism to Relativism to Commitment. The developmental scheme is characterized by the progressive negotiation of the domains of Multiplicity and Authority. This occurs as relativism expands into the domain of authority through the encounter with multiplicity. I would place the Khan of the passage cited above at "position four," in which "the student had assimilated Multiplicity and Relativism into the framework of a world he still assumed to be dualistic."[16] Calvino's novel is about the mysterious transformation that the Khan goes through to bring him to "position six," where the student is able to "apprehend the implications of personal choice in a world he assumes to be relativistic."[17] Perry speaks of this transformation as a revolution that arises with the failure of a dualistic framework in the face of an expanding generalization of Relativism. It is of great significance that Perry can find no explicit description of this kind of transformation as a phenomenon in human personal development (except in certain descriptions of psychotherapy). I shall return to this transformation in my conclusion; but if you sniff out a bit of religious faith here, you are right.

*   *   *

Kublai Khan had noticed that Marco Polo's cities resembled one another, as if the passage from one to another involved not a journey but a change of elements. Now, from each city Marco described to him, the Great Khan's mind set out on its own, and after dismantling the city piece by piece, he reconstructed it in other ways, substituting components, shifting them, inverting them.

Marco, meanwhile, continued reporting his journey, but the emperor was no longer listening.

Invisible Cities, p. 43

---

[15]Ibid., pp. 125 and 131. This passage is repeated twice in the text.
[16]William G. Perry, Jr., *Forms of Intellectual and Ethical Development in the College Years: A Scheme* (New York: Holt, Rinehart and Winston, Inc., 1970) p. 110.
[17]Loc. cit.

Marco tells the Khan of city after city, each named after a woman; and the Khan begins to suspect a pattern, something that is withheld, something that cannot be spoken. There is no plurality of cities; there is but one city.

The concept of city functions much like our concept of religion as the organizing focus: a second-order generalization that makes our discourse possible, but which can never be found outside the academy. There is no religion, only religions. We are accustomed to considering our category of religion like our category language. The analogy has contributed two central themes to the study of religion: the notion of structure; and the stress on religion as communication. The analogy of language allows us to distinguish between surface phenomena and deep structure, and to affirm the unity of structure in the face of multiplicity of expressions. It also has led us to stress that above all, religious expression is communicative. Religious people are saying something with their words and with their actions.

What would happen if we were to take the notion of the city as our analogy to religion? Just as there is not language, only languages, there is no city, only cities. Seeing religions as cities might win us some new approaches to our object.[18] Rather than the image of *homo religiosus* as competent speaker, we can also see him/her as resident of a particular city.

The notion of the city makes impossible the isolation of structures from function (speech) that is central to the language analogy. When we look at cities we always see a living whole: an organization of space and definition in time that is in a process of continual change that can never be abstracted synchronically. Moreover, the city is always an embodiment, a material reality in space and time that allows of no abstraction into a nonmaterial and largely intellectual essence. It is simply always a thing.

In addition, the city is always an imposed organization of sometimes serpentine, sometimes fixed walls that must constantly be maintained. A city is an act of power in the laying of its foundations and in its continuing struggle to survive. Its boundaries are always being breached by the outside—be they the enemy, the suburb, or the trader. It is not only the external boundaries of the cities that are always in danger of being breached, but the internal ones as well. The sewer, the rat, the dead are constantly present below, and always in

---

[18]Of course, the urban form has religious origins as illuminated by Paul Wheatley in *The Pivot of the Four Quarters: A Preliminary Enquiry into the Origins and Character of the Ancient Chines City* (Chicago: Aldine, 1971) and Joseph Rykwert, *Idea of a Town: The Anthropology of Urban Form in Rome, Italy and the Ancient World* (Princeton: Princeton University Press, 1976). These studies make clear that this is not a particularly innocent analogy. I owe Charles Long thanks for reminding me of these references.

interaction with, the living city.[19] The city must organize itself, define itself and protect itself from the manifold others that threaten it both from without and within.

Further, the city always represents itself to itself and celebrates that representation. Each city has its master symbol which at once affords self-definition as well as a definition for the visitor. This is what makes the tourist possible. The tourist is beckoned by the master symbol, be it the Golden Gate, the glass flowers, the Sears Tower or the Piazza San Marco.

It has been one of the hallmarks of this project to examine critically the appropriateness of the master symbols we give of the traditions we are teaching. Do we misrepresent when we present the Zoroastrian before the fire, the Muslim in huge concentric circles around the Kaaba, the Buddhist in meditation, the Hindu in Benares? I am in complete sympathy with the ethical imperative of this question, but not convinced of its appropriateness. After all, it is in the character of the city to produce the master symbol: the city literally erects and mandates its specific symbol, and invests it with a multiplicity of meanings. I do not know how we as tour guides of avid tourists can avoid showing these traditional sights; our task cannot realistically be to find more accurate sights, but rather to interpret with our students the layers of meaning that adhere to the master symbols of the traditions we study.

Finally, conceiving of religion as city may give us one more insight that arises when Piazza San Marco is inundated with water, when Venice is uninhabited by anyone because they cannot afford to live there, when only tourists come and have now so inundated the city, that even their entry must be restricted. Transformations and endings of a city and its symbols, of a religious community and its representation, are also what we are in the process of studying; and the image of the city that is no longer a city may give us insight into the death of religions and the experience of homelessness, of having lost our identity in travel, of having our home lost in translation.

*   *   *

"Sire, now I have told you about all the cities I know."
"There is still one of which you never speak." Marco Polo bowed his head.
"Venice," the Khan said.

---

[19]As the problem of memory recedes in Calvino's early accounts of cities, the presence and character of the dead becomes the central issue. My comments on the internal subversion of the city is much informed by Peter Stallybrass and Allon White, *The Poetics and Politics of Transgression* (Ithaca: Cornell University Press, 1986).

Marco smiled. "What else do you believe I have been talking to you about?"

The emperor did not turn a hair. "And yet I have never heard you mention that name."

And Polo said: "Every time I describe a city I am saying something about Venice."

"When I ask you about other cities, I want to hear about them. And about Venice, when I ask you about Venice."

"To distinguish the other cities' qualities, I must speak of a first city that remains implicit. For me it is Venice."

"You should then begin each tale of your travels from the departure, describing Venice as it is, all of it, not omitting anything you remember of it."

The lake's surface was barely wrinkled; the copper reflection of the ancient palace of the Sung was shattered into sparkling glints like floating leaves.

"Memory's images, once they are fixed in words, are erased," Polo said. "Perhaps I am afraid of losing Venice all at once, if I speak of it. Or perhaps, speaking of other cities, I have already lost it, little by little."

Invisible Cities, pp. 86-87

The instruction of the Khan progresses and becomes increasingly personal. The student may not become a traveler, but he now begins to see through his teacher. It is this, above all, that should be the goal of our enterprise as teachers. In view of this goal, I would like to propose—albeit in a most preliminary sort of way—that what religious studies have to offer to the academy is insight into three issues central to its concerns: the character of teaching and student-teacher relations; the character of canon; and finally, the character of memory.

Bourdieu and Passeron have shown that education is always symbolic violence in two distinct, but related, senses.[20] It is always a double arbitrary. First, in the sense of a cultural arbitrary, a curriculum cultivates meanings, skills and attitudes deemed by a culture to be conducive to truth. Second, in the sense of arbitrary powers, the power relations in a society give to one group or set of groups the authority to declare what will count as true, relevant and appropriate to know. The teacher stands within these two arbitraries and, with the authority lent by a society, is charged with the task of negotiating the symbolic violence of education on the young.

It is remarkable how rarely we religionists talk comparatively of the styles and character of the educational systems that reproduce and adapt knowledge in the traditions we study, especially in view of the fact that we all function in one such system. This is probably because we are turned off by the appearance of a lack of creativity, and by the emphasis given to memorization, which we take to be hall-

---

[20]Pierre Bourdieu and Jean-Claude Passeron, *Reproduction in Education, Society and Culture,* trs. Richard Nice (Beverly Hills: Sage Publications, 1977).

marks of other educational systems. The lack of comparative discussion at this juncture might also be traced to the extent to which our notion of "holy man" restricts our view of religious educators to the highest elite of exemplar teachers, not the more everyday teachers who preserve and transmit their traditions.[21] We are now beginning to explore the history and character of the Islamic madrasa, the Jewish yeshiva, the Tibetan debating forum, the Chinese academy and the philosophies of education that they embodied. In such mirrors we can perhaps learn much about our enterprise.

The relation of teacher and student is a rich theme. To take one example, Eugen Herrigel's account of his training as an archer gives us precious insight into the features of the relation between himself and his master.[22] The authority of the teacher, the teacher's apparent disinterest in the student's progress, the sheer work of the training, the teacher's unexpected but absolute willingness to flunk him out when he cheated, Herrigel's unwillingness to talk about the character of the teacher, and finally the experience of the pupil and the master having become one are rich images which allow students to reflect on the character of their expectations of their educational system. Perhaps these images go further in allowing students to catch a glimpse of the sacrality that at least nostalgically attaches to the profession we are all engaged in.

Entry into the educational systems of the traditions we study also allows us to raise the question of canon. What is to be read? How is it to be read? In what order should things be read? What should not be read, except by the most advanced student? These are all questions that resonate through our traditions. Changes in the canons of the educated individual have repeatedly occurred in human history. Three prominent examples are the debate in both the Christian and Muslim worlds over the place of Greek philosophy in the time period from Muhammad to the Mongols; the neo-Confucian reappropriation of the classics before the Mongol invasions and rise of neo-Confucianism to state power; and the full embrace of Persian poetry in the Persianate world which, after the Mongol conquest, came to be recognized as a legitimate cultural good equivalent in some ways to the Qur'an.

Recent work on scripture, above all that by William Graham, has illumined for us how ill-equipped we contemporary Americans are to understand the canonical worlds in which texts are embodied, rather

---

[21]An unforgettable such teacher is to be found in Cheikh Hamidou Kane's *Ambiguous Adventure*, trs. Katherine Woods (London: Heinemann, 1972).

[22]Eugen Herrigel, *Zen and the Art of Archery*, trs. R.F.C. Hull (New York: Vintage Books, 1971).

than passively read.[23] I confess myself to be a bit uncertain about
what it means to go beyond the written word, since I am not quite
sure where the written word ends and the oral embodiment of texts
begins. The image of the Khazar envoy in Pavic's *The Dictionary of the
Khazars* (the best book on the encounter of religions ever written),
who dies with the history of his people tattooed on his body, makes
me suspicious if oral embodiment ever allows one to escape writing.[24]
But otherwise, Graham has laid the groundwork for an ex-
traordinarily interesting comparative discussion of the character of
canon, scripture and interpretation. In providing a set of issues to address in the study of educational institutions, we may also have a tool
for understanding how traditions reproduce themselves and at the
same time adapt to changed contexts.

In both the discussions of teacher and canon, the role of memory
has been briefly glimpsed; and it is with the question of memory that
I want to conclude. These final thoughts are inspired by Peter
Homans' suggestion concerning the interconnections between psychoanalysis, religious healing and mourning.[25] Central to the
mourning process is the multiplex operation of memory. Memory
may in fact be the real object of our study. I do not have the space
here to develop this thought, but several issues are important.

The first is the obvious one. We need to be careful neither to over-
rate nor underrate the importance of memory in the societies we
study. Nothing more immediately reinforces the prejudices of our
students than the impression that the character of other educational
systems consisted simply in vast amounts of memorization. We need
to emphasize that in all cases, memorization was the basis for further
education and the development of literary skill, dialectical debating
techniques and exegetical genius. We may use this occasion to query
whence the profound prejudice against memory in our society, and to
venture the hypothesis that there may be a close connection between
the loss of the value of memory and the loss of religion and identity.
The role of memory in the establishment of personal identity and the
interconnection between personal and cultural/ethnic identity is

---

[23]William A. Graham, *Beyond the Written Word: Oral Aspects of Scripture in the
History of Religion* (New York: Cambridge, 1987).

[24]Milorad Pavic, *Dictionary of the Khazars: A Lexicon Novel*, trs. by Christina
Pribicevic-Zoric (New York: Alfred Knopf, 1988) p. 73-78. "He passed away, because his skin inscribed with the Khazar history began to itch terribly. The itch
was unbearable, and it was with relief that he died, glad to be finally cleansed of
history."

[25]Peter Homans, "Once Again, Psychoanalysis, East and West: A Psychoanalytic Essay on Religion, Mourning, and Healing," *History of Religions* 24:2
(November, 1984) pp. 133-154.

centrally at issue here.[26] For example, no act is more central to the Islamic vision than the act of remembering, *dhikr*. The individual and the community are continually exhorted to remember God's warnings and beneficence; and in that act, the framework for Muslim identity is laid. This is familiar stuff. The model of religious activity as *anamnesis* is a commonplace. But there are issues here which we have not fully thought through, issues having to do with the connection between memory and the phallus, the member that is agent in the re-membering process, a connection also made in the Hebrew and Arabic root *dh-k-r*, which has to do both with the phallus and memory.

*   *   *

> And Polo said, "The inferno of the living is not something that will be; if there is one, it is what is already here, the inferno where we live every day, that we form by being together. There are two ways to escape suffering it. The first is easy for many: accept the inferno and become such a part of it that you can no longer see it. The second is risky and demands constant vigilance and apprehension: seek and learn to recognize who and what, in the midst of the inferno, are not inferno, then make them endure, give them space."
>
> *Invisible Cities*, p. 165

So ends Calvino's account. In the end the professor has the last word to the student. It is preachy; and it is potentially not convincing, because the student still has the choice of either forgetting what he has learned and plunging into the inferno, or of stepping back and remembering. What he remembers is a hint of an origin that can never be spoken because to do so is to be in danger of losing it. What he remembers is the ability for commitment to the task of one's life even though there is no apparent value to the goal, no clear reward that means something. What he remembers is that mysterious power that sustained him from "position four" to "position six" in Perry's scheme, or what carried him from Burkhalter's mode four further on, which we now understand more in the psychoanalytic than the religious context. By occupying the space created by the dearth that memory both clears and fills, the student can experience duration, transformation, and meaning in the face of the surrounding inferno. This is what I believe a liberal education to be about, and what we as teachers are all about.

---

[26]Michael Fischer provides a very useful introduction to this issue with his article, "Ethnicity and the Post-Modern Arts of Memory" in *Writing Culture: The Poetics and Politics of Ethnography* (Berkeley and Los Angeles: University of California Press, 1986) pp. 194-233.